Surviving
A Cheating Man's
Heart

A True Story

By

Da'Naia Jackson

I dedicate this book to 'I AM' the Most High God, the Author and Finisher of my faith.

And the Lord said to me, "Hear O you generations, for you have forgotten the ways of the Lord your God, and I have sent my servant to reestablish my name on the earth in preparation for My second coming. Write this on the tablets of your heart: "The LORD our God, the LORD is one! You shall love the LORD your God with all your heart, with all your soul, and with all your strength. And these words which I command you today shall be in your heart. You shall teach them diligently to your daughters and shall talk of them when you sit in your house, when you walk by the way, when you lie down, and when you rise up-. Deuteronomy 6:4-7

As the deer pants for the water brooks, so pants my soul for You, O God. My soul thirsts for God, for the living God. I will say to God, my rock, You are worthy to be praised because You heard my cry and rescued my soul from the pit of Sheol.

I SATURATE EACH PAGE AND WORD OF THIS BOOK IN THE POWERFUL BLOOD OF JESUS CHRIST

Table of Contents

Introduction

A *Cheating Man's Heart* is saturated in deep-seated rejection, pain, hurt, a lying tongue, manipulation, haughty eyes, bribes, schemes, hatred, and the intention to shed innocent blood. The bloodshed of a woman who doesn't know her worth and loves the idea of a relationship and marriage more than she loves God. A woman who never takes the time to heal from past trauma and buries the current trauma dished out to her at the hands of a cheating man and his "heart" for a cute family Instagram picture, status upgrade, and bragging rights because he put a ring on it. I know that several of you are reading this book only to get "tea," so let me be the first to thank you for paying the total price for your tea with a reminder of 1 Thessalonians 4:11(NKJV), which states you should *"make it your ambition to mind your own business and work with your hands."*

Therefore, your takeaway from this book should be the reality of demonic oppression plaguing marriages and romantic relationships worldwide. All the details in this book are accurate to my experience (Jn8:32 NKJV), and the actual first names of the individuals who played a role in this story are used; I have omitted some of their last names. I need to tell this story for several reasons, the first being that it is a testament to how the Lord saved me from myself and the snare of *"A Cheating Man's Heart"* by making me the head and not the tail after two public cheating scandals.

As the adage goes, only God can turn a mess into a message, and my hope is that women across the world will gain insight into their situations so that they can be free from the demonic entanglement of the heart of a man who cheats. Second, I pray that the story of my life that rose to fame through scandal and deceit will serve as a blueprint of hope, showing how *"all things work together for good to those who love God, to those who are called according to His purpose"* (Rom 8:28 NKJV) so that more women can rise and reclaim their voice. Third, my prayer is that men and women currently in the deadly cycle of infidelity become educated, equipped, and empowered to war after the principalities, powers, rulers of the darkness of this age, and spiritual hosts of wickedness in the heavenly places (Eph 6:12 NKJV) directly behind the behavior and turmoil feeding the man who chronically cheats and the woman who stays to "try and make it work" because they don't want to disappoint God since we all know *"He hates divorce, For it covers one's garment with violence"* (Mal 2:16).

The nagging question that must be answered is why 'I AM' hates divorce? Followed by why would He call you to stay in an adulterous marriage? In conclusion, will He ever release you from the marriage? All these questions had no answers that made sense or resonated when I was amid the fire in the very public cheating entanglement. However, through faith, the Holy Spirit became my teacher, imparting seeds of wisdom as I went through the storm. The first word of wisdom He gave me is that I had made an idol out of the man and was in direct violation of the law as it is written in Deuteronomy 6:4-7 *"You shall love the Lord, your God with all your heart, with all your soul and with all your strength"* which became the hindrance and open door of a negative soul tie that kept me wanting to "try and make it work" for fourteen years in which five of those years became a legally binding covenant agreement in the eyes of God. Once I became aware of this open door, the man idol of my youth began to be torn down in my heart, soul, and body, allowing the Holy Spirit to reclaim His rightful position.

Moreover, allowing Him to change my beliefs concerning the standard of acceptable treatment by a man. My first book, *Healing God's Way: The Art of Spiritual Warfare, Deliverance and Healing* devotional/journal, manifested from the process of tearing down the idol of Derrick as my provider, protector, and ultimate savior. As I leaned more into the word of God to reestablish Him as my personal Lord and Savior, the more my marriage blew up in flames, eventually becoming as hot as the fiery furnace that Shadrach Meshach and Abednego were thrown into. But GOD saved my life in the ultimate blow-up as the headline surfaced, "Relationship Coach Derrick Jaxn Announces Divorce from Wife- "My Family and I Have Gone Through Many Changes," making it to every major platform worldwide.

December 10th, 2022, 8:16 a.m. I woke up to a text message from Derrick with a screenshot of his statement announcing the divorce along with the question, *"Do you have any thoughts before I post?"*.

"Over the past several months, my family and I have gone through many changes. Some of you have speculated, while others of you have reached out to offer support as we privately established this new normal for ourselves and our beautiful children. Earlier this year after much prayer, counseling, and deep consideration, we decided to go our separate ways and filed for divorce. Making the decision to file was one of the hardest decisions of my life, but I've found peace knowing that our mission of raising healthy children, starting with healthy and whole parents, is still being accomplished. From falling in love as just teenagers, to becoming spouses and now co-parents, I'm grateful for the years we've spent together and wouldn't trade them for anything. I was blessed to have such and amazing person in my life and will forever be thankful for all she's meant to our family. We ask that if you pray, to please pray for us. If not, please respect our privacy."

I replied at 8:25 a.m.

It wasn't earlier this year. It was three months ago. We did not make the decision. You did September 29th in a text message.

Derrick replied at 8:33 a.m.

Feel free to clear that up on your page. I reserved specifics to give us privacy as, much as possible. Making our private business a public thing has never been my flow, but I wanted to honor you best as possible."

So here I am, clearing it up in pages! In a book series form to educate, equip, teach, and warn women worldwide about the dangers of dealing with *"A Cheating Man's Heart"* and how to SURVIVE in God's way. The following story is a true story of my life and my point of view as it happened, and the only way to tell that story with the utmost accuracy is to go back to the beginning. The Lord the Father, Son, and Holy Spirit said to me to begin with: Malachi 2:10-17

Treachery of Infidelity

"Have we not all one Father? Has not one God created us? Why do we deal treacherously with one another By profaning the covenant of the fathers? Judah has dealt treacherously, And an abomination has been committed in Israel and in Jerusalem, For Judah has profaned The LORD's holy institution which He loves; He has married the daughter of a foreign god. May the LORD cut off from the tents of Jacob The man who does this, being awake and aware, yet who brings an offering to the LORD of hosts! And this is the second thing you do: You cover the altar of the LORD with tears, With weeping and crying; So He does not regard the offering anymore, Nor receive it with goodwill from your hands. Yet you say, "For what reason?" Because the Lord has been witness Between you and

the wife of your youth, With whom you have dealt treacherously; Yet she is your companion and your wife by covenant. But did He not make them one, Having a remnant of the Spirit? And why one? He seeks godly offspring. Therefore, take heed to your spirit, And let none deal treacherously with the wife of his youth. For the LORD God of Israel says That He hates divorce, For it covers one's garment with violence," Says the LORD of hosts. "Therefore, take heed to your spirit, That you do not deal treacherously." You have wearied the LORD with your words; Yet you say "In what way have we wearied Him?" In that you say, "Everyone who does evil is good in the sight of the LORD, And He delights in them," Or, "Where is the God of Justice?"

Welcome to the days of my life...

PART I:
Bitter Roots and Satanic Deposits

In the beginning, "Shawn" met "Danielle" according to the original novel "*A Cheating Man's Heart*" by my soon-to-be ex-husband Derrick Jaxn. Luke 8:17 states, "*For nothing is secret that will not be revealed, nor anything hidden that will not be known and come to light.*" The Cheating Man's Heart Series is not "a work of fiction, names, characters, places, and incidents" as it is written in the publisher's notes. Shawn's character, actions, and behaviors are a cover for the identity of Derrick Jaxn, the man, and the brand. "Likewise, Danielle's character, actions, and behaviors are a cover of my identity, Da'Naia Jackson, formerly known as Da'Naia Broadus, at the time these events and incidents took place in the trilogy's first book. Looking back on this portion of my life, I've come to realize how vital it is to know your identity in Christ Jesus and teach this to my generation and our children so that they do not repeat the same cycles and demonic bondages that come with *A Cheating Man's Heart*. Furthermore, healing God's way requires identity recovery mentally, emotionally, physically, and spiritually to survive and thrive in the promises of the Holy Spirit after the treachery of infidelity.

Derrick and I met on January 13th, 2009, in business calc at the prestigious Tuskegee University in Tuskegee, Alabama. Three weeks before we met, I was raped, and I never told a soul, which you will learn about later in the story. Introducing the rape in brief here is important because it exposes the broken consciousness that I had before I entered a fourteen-year relationship with Derrick. Wisdom gained through the treachery of infidelity showed me that bitterroots preexisted my relationship with Derrick and greatly influenced how I viewed men and my worth to a man. Healing God's way began with battling the need and right to blame Derrick for ruining my entire life and my ability to give and receive love. Unfortunately, I did not heal God's way in the beginning, and the history of my famous relationship is the training material that will be used in this book to expose, correct, and direct men and women to whole person healing in their relationships. Silence concerning the sexual trauma I experienced before Derrick manifested in my behavior, my beliefs, and my acceptance of mental and emotional abuse that both of us inflicted on each other throughout the course of our union. Admission of both of our abusive tendencies is in no way a justification for Derrick's behavior and choices from the beginning to the end of our relationship. I can only take accountability for my part along with the harsh realities of his part, for which I pray that he takes true accountability and responsibility without excuses.

As previously mentioned, I did not heal God's way initially. My first mistake was violating 2 Corinthians 13:5, which reads, *"Examine yourselves as to whether you are in the faith. Test yourselves. Do you not know yourselves, that Jesus Christ is in you- unless indeed you are disqualified."* I failed to even consider how the sexual trauma that I swept under the rug affected how I valued myself, and that became the open door for what I allowed and accepted from the toxicity of an undisciplined sex drive of a man who is broken from his own childhood traumas. Please pay attention to this part so that you can pluck out the root that is keeping you in a cycle of being the cheating man or the woman "trying to make it work" with chronic infidelity. If you do not kill a weed at the root, it will grow back faster and stronger and bring friends with it. This concept resembles the story of the unclean spirit that goes out of a man and returns to the house after he finds it empty, swept, and put in order. He goes and takes seven other spirits more wicked than himself, and the last state of that man is worse than the first (Matt12:43-45). This scripture's knowledge and practical application do not influence the situations and circumstances in our early relationship.

Now that I have gone through the first level of healing and writing this book as the next level of healing, I'm inserting this as a corrective teaching point for every woman who has been cheated on or is being cheated on by a man. Reflect on what you experienced before you met that man, and ask whether you have healed from it or swept it under the rug and keep pushing forward as if nothing ever happened? If you fall on the later end of the spectrum, you have what Bishop R.C Blakes coins "the broken consciousness of a woman." According to Blakes, "broken consciousness is when the world intentionally drains the queen of her awareness relative to who she is and when the world is through with her, she does not recognize her crown, she does not own her throne, and she relinquishes the power over her kingdom." Bishop Blakes goes on to say "A lot of these issues that generations of women struggle with are not necessarily directed by the hands of men all the time; sometimes it's the older generation whose consciousness has been broken, and self-esteem has been drained, and they pour these deficiencies onto the coming generations".[1] Therefore, a woman must repair the damage done to her. The root cause of a woman's condition in question form is, Do I have value and worth, which often comes with another question of whether I am good enough?

Jesus answered and said YES, *"For I know the thoughts that I think towards you, says the Lord, thoughts of peace and not of evil, to give you a future and a hope."* The problem is that I didn't know or believe that when I entered a relationship with Derrick. On top of that, I had a daddy issue as I had unhealed trauma from the death of my father, who passed away at the age of 30. My father's death fragmented me mentally, emotionally, and spiritually. I had no idea of the effects of that until I was thirty years old and on the brink of death myself 18 years after his death. I will not go into detail about this in this section; however, it is essential to note this as I pinpoint the manifestation of demonic, toxic, and abusive cycles in my relationship with Derrick. When a woman has unhealed traumas of any kind, and she is in a relationship where chronic infidelity is taking place, she needs to keep her heart with all diligence with the word of God, or out of it will spring the issues of life (Prov 4:23) until she's so broken and fragmented that she will not want to live. Exposing the bitter roots of the pre-public scandal sets the stage and tone for how the living God heals the individual and, in some cases, the marriage of those ensnared by cheating hearts.

Moving forward, after exposing the demonic taproot of my life pre-relationship, twelve days after Derrick and I met in business calc, I found myself bent over doggy style in his Russel Hall dorm room late at night while his roommate was "sleep" on the other side of the closet like room. Yes, welcome to the whorish ways of my former self, but the truth must be told that I was not saved and sanctified in the beginning though I thought I was saved. Immediately after this sexual encounter, the relationship went warp speed, and this was an increase from the three days it took for us both to fall in love after just meeting in class. What I learned is that any relationship that moves as quickly as ours did should be a big red flag for the things to come as you get deeper into a sexual relationship. Next, I learned that a negative soul tie is created and keeps you in bondage. Even when you want to leave, you feel like you can't, or you always come back because of this soul tie created during sexual sin. This is why 1 Corinthians 6:18 tells us to *"flee sexual immorality"* because the snare of these ungodly soul ties is destructive to everyone in its path. Last, I learned that the spiritual state of each person changes for the worse because of the transfer of spirits that are exchanged during each sexual encounter. So, every person's spirit and demons that Derrick had ever had sex with up until we had our first sexual encounter had entered me, adding to the demons that preexisted our spiritual union. Likewise, every person's spirit and demons that I had ever had sex with up until we had our first sexual encounter had entered Derrick, adding to the demons that preexisted our spiritual union. The spiritual impact of my relationship with Derrick is significant to the manifestation of what you, the world, have seen so far play out in the public eye.

In the beginning, I had no awareness of the seriousness and catastrophe of my sexual sin that would open the door to a world full of heartache. In that ignorance, I also developed a spirit of pride which manifested every time I caught Derrick with another girl with the thoughts, belief, and words, "I'm not the one who's been whoring in the relationship," so that makes me better than him morally. Later, after we had already been in marriage three years, I found out that his being a whore automatically made me a whore because *she who is joined to a harlot is one body with him for the two became one flesh* (1 Cor 6:15-17). Therefore, as I write what you are reading today, you won't hear me bash him for his harlotry because I became a harlot with him when he decided to defile the marriage again. However, in the past, I absolutely, without a doubt, called him a whore and referred to him as "community dick" according to his own words of warning to women about a man who is still reserving his right to have options. And yes, I told Derrick to his face that he was giving me his wife at the time "community dick," and he blew up on me. I want to stay within reach of myself, but you will learn more about that in part three of this book series.

The sex between Derrick and I became the focal point of the entire relationship in our early college days. Nearly every encounter started or ended with some type of sexual exchange, but it felt right at the time. Looking back, I know there was too much time and energy spent on the relationship's physical component, leaving little time and energy spent on getting to know each other. Not too long after our first physically intimate encounter, I left my cell phone in Derrick's black 1999 Grand AM, creating one of the major issues we had leading to the September 29th, 2022, text message that Derrick sent me with his solo decision to end the marriage. Upon discovering that I had left my phone in his car, he told me that my mom had called the phone, and he answered it, and she began asking lots of questions about how he received my phone, how he knew me, and the like. In his "defense" of me, Derrick did not answer these questions, sparking a 14-year war between him and my mother and earning him the name "that boy," which my mother referred to him as from that time forward. On the other hand, my mother recounts that Derrick called her from my phone asking which dorm room I was in because I left my phone in his car; at that point, she began "asking all the questions" because I had not yet told her anything about Derrick or my dealing with him at that point. She said he refused to answer the questions, and she refused to give him my dorm room information for obvious safety reasons. Ever since that day, I was in the middle of a feud that became even bigger in February 2020 when my mother helped me leave Georgia after finding out about Derrick's "eleven" admitted affair partners.

Over the years, the beef between them grew and will be unraveled in these pages throughout the series. I handled this situation early on by creating distance between my mother and me. I took on having beef with her to defend my adulthood and make my own decisions. However, if you let Derrick tell it, this never happened over the 14-year relationship, and I've always chosen my mother over him. I learned from this experience that there is a healthy balance of making your own decisions as an adult with healthy boundaries and pushing away valid concerns and words of wisdom from people who care and love you. A few days after this rift, Derrick and I found ourselves in the Union, sitting on the couch, chatting, and watching others play recreational games. Jasmine, one of the girls Derrick had been dealing with when we met, saw us and was very upset, walking up to us and requesting to speak to him. He got up and went with her; after about 15-20 minutes, he returned and sat down as if nothing had ever happened. I looked at him and asked, 'What was that about" he said, "I was dealing with her before we met, ended it, but she doesn't want to let go; I took care of it." Jazmine is not only a real person that is the third party to the original *A Cheating Man's Heart* "fiction" trilogy, but her character in the original text is also a cover for the hundreds of women Derrick has dealt with mentally, emotionally and sexually over the 14 years that I was in a relationship with him. Jazmyn's character in Derrick's version of the *Cheating Man's Heart* series changes depending on the women in the Rolodex when each novel is written.

Since I am starting in the beginning, about the first of Derrick's trilogy, the women that make up the identity of Jaz are Jazmine, Dunnie, Iman, Jade, Christina, Daysha, Megan, Latrece, Kirsten, Desiree, Januar, Ciera, Rochelle, Nikki, Kirsten E., and a host of other women who would fill the rest of this chapter if I continued to list them. It was with the women listed that Narcissistic triangulation began as Derrick and I had a conflict, and one of these hitters would be right there to pick up his broken and damaged heart, fulfilling an emotional need that I never met, according to his addiction to go back to them year after year. What I learned from this is that Derrick has a massive wound of rejection, abandonment, and neglect dished out by his absent Jamaican father and his New York bread mother, who was using cocaine during her nine-month pregnancy down to the day he was born. According to Frank and Ida Mae Hammonds, *A Manual for Children's Deliverance*, addictive drugs used by the mother pass right through the placenta into the baby. Therefore, a baby can be born with fears and insecurities through the parents as demon spirits gain legal rights to the child while in the mother's womb. It is helpful to keep in mind that demons establish themselves in an individual's life in a systematic and organized way.

In every situation, one is dealing with a network of spirits with a "strong man" in charge. A ruler's spirit is at the root of the problem.[2] In Derrick's case, the strong man and ruler spirits entered him in his mother's womb from the inherited generational taproot of both parents' decision-making from conception. Enlighted by the wisdom of Frank and Ida Mae Hammond's deliverance ministry, I have a level of compassion for Derrick because of the inherited demons passed from his parents in the womb, which have engrained themselves so much into his DNA and personality that he and those who are not awake in Christ cannot make a separation between the demons that he has come into agreement with and the spirit our heavenly Father created. The demons in Derrick that are operating in him and influencing his sexual appetite to devour women with his sexual attraction have become strong men and rulers because they have been able to inhabit his body from conception to the present day. I have learned the significance of Ephesians 6:32 command with this understanding, which calls us to be kind to one another, tenderhearted, and forgiving one another, even as God in Christ forgave you is the key to freedom from hell and destruction that I have gone through in the relationship with Derrick.

Derrick's addiction to women and his choice of drugs like alcohol, sex pills, and other recreational pills of molly and ecstasy seemed to increase when he would be triggered and spin off into his own destructive pattern of behavior, leaving me crushed again as he ran through women to fill the void left by his parents. The void is deep and wide, unraveling another layer of unhealed rejection, being the time Derrick's mother chose another man over nurturing him when he was six years old and really needed her to be there for him emotionally. Instead, she chose to be with her man at that time. This incident is rooted in the unconscious hate that Derrick has for women and why he finds comfort in soothing between the legs of many women in hopes of filling this void of emotional rejection and abandonment dealt by this blow in his youth. Another major problem rooted in his early childhood trauma that he often would project onto me is choosing another man over him, whether it was a Pastor, friend, or acquaintance. Contempt and rage would fill his heart, thoughts, and dreams, and all kinds of accusations would be hurled at me, beating me down mentally, emotionally, and spiritually until I would spin off into my own pattern of destructive behavior. I later learned that this is a narcissistic tactic used to gain control and keep the person on the receiving end bonded to the person, also known as a trauma bond. And like clockwork, the second I started down my own path of destruction with lying and manipulation, Derrick would begin showering me with gifts and practicing giving me "more" uninterrupted quality time, giving me tidbits of motivational and encouraging advice, all of which I would reject spinning him back into a cycle of soothing in-between the legs of another woman.

The cycle continued for fourteen full years of our relationship, with the last two of those years being educational years in which I became aware of the demonic cycle and began working on learning my triggers and what pulled me into a destructive pattern of behavior. The first step to breaking the stronghold of demonic cycles and patterns in my relationship was asking myself why specific actions, words, non-verbal cues, and lack of action bothered me so much? I must admit while asking this question, I did not seek the answer first from the Holy Spirit; I would be asking the question while simultaneously complaining to my mother, her best friend Tabitha, and Tabitha's mother, Marcella, along with anyone else who would take the time to listen to what I had to say. In fact, in the beginning, I wasn't even in a place to assess my own "vulnerability inventory" or "resentment/childhood trauma vulnerability inventory" (Teahan)[3] to gain clarity on my role in allowing such spiritual destruction to stay in my life for over a decade. What I know now after practicing healing God's way for the last three years and continuing with healing after divorce is that I idolized the idea of having a marriage, and my expectations were higher for Derrick as a man than they were in God as Author and Finisher of my faith.

Acknowledging this was the first step to healing the untouchable soul pain that I felt a few short days after learning publicly that Derrick had been having affairs again based on his inaccurate statement announcing our divorce on his social media. In the time I spent in silence on social media writing this book and watching the ruthless media wolves gnashing at the teeth to get the scoop on what I am doing and feeling, it's been revealed to me my story is familiar to women around the world who are suffering and battling the same demons while "trying to make it work" because they want to save their marriages and relationships. Still, their soul has an indescribable pain they don't know how to fix. Revelation struck me as a new infilling of the anointing has rested upon me in a new way, allowing the Lord to reestablish me as a leader in the body of Christ for my generation to lead by example how to heal and *Survive A Cheating Man's Heart* in these last days.

As I shed the old wineskin and step into the new, I'm reminded of the classic quote of the late Dr. Maya Angelou that says, "Each time a woman stands up for herself, without knowing it possibly, without claiming it, she stands up for all women." Therefore, I arise and shine, accepting a greater portion of the anointing and standing up for all women who are experiencing the same thing privately that I'm experiencing publicly and globally. As Moses was called by God to lead the Israelites out of Egypt into the promised land, so have I been charged to lead the women around the world out of "A *Cheating Man's Heart*," which is the modern-day Egypt enslaving the daughters of the Most High God. Get ready; this is our exodus.

Chapter One:
Young Love

The Lord has been witness between the cheating man, his heart, and the wife of his youth (Mal2:14). Therefore, nothing is secret that will not be revealed, nor anything hidden that will not be known and come to light. I had to learn this by going through the fire of the cheating scandals and recognizing that they were indeed secret and hidden things the Lord revealed to me after much prayer and supplication. A key takeaway that I impart to you is that when the Lord gives you the answer to your prayer, recognize it, give thanks to Him for the answer, and submit to Him the pain of the answer, especially if it ends up being the outcome of divorce caused by adultery and leading to personality conflicts that are no longer able to be resolved. *A Cheating Man's Heart* is rigged with all kinds of trapped doors and snares ready to entangle everyone who agrees with the deception of exuberant charm radiated by the man. Once a person comes into agreement with the lies running in the unfaithful consciousness of a man's heart, they become a slave to them mentally, emotionally, and physically, forming a negative soul tie that is impossible to break without the power of the Holy Spirit and the authority of the blood of Jesus.

The amplified version of Romans 6:16 says, *"Do you not know that when you continually offer yourselves to someone to do his will, you are the slaves of the one whom you obey, either [slaves] of sin, which leads to death, or of obedience, which leads to righteousness (right standing with God)?* In this passage, the answer is revealed to us concerning the sin cycle of the chronic unfaithfulness of a man and the chronic addiction of the woman who stays regardless of how much she may want to leave or even has left but comes back. We were all born into sin because of Adam and Eve's mistakes. To sin means to miss the mark or to trespass, but the type of sin that causes enslavement is bigger than just missing the mark. Sin cycles are categorized as iniquity. Iniquity is when you know that what you are doing is a sin, but you won't or can't stop it. Many Christians confess their belief in Jesus Christ and claim to follow Him, but they are still enslaved to sin cycles. When Christ died on the cross, He eliminated the power that sin had over us. Any time you find a believer who has fasted, prayed, and cried out to God but can't seem to be separated from a particular sin, you will find a demon at work.[4]

Derrick is the perfect example of a slave to sexual sin with repetitive adultery as he has presented himself to profess that he became a born-again Christian on February 4th, 2020. However, since that time, he has struggled the same way he did in the earlier years of our relationship with letting go of women who were more than just friends. In fact, several months leading up to the divorce, he stated to me directly and in front of spiritual and secular counsel that he didn't understand why he had to give up all the women, but I didn't have to give up my mother. Later in this series, this complaint will be unpacked more. However, this consistent complaint over the two-year attempt to reconcile is the perfect example of oppression rooted in unforgiveness and manifested in a pattern of repetitive and senseless acts of adultery in which Derrick has become a slave. This thought process can be difficult to overcome without the Ministry of Deliverance, followed by therapy to help retrain the thought life of a person. There is an open door to the kingdom of darkness to the soul of the man with unfaithfulness in his heart that must be shut.

Cheating is not a natural world-only thing; the spiritual component weighs heavily in the sin cycle of men and women who are filled with the lust of the eyes and flesh. Once a cheater, always a cheater is an adage that's repeated among the old, middle-aged, and young people of this generation; however, that is not entirely correct. Infidelity, cheating, adultery, whichever word you choose to use, is a sin cycle caused by addiction. Proverbs 25:28 calls it out this way: *"Whoever has no rule over his own spirit is like a city broken down, without walls."* A chronic cheater is an infidel, and much like the snake that deceived Eve in the garden of Eden, they are craftier than any other person the Lord God has made. The craftiness of an unfaithful heart is not limited to infidels; it also has a reach within the religious communities, which is why we see several pastors' men and women of God who know the word as it relates to sexual immorality, but their private lives are not aligned with the word, therefore, opening the door to infidelity in the church. When you combine oppression and sin cycles, you get an addiction. Any form of addiction is tied to a very strong demonic influence. The American Heritage Dictionary describes addiction as a compulsive physical or mental need for habit-forming substances, activities, or experiences. Addiction is also characterized by a behavior performed in response to an obsession. Here is a list of common addictions that can be broken through the power of deliverance.

1. Substance: alcohol, heroin, tobacco, solvents, cocaine, crack, cannabis, caffeine, steroids, tranquilizers, hallucinogens, amphetamines, ecstasy, painkillers, barbiturates, etc.

2. Social: Overexercising, sex, sexual perversions, pornography, eating disorders (anorexia, bulimia, overeating), techno-addictions (computer games, cybersex), work, gambling, etc.[5]

Derrick's addiction from the beginning of our tumultuous relationship has been over-exercising, sex, sexual perversion, pornography, cybersex, and social drugs like ecstasy, sex pills, and the like. I did not understand or even want to understand this harsh truth for twelve years. However, knowing what I know now, it all makes sense. Remember, I spoke about the bitter roots and satanic deposits of Derrick's childhood. Martha, his mother, had an addiction to cocaine and used the full length of her pregnancy with Derrick, with her last day being the day that he was born, according to what Derrick knows about his birth. The demon of addiction transferred into Derrick in the womb due to his mother's personal sin and addiction to a substance. Undetected due to a lack of knowledge (Hos 4:6), the demon of addiction intertwined itself into the personality and moral compass of the man we know today as Derrick Jaxn, becoming a stronghold that keeps him in a sin cycle of reckless sex at the expense of other people's feelings and emotions.

And this is the danger and result of unhealed generational curses and tap roots. The same demon of addiction manifested itself in different ways in two distinctly different people in the same family because they made the mistake of thinking that because the addiction to cocaine stopped, Derrick's mother overcame it when, in reality, the demon has been lying dormant and made itself manifest in her offspring in a different way which created the cheating man's heart in my life. Demons don't just leave; they have to be cast out, and if they are not cast out, they are still there, destroying whole families. It doesn't stop there; this demon of addiction hiding at the root of Derrick's chronic unfaithfulness also manifested itself in his sisters. One of them is the sister closest to him in age, Yonnie, who became the mistress in the marriage of a deacon in their enterprise Alabama hometown. The addiction in this snapshot of Yonnie's life manifested as she dealt with, waited for, and slept with this deacon who was married, resulting in her not being able to move forward with her life for over 10 years waiting for this man to leave his wife. He did not leave his wife in the time of her waiting, hoping, and wishing, but she would ruminate on their interactions and try to make sense of them, leaving her addicted to what could and should have been. But God does not give you someone else's husband. Are you able to see the pattern?

Moreover, the Bible says that *we do not wrestle against flesh and blood, but against principalities, against powers, against the rulers of the darkness of this world, and against spiritual wickedness in high places* (Eph 6:12). The attack is in the mind, the values, the beliefs, and culture of all families on the earth and it takes someone in the family to wake up and become aware of these cycles so they can break these generational curses. Derrick's mother stopping her need to shoot up coke did not get rid of the demon of addiction; her will to stop allowed her to stop and move forward in that area of her life, but the demon has legal rights to the family because it has not been cast out. Anytime you are dealing with repeated unfaithfulness, you're dealing with a demonic presence, and demons don't leave on their own. You must take the authority of Jesus and cast the devil out of your life and your family's lives.

The challenge to this is that you must have willing participants who acknowledge that demons are real entities that can inhabit the bodies of people and that there are demons at play in them or in the family bloodline. 1 John 2:4 says, *He who says, "I know Him," and does not keep His commandments, is a liar, and the truth is not in him.* As to Derricks claim to know Him the Father, Son and the Holy Spirit I didn't believe that he really had an encounter with the Holy Spirit to help Him to change. How things played out with his decision to divorce me and the public spectacle he made with the other women it's hard to say that this is not a true theory. However, as someone who did not believe in Jesus, have knowledge or understanding about demons before February 4th 2020 I've reconsidered my unbelief and outward expression of that unbelief of his salvation which I believe hindered his ability to grow in that area so that the seed of faith and hope in salvation could take root and produce fruit of the spirit.

Death and life are in the power of the tongue, and those who love it will eat its fruit (Prov 18:21). What I learned is that everything that comes to my mind based on what I've observed or sense does not need to be said out loud and when I learned to submit my concerns , observations and senses to the Holy Spirit concerning Derrick's path to righteousness, He sharpened my discernment and revealed more to me about what I should do and how I should do it to preserve the dignity of Derrick, which I did not do in the beginning. I stayed in the two-year attempt at reconciliation because I loved the man Derrick more than I loved God and I had more belief that something miraculous could happen in our marriage and was encouraged by spiritual counsel to weather the storm. However, even spiritual counsel was limited to all the ins and outs of fourteen years of turmoil and cycles between Derrick and I except for what the Lord revealed to them directly about the situation.

Bitter roots if not dealt with *defile a man because it will spill out of him and as a result it will defile many* (Heb 12:15). It is important that I assert very clearly that there is a difference between the person and soul that God the Father created in Derrick and his family and the demonic presence operating within Derrick and his family. Derrick and his family are not demons; however, they are oppressed by demons that need to be cast out by the power of the Holy Spirit. Ignorance and refusal to acknowledge the truth of the spiritual component of infidelity and bitter roots is a deadly mistake that we have been making for generations. Derrick and I's story is no different, but what is different is the choosing to seek and understand how the demonic forces play a significant role, understanding that we are not wrestling after flesh which eliminates the natural urge to blame and shame while moving forward in life through forgiveness which is not contingent on a restored relationship.

Two Sides to Every Coin

He who is without sin cast the first stone (Jn 8:27). Before I get too far ahead of myself with unraveling the toxicity of my infamous marriage, I must take a deep dive into my family's bitter roots and demonic strongholds. Yes, my family has demons, and so did I until I went through the process of Healing God's Way by taking my bloodline demons to the courts of heaven. Since God is a just God, He is not partial to one over the other, so I must examine myself (2 Cor13:5) and my family's hidden secrets for the purpose of teaching, rebuking, correcting, and training in righteousness concerning how to *Survive a Cheating Man's Heart* (2 Tim3:16-17).

I will begin with my parents, Leslie and A'Nedria, who conceived me as teenagers who were supposed to be playing video games instead of having premarital sex. All of this took place on March 23rd, 1989, during spring break, according to my mom, and nine months later, I came into the world as a Christmas gift to my father. I say this literally as my father was not present at the time I was born but came hours later with my two uncles, Kris, and Reggie. According to my mother, the conversation upon his arrival consisted of my dad's first words being, "I just wanted to see how you and the baby are doing," and my mother's response was, "nigga you just came to see if she looks like you."

Let us fast-forward and note a pattern at the births of my son and my third child, who look more like me than Derrick. Ironic or not, a similar expression to my mother's response to my father flew out of my mouth with the births of my last two children with a question or doubt as to their paternity raised by their father? I will go deeper into this later in the text. Apparently, while they were exchanging these words, my uncle Kris was looking at me, picked me up, and then handed me to my father. At that point, it is noted that my father's words upon looking at me were, "She's white; she looks Spanish. Are you sure this is the right kid?" My mom recalls my uncle Reggie saying she is white, but she looks just like Janay. Janay is my older cousin, the daughter of my dad's older brother Clifton.

At this point, my dad had not yet told his mother about me, though he anticipated my birth all nine months, which had now come. Again, I was a Christmas gift, literally, so he took me to his mother on Christmas day just four short days after my birth, in my car seat, which had a blanket covering me, sat me down in front of his mother, and said, "Merry Christmas."

She said, "What?"

He said, "Merry Christmas".

In perfect timing, I began crying; she pulled off the cover and said, "Whose baby is this?"

And my dad said, "mines."

My grandma Broadus then had my dad call my mother so she could speak to her, and her first words were, "why aren't you here right now with your baby?"

Let us rewind even further to the nine months of my being in my mother's womb before being born into the world. After the "hit it" and "quit it" situation between my parents, my mother walked away from the experience immediately, having thought she was pregnant but dismissed it. Roughly three weeks later, on her 16th birthday in April, she was having morning sickness and vomiting everything that she consumed. Approximately a week after that, my mother found herself in Strasburg, Colorado, in a thrift store with my grandmother Gertha and her mother Lela. At the thrift store, she saw this twin-size comforter that was purple with hearts all over it, which she asked my grandmother to get for her. Immediately after seeing the comforter, she looks and sees an early pregnancy test on the shelf. My mother recalls grabbing it and stuffing it in the comforter, thinking my grandmother would buy it immediately so she could see if she was pregnant. However, my grandmother put it on layaway and told my mom she would get it out in mid-May. When mid-May came around, my grandmother paid off the comforter and gave it to my mom. My mom then took the comforter in her room, took out the EPT, and went to the bathroom to take the test. The results of the test revealed PREGNANT with a deep pink plus on it, which was undeniable confirmation that she was with child, but she still could not believe it, though she was sick as a dog, so she dismissed it. She then had to smuggle everything out because she could not just leave it in the trash to be discovered by my grandmother or one of her five siblings who would rat her out.

Let us pause here and examine my mother's behavior in this situation from the beginning.

1. My mother broke God's law by having pre-marital sex with my dad, who was equally as guilty of this sexual sin.

2. My mother was in complete denial for the first 3-4 months of my gestational age, which led her to break the eighth commandment by stealing an EPT that she stuffed in a comforter that was purchased by my grandmother.

3. My mother dismissed the signs and symptoms of pregnancy, though she took an early pregnancy test, which revealed a deep pink dark plus sign, indicating a positive pregnancy test.

On the surface, it seems like these details are trivial, or that I am just babbling about something irrelevant to why you really bought this book as it relates to my infamous marriage. However, all these details are bitter roots that contributed to me staying bound to a man who struggled with a cheating heart for fourteen years. Bloodline and generational curses influenced my life just like they influenced everyone else, regardless of whether I was aware of it or not. In my case, I was not aware of it until the marriage was over.

All Christians need to understand the spiritual impact of bloodline and generational curses and their effect on everyone in the family regardless of whether any one family member is known or has met others in the family. Abraham, the father of faith (Rom 4:16), is the best biblical reference for my life story's spiritual impact and relevance. In Genesis 20:2-12 it is recorded that Abraham lies by saying that Sarah is his sister out of fear for his life, when in fact she was his wife. Isaac, the son of the covenant promise that God made with Abraham birthed through his wife Sarah (Gen 18), then lies by saying that Rebecca is his sister out of fear for his life, when in fact she was his wife (Gen 26:8-9). Jacob, son of Isaac and grandson of Abraham, then deceives his twin brother Esau into giving up his birthright and lies to his father Isaac on his deathbed about being his brother Esau in order to receive the firstborn inheritance right (Gen 27). Do you see the pattern?

Father, son, and grandson all had a problem with lying. Abraham and Isaac committed the same lie several years in between each other. Jacob lied, but the form of his lie looked different because his lie involved his brother and father and was not a romantic partner like his father and grandfather. The spiritual impact is that if the father does not repent, renounce, and announce an agreement with the truth of God's word, the son will battle the same demon. Likewise, suppose the son does not repent, renounce, and announce agreement with the truth of God's word. In that case, his son will battle that same demon; though the manifestation of that demon may have transformed and is operating in a different set of circumstances in the son's life, the behavior is the same.

Derrick's family and my family are no different, and each of us, blind to the bitter roots and generational taproot of our families, willingly engaged in a relationship turned situationship turned marriage. Exposing these bitter roots reveal foundational cracks in the character, integrity, and intent of the heart of each person in the marriage. Since I am using my life as a training ground, I am exposing foundational problems in myself and Derrick, which was one contributor to the overall dysfunction and cycle of toxicity in the relationship from start to finish. Do not confuse this contributing factor with the justification of Derrick or my personal and individual decision-making in the failed marriage. The bitter roots simply serve as findings worthy to be noted as a factor leading to the cause of death of my marriage through this written autopsy.

In other words, there was something wrong with how the marriage was built. Pastor James Morris of Gateway Church said it best in a collaborative sermon series with his father, Robert Morris, who called Jesus at the center when he said, "It needed to be broken." Pastor James goes on to say, "Not all brokenness is a bad thing, and not everything that breaks in our lives is a bad thing. God can use brokenness to work something out of us."[6] I had several things that needed to be worked out of me during the public breaking of my marriage through the cheating scandals that went viral around the world. In other words, God removed the *dross from silver and was able to produce a vessel to set the captives free* (Prov 25:4). The Amplified Bible says it another way in Job 23:10 *But He knew the way that I took [and He paid attention to it]. When He tried me, I came forth as [refined] gold [pure and luminous].*

My marriage and relationship with the self-love ambassador Derrick Jaxn needed to be broken, and it was not a bad thing. In fact, it was the ultimate test of my faith (Deut 8:2-3). The bitter roots shared thus far about Derrick and my life paint a picture and provide a reason why God needed the marriage to be broken. Matthew 21:42-44 supports what I mean when I say God needed the marriage to be broken. Jesus says to the chief priests and the teachers of the law in verse forty-two, *"Have you never read in the Scriptures: "The stone the builders rejected has become the cornerstone; the Lord has done this, and it is marvelous in our eyes?* Jesus goes on to say in verse forty-three *Therefore, I tell you that the kingdom of God will be taken away from you and given to a people who will produce its fruit.* My marriage was not producing any fruit worthy of the kingdom of God. In fact, it was continuously producing bad fruit as the bitter roots of Derrick and myself had not been individually and collectively examined to be plucked out and replaced with good fruit. Due to this, no matter how much good seed was planted into the restoration process of our marriage by ministers, the tree of our marriage could not produce good fruit because *bad trees cannot bear good fruit* (Matt 7:18). Here is where Matthew 21:44 comes into play when it says, *"Anyone who falls on this stone will be BROKEN to pieces; anyone on whom it falls will be crushed."* While I was hard-pressed on every side and suffered much loss, I was not personally crushed by public scandal, though I was broken (2 Cor4), my marriage was crushed because it was not built on the rock. And we did not agree to rebuild it on the firm foundation.

All of this completely shatters and goes against the doctrine and theology that says God hates divorce, in which Malachi 2:16 is used to keep marriages together. Even the toxic and horizontally cracked-in-foundation marriages like mine. Do not hear what I did not say! God loves and honors marriage His way, but when the foundation of that marriage is built on sand and not on solid rock, the marriage falls and crashes hard like mine (Matt 7:24-26). This is where I step up and advocate that ministers MUST care for each individual person in mind, body, soul, and spirit before trying to repair a faulty marriage. Suppose we continue to minister according to the traditions of men. In that case, we will miss the signs and symptoms of emotional, psychological, and physical abuse, which often occur when you are dealing with *A Cheating Man's Hea*rt.

SURVIVING A CHEATING MAN'S HEART

Trauma-informed care, which I advocate and argue needs to be added to the ministry programs in every local church, is critical in the spiritual formation of the traumatized believer.[7] Women entangled in the dark vessels of *A Cheating Man's Heart* are traumatized. The only way out of the dark chambers of this heart is through the wounds and trauma of Jesus Christ. When a woman or man can study the toxicity of their relationship thoroughly using a timeline of events that led up to the toxic union, along with studying their trauma and various responses to the trauma, they engage in the hard work of wrestling with the complexity of Jesus Christ's suffering on the cross for our sins [8]. It is in this space where victims are transformed into survivors by the power of the Holy Spirit, who is the only one who can perform this heart, mind, body, soul, and spirit transplant. This is why I am exposing the two sides to the coin in my failed marriage that has captured the attention of millions around the world.

Simply, being alive after such trauma that has played out publicly does not make me a survivor. I was made a survivor going through the transformation process of identifying and acknowledging my toxicity, Derricks's toxicity, and the toxicity from which we came in our bloodlines. I then had a road to Damascus encounter with the one true living God (Ac 9:1-9), and you do too if you want to survive *A Cheating Man's Heart* with all your mental faculties intact.

Clinical Psychologist Diane Langberg explains the spiritual impact of trauma like cheating on a person as being so significant because the messages received through the trauma are about the identity of the person who has experienced the life-threatening event and, therefore, the identity of God whom the offender(s) represent to the victim. In the case of a wife who is chronically cheated on by her husband, like I have been, personal identity becomes even more confused when you add in the subtleties of psychological and emotional abuse. I had no idea what any of these terms were or that they even existed throughout the

66666

majority of my tumultuous relationship with Derrick. However, as I began the healing process in 2020, during the 8 months I spent on my mother's couch, I began to learn and see clearly that I was not only dealing with the heart of a cheating man but also a man who suffers from toxic entitlement.

Toxic entitlement is at the core of oppression. I was in an oppressive relationship, and marriage and bitter roots played a part in the overall toxicity. Oppression means an unjust or cruel exercise of authority or power; something that oppresses, especially in being an unjust or excessive exercise of power; a sense of being weighed down in body or mind, according to Merriam-Webster Dictionary. Men who suffer from toxic entitlement oppress their relationship partners over time until they begin seeing the signs and symptoms of the woman being weighed down in mind and body. In my case, my mind and body were affected as I reached my heaviest weight of 273 lbs., and my mind needed so much help that I solicited the services of three clinical therapists just to stay sane in 2017. But how could I stay stuck in this cycle of toxicity for so long? Well, we must continue peeling back the layers of the bitter roots from which I came.

Dr. Simpson's office is where my mother ended up after weeks of being physically ill, which was now noticeable to the entire family. Sitting in the patient's room with my head in the waste basket, vomiting, my mother was able to get a few seconds' worth of break as Dr. Simpson walked in the room carrying what appeared to be a pill. A deep baritone voice filled the room as Dr. Simpson reached out his aged and wrinkly hand towards my mother, saying, "Here, this should help with nausea. Ignorant to the Doctor's order, my mother took the pill, tramadol. Tramadol is a pill that will cause a woman to abort a baby. Immediately after taking the pill an uneasiness and feeling of death fell upon my mother. The discomfort from the shadow of death (Psa23:4) hovering over her made her so uncomfortable it prompted her to go to the library to read about the drug. What she found sent panic, terror, and rage like violent waves crashing on the seashore in the middle of the storm through my mother's body. Abortion, birth defects, and adverse reactions in babies flooded the page concerning taking tramadol in early pregnancy. Without any further hesitation my mother jammed her index finger down her throat to invoke vomiting in the middle of the library medical book section. Upon the third upheaval, the oblong tramadol pill was spotted amongst the debris, which relieved my mother. Even after all of this drama, my mother still had the nerve to be in denial about being pregnant. Yes, I know it makes no logical sense that there was any confusion concerning her carrying life at this point.

Again, I want to interject by pointing out a pattern in toxic thinking that plagues the traumatized mind. Please note that my mother was still in denial of being pregnant after:

1. Taking an early pregnancy test that revealed a dark pink plus sign confirming a positive pregnancy.

2. Experiencing consistent and persistent vomiting and sickness for two months at this point in the timeline of my life. Which also proves that life begins in the womb in the eyes of GOD.

3. She went to great lengths to vomit a pill that would cause birth defects and fetal fatality, though she still refused to acknowledge and accept that she was pregnant.

The Category of Trauma: The word trauma refers to the emotional, spiritual, and psychological disruptions that occur when a person is overwhelmed by extreme suffering. Their relationships with God and others are often significantly impacted by what happened. People use the word traumatized to describe a person severely affected by a terrible event such as rape, a natural disaster, or a car accident. An event rises to the level of a traumatic experience when it is sudden and unpredictable, involves a threat to life, or profound violation of trust. Adolescent pregnancy falls under the category of being sudden and involving a threat to life as adolescent mothers (aged 10-19 years) face higher risks of eclampsia, puerperal endometritis, and systemic infections than women aged 20-24 years, and babies of adolescent mothers face higher risks of low birth weight, preterm birth, and severe neonatal condition.[9]

According to the American Association of Christian Counselors training course Youth Mental Health 201: Childhood Trauma and Adverse Childhood Experiences, trauma is an overwhelming event or experience that exceeds one's capacity to cope. The impact of childhood trauma experiences, which teen pregnancy falls under, is that which produces lasting and disintegrating effects on the mind and body. I add to this by stating it also affects the soul and spirit of a person. Since trauma is an event that overwhelms the emotions of a person, you have to be able to tolerate a certain level of emotion for trauma not to be so devastating.

Research shows that the older you are, trauma will tend to have a lesser effect than if you are a child or adolescent in a younger developmental phase. Age and developmental phases are critical when you're talking about trauma. Children and Adolescents are at much greater risk of developing long-term post-traumatic effects to the same type of trauma that an adult does because their brains are not completely formed yet, and they do not have the mental capacity to cope or understand what is happening. Your challenge as a reader is to confront your personal beliefs about what a teenager or adolescent can cope with regardless of their personal decision to engage in pre-marital sex or what they understand when it comes to the trauma of teen pregnancy. Does your personal belief trump the findings of the clinical professional and mental health science research provided by the American Association of Christian Counselors on Youth Mental Health?

While, to a degree, there is a basic understanding that if you have sex, you run the risk of getting pregnant, it does not change or negate the sudden life-threatening and life-changing reality that comes when a child is conceived in the womb of another child. Understanding this reality of trauma does not justify or dismiss the personal accountability for the poor decision-making that transpired between my parents, who were teens. Nor does it justify or dismiss Derricks or my poor personal decision-making when we conceived our first and second child out of wedlock, though our second child was born in wedlock.

Understanding secular literature on trauma sharpens observations and descriptions in our evaluations of relationships and marriages like mine, along with the complexities and various ways in which trauma affects a person reaching back to their childhood.[10] In my case, Derrick's case and the cases of our parents we all had various effects of trauma passed down from one generation to another. Research shows that for trauma not to be so devastating to the psyche of a person, the measure of trauma that they are able to cope with must be within their mental and emotional capacity. Anything above that is too much and results in a cycle of trauma responses, which includes dissociation.[11] Dissociation is a mental process that causes a lack of connection in a person's thoughts, memory, and sense of identity.[12] Going back to my mother's consistent and persistent denial and dismissal of being pregnant, it becomes apparent that the news of her carrying me in her womb exceeded the measure of trauma she was able to cope with thus making it too much and resulting in a cycle of denial and dismissal of the reality of her situation.

It is vital that we, as believers in Christ Jesus, stop looking at teen pregnancies and cheating scandals like normal everyday occurrences, with discussions saying that those who are involved should just get over it or judge the situation based on their lack of better decision-making. Understanding victim blaming and why it's harmful to victims and survivors must then be addressed. When someone speaks out publicly about personal experiences of violence or abuse or a high-profile case is covered in the media, similar comments and responses come up time and time again. These include.

"Well, they should have left the relationship sooner."

"What did they expect, walking home alone at night?"

"They probably shouldn't have drunk so much."

"But what were they wearing?"

"She deserved him cheating on her. Look at how she looks."

"I see why he cheated on her."

These are all examples of victim blaming. What is victim blaming? Victim blaming is any response that explicitly states or implies that the victim is to blame for the abuse they have experienced. Cheating on a person is psychological, emotional, and physical abuse. Like the examples above, victim blaming often revolves around actions that a victim could have taken (or not taken) to avoid experiencing abuse. In reality, violence and abuse will happen regardless of the victim's choices. Whether intentional or unintentional, victim blaming can cause serious harm to people who have victim mentalities and survivor mentalities, leaving them feeling responsible for their abuser's actions, therefore increasing feelings of shame and guilt.[13]

The scars left from trauma in its various forms, which include victim blaming, are not just physical. Experiencing emotional, physical, sexual, and betrayal trauma can have long-term psychological impacts on a person, including self-doubt and low self-esteem. This is why a supportive response to a disclosure of trauma or abuse in all its various forms is so important. However, the key and foundational response to these disclosures is leaning on the truth of God's word that He is closest to those who are brokenhearted and in a contrite spirit. Victim blamers are no different than the abusers themselves, and often, they are just as dangerous to the psyche of those around them because they do not see or hear the subtle abuse that comes with speaking on issues that produce real trauma in the lives of people regardless of their personal decision making. One of the greatest barriers to seeking help for traumas such as abuse, rape, teen pregnancy, betrayal trauma, and other traumas is the victim feeling they are to blame for what has happened to them. When people speak or behave in ways that reinforce this feeling of self-blame, the impact of the abuse may be greater, leading to a longer recovery.[14]

The curiosity that surrounds my marriage, its betrayals, and symptoms of abuse sparks the question, if Derrick was such a bad person, why didn't I leave him earlier? Often, this question is followed by victim-blaming statements that dismiss, devalue, and degrade me as being nothing more than a hopeless, helpless, conniving woman who helped her husband successfully deceive the world on the topics of healthy and loving relationships and marriage. All this commentary, along with similar schools of thought, generally leads a person experiencing this type of trauma to a longer healing recovery time. However, in my case, the recovery time was dramatically shortened, and thoroughly healed by the power of the Holy Spirit. John 15:15 makes it very clear that Jesus Christ of Nazareth *is the vine, and we are the branches. If we remain in Him and Him in us, we will bear much fruit; apart from Him, we can do nothing.* I've lived, breathed, and clung (Rth 1:14) to this life-giving word before, during, and after the public scandal. The active and living word (Heb 4:12) from this scripture also makes up the foundational components of the **HELMET of SALVATION** (Eph 6:17).

How did I access this accelerated healing and deliverance by the power of the Holy Spirit? The Apostle Paul articulated it best under the inspiration of the Holy Spirit when he said *for, we are co-workers together with God* (1 Cor3:9). The Holy Spirit didn't just heal me in mind, body, soul, and spirit because I believed alone that by His stripes I am healed (Isa 53:5). It was through the complex, scary and brutal work of identifying the bitterroots in my life, Derricks life and foundations of my marriage, day and night, week after week, year after year which was my co-laboring work together with the Holy Spirit that accelerated my healing and earned me an extra portion of God's divine wisdom, knowledge and understanding when it comes to healing God's Way after being ensnared by *A Cheating Man's Heart*.

I am not just telling you a portion of my life story just to tell it; I am laying a spiritual blueprint and biblical road map for millions of women and some men to be delivered, healed, and set free from the same bondages that once held me captive. In order to go deeper on this, we must continue to unearth the network of bitterroots that plagued my life, Derrick's life, our marriage, and our family bloodlines, which contributed to a spiritual battle from hell that nearly killed me, him, and our children.

After the encounter with Dr. Simpson, Cousin Jr., my mother's second cousin on her father's side, girlfriend named Brenda, was concerned about how my mom was so sick for weeks and encouraged Cousin Jr. to take my mom to Denver General Hospital (DG). The hospital began to run several tests and took blood and urine samples. After a couple of hours, my grandmother arrived to be with my mother, relieving Cousin Jr. and his girlfriend from duty. The on-call doctor asked my grandma Gertha to leave and told my mom that she had extra oxygen in her blood and that the urine/blood test results showed she was pregnant.

The doctor then says, "Legally, I don't have to tell your parents, but you should tell your parents."

He then asked her if she knew who the father was.

She said, "Leslie K. Broadus."

My grandmother comes back in the room, and my mom blurts out "I'm pregnant" before my grandmother can get her left foot fully over the threshold of the door.

My grandmother replies, "Well, you are going to tell your father."

My mom nonchalantly says, "That's fine, but I am not telling my momma."

Now, my grandmother, Gertha, is my mom's stepmother, who loved her and cared for her as if she were her own, and my mom's biological mother is Linda Faye, who was previously married to my grandfather.

Immediately after the doctor left the room and my grandmother was told of my being in the womb, my mother called my father and told him. By this time, she was nearly 4 months pregnant with me and showed no baby bump.

His first words were, "Is it mine?".

Fast forward to when I found out I was pregnant for the first time by Derrick at 19 years old and told him, his first words to me were, "Is it mine?" I will unpack this further, but these words are essential to note here.

Back to my father's response to my mother, "Is it mine?"

As the story goes, according to my mother, he followed that statement arrogantly by saying, "I knew you would be because it was just too good."

In a snappy reply, my mom replied to my dad, "When she comes, you can get a paternity test."

Silence fell over the phone line. However, a perceived glare glossed my father's face, which could have been felt through the phone by my mom. Continuing the story, my dad then tells my uncle Kris, who went to my mom at school the next day and said, "Are you seriously pregnant."

Irritated, she said, "Yes."

At school in the days following, my dad didn't say anything to my mom. He tried to stay far away from her but couldn't avoid her in every area because she was the basketball manager, and my dad was on the basketball team. Les, my father, like many others, did what most other teen boys do when a girl is knocked up and claims it is his baby; he surrounded himself with other girls, one in particular whose name is Lashaundra, and pretended my mom didn't even exist.

I must interject here with teaching, correcting, and rebuking regarding these interpersonal transactions between my teen parents that impacted my view on love and relationships, which ultimately showed up in my marriage. I learned toxicity in the womb before I was even born through the emotional disruptions, dissociation, dismissiveness, avoidance, and contemptuous speech that took place between my teen mother and father. Again, teen pregnancy is a traumatic experience. Both of my parents experienced this trauma in their adolescent developmental phase, producing traumatic effects that completely and

SURVIVING A CHEATING MAN'S HEART

suddenly shattered the vision my parents had for their lives. My father's avoidant and anxious attachment style ultimately transferred to me and became full grown, well, and living in my life when he died when I was twelve years old. When we see someone who has endured trauma like me and my teen parents, we really have to watch and sense how they are individually coping with it.[15]

Remember what I've disclosed so far about my parents' interactions while I was still in the womb in the first 4 months of gestation? Track with me how each of my parents was coping with the traumatic experience of teen pregnancy.

Let us revisit my mother again:

1. She denied and dismissed the signs, symptoms, and blatant positive EP.

2. She willingly participated in pre-marital sex which breaks God's law and perfect design for sex.

3. She stole the EPT and deceived my grandmother, causing her to sin unknowingly because my mother stuffed an EPT into the comforter at the thrift store.

4. Her responses and actions toward my father became increasingly irritated, snappy, and contemptuous.

5. She displayed signs and symptoms of dissociation, which displayed as a protective mechanism from rejection of my father's questioning of my paternity and his blatant avoidance of her complete existence.

This short list of observations in my mother's response to teen pregnancy shows, from a clinical youth mental health perspective, a negative severe impact that exceeded the trauma threshold or capacity my mom had to cope with teen pregnancy. Resulting in the fracturing of the mind through dissociation. Genetic factors of mental health disorders in the bloodline contribute to this, which I will disclose at a later time. However, it is important to understand that genetic factors increase the negative effects of traumatic experiences that individuals have and how they respond to that trauma, according to the American Association of Christian Counselors professional trauma experts. My father's avoidance and blatant ignoring of my mother's entire existence adds another layer of trauma, otherwise known as complex trauma. Not only is complex trauma a factor here, but specifically little T trauma, which is comprised of upsetting experiences such as divorce, financial difficulties, romantic breakups, and losses. Since my parents were never technically in a romantic relationship, little T trauma best describes the highly disturbing emotional experience displayed in my mother, which reveals her toxic traits that I picked up and carried into my marriage.

Let us now turn our attention to my father and see how he was coping with the trauma of teen pregnancy and fatherhood:

1. Immediately after my mother called him from DG with the news, she was pregnant, he went into avoidant behavior by saying, "Is it mine"?

2. After the initial avoidant response, he immediately followed with arrogance, pride, and puffed-upness by saying, "I knew you would (get pregnant). It was just too good."

3. He went back to his avoidant behavior and added a dismissive component when he blatantly dodged my mom at school as much as he could and pretended, she didn't exist or that he even knew her.

4. He was intentional about being spotted with, flirty, and 'hugged up' with other girls (Lashaundra) when he could no longer avoid my mother's presence.

5. He willingly participated in pre-marital sex breaking God's law and perfect design for sex.

This short list of my father's response to teen pregnancy shows, from a clinical youth mental health perspective, a negative severe impact that exceeded the trauma threshold or capacity my father had to cope with teen pregnancy. Resulting in the fracturing of the mind through dissociation. In my father's case, biological vulnerability was a risk factor as temperamental differences displayed themselves in a cyclical pattern when he went from avoidant, dismissive, arrogant, and back to avoidant behavior. The youth mental health risk factors displayed by both of my parents individually show the inability for both of them to emotionally cope resiliently initially with the trauma of teen pregnancy. Since trauma is an event that overwhelms emotionally, we see a variety of different trauma responses in both of my parents, who are experiencing the same traumatic event.

My parent's responses to trauma affected my life in many ways I had no clue about until the divine wisdom of God through the Holy Spirit pulled me up and out mentally, emotionally, spiritually, and nearly physically space of death. In their book, *A Manual for Children's Deliverance* Frank and Ida Mae Hammond discuss when the womb is unsafe. The Hammonds go on to say, the devil is a strategist." He devises a plot and plan for each person whom he attempts to capture. How early in one's life can he begin to execute his plan? We are convinced that he initiates his evil scheme the moment one is conceived in his (her) mother's womb. No new life goes unnoticed by Satan. It is the devil's intention to destroy each life, if possible, or to cause as much harm as he can.[16] Satan is called Apollyon the Destroyer (Rev 9:11).

The devil's options are limited. He must operate within the bounds of his legal rights. In other words, he must have an opening before he can get into a person's life. God's word exhorts us; *do not give the devil an opportunity* (Ephesians 4:27). How can the devil get a foothold in the life of a child still in his mother's womb? What would open that door of opportunity? In the *Inherited Curses* section, the Hammonds answer with, first of all, inherited curses give the devil a legal right. God has decreed:

I, the Lord your God, am a jealous God, visiting the iniquity of the fathers on the children, and on the third and the fourth generations... (Deut 5:9). Children can be born with anywhere from a few to many curses due to "the iniquities of the fathers" (Exo 20:5).[17]

Iniquity is when you know what you are doing is sin, but you won't or can't stop it.[18] Parents, grandparents or great-grandparents have transgressed God's commandments, and the curse has passed down. I referenced this earlier in this book section with the biblical references of Abraham, Isaac, and Jacob. Perhaps there has been idolatry, witchcraft, occult practices, incest, fornication, illegitimacy, adultery, bestiality, or other transgressions in the family tree. Unless these curses have already been disallowed, the atoning blood of Jesus accepted and the demon's curse expelled (cast out in the name of Jesus) by the power of the Holy Spirit, then the devil has a right to perpetuate the curse to another generation.[19]

In my case, my parents and grandparents transgressed God's command to abstain from pre-marital sex and birthing children outside of the legal covenant of marriage. Another right that gave Satan access to my life, marriage, and children is described in the next section of the Hammonds *Children's Deliverance Manual* under the section entitled *Prenatal Rejection*. It begins by asking, "What other right does the devil have?" It then goes into a story of a young woman who approached Frank and Ida Mae by the name of Phyllis, a young woman, who came concerning deliverance for her child. She said, "My baby needs deliverance." Since she had no baby in her arms and was obviously pregnant, they queried, "Do you mean the one in your womb?" She said, "Yes," and began to explain why her unborn child needed deliverance.

When the baby was conceived, Phyllis did not want a child. She had since learned that rejection of a child in the womb creates an opening for a spirit of rejection to enter the fetus. The baby was at a six-month gestational age, and the mother had gotten her heart right with the Lord. She now accepted the baby and dedicated him to God. She asked that the Hammonds deliver her little one from the spirit of rejection. At the time this was new ground for the Hammonds. Their question was, "Is a child in the womb subject to spiritual influence?". In an instant, they were drawn to the account of John the Baptist, who was influenced while in the womb. Hadn't an angel of the Lord appeared to Zacharias, the father of John the Baptist, and announced that John would be filled with the Holy Spirit while yet in his mother's womb? (Lk1:15). John's filling of the Holy Spirit was evidenced when Mary brought salutation to Elizabeth, and the baby *"leaped in her womb."*

Since the Holy Spirit can enter a person before birth, why couldn't an evil spirit also enter a person still in the womb? It was this question from these deliverance ministers that came before me and others that has shed light on the spiritual impact of trauma on a person in the womb along with that of the parents. My father rejected me in the womb when he said, "Is it mine"? My mother and father also discussed having an abortion, which they came to an agreement to execute but did not immediately have the money to take action to complete. Adding yet another core wound of rejection of me from my mother, who came into agreement with my father. Though they clearly did not abort me since I am here writing this book to talk about it. The agreement they made added yet another legal opening for Satan to lay claim to my life and infect me with demons in the womb of rejection and murder. Later on, in my late teens/early adulthood, the demon spirits of rejection and murder would come into maturity and full manifestation within me, influencing my execution of three completed abortions that took place back-to-back in 2010 and again in 2012.

According to Frank and Ida Mae, a child that is rejected from the womb is usually fretful, cross, and irritable. He or she is prone to being stiff rather than relaxed in the mother's arms. The child usually resists being held or cuddled. Torace D. Solomon adds to this by stating that demons manifest in people's lives in many different ways. Their objective is to stay hidden so that they can complete their work. They are the source of many cases of mental trauma, physical pain, and emotional health issues. He says he has seen many healings and miracles through the deliverance ministry because when the root is cut out, the bad fruit has to dry up!

Recognizing demonic influence is a powerful skill that every believer should develop. In the case of Phyllis, who visited the Hammonds for deliverance on her unborn child, after the child was born, Frank and Ida Mae received a report that he was a quiet and peaceful baby who was very much loved. This child's tranquility was in marked contrast to others who are rejected from the womb and who receive no deliverance. The enemy is masterful in the art of deception, so the discerning of spirits is a gift that you need to ask God to give you! I am not talking about discernment of suspicion. I am talking about the authentic gift of God that is rooted in love. Suspicion tries to come to conclusions through carnal senses and memories, like many of you did when adultery in my marriage went public. The true gift of discerning spirits gets to the root of the matter quickly and doesn't hesitate to show the love needed to set someone free! Suspicion judges the person. Discerning of spirits judges the enemy of that person's soul![20] In love, I am exposing, correcting, rebuking, and teaching under the gift of discerning of spirits by judging the enemy of me and Derrick's souls.

Earlier, I provided a description of trauma; with that in mind, let me make a few clarifications about the experience. Not everyone who experiences a horrible or life-altering event will be traumatized by it. And for those who do, some will have symptoms that resolve after a few weeks, while others will wrestle with the long-term effects. Although symptoms of trauma often share similarities, the response to individual events can vary widely. Therefore, we must learn how an individual person has been affected. We want to know how a person- body- mind- soul, and spirit has responded to and processed their experiences.[21]

After I was born, my dad went to my mom's house on Randolf street in Montebello after getting into a confrontation with my mom's ex-boyfriend Ernest, telling her that I was not his baby because of a head-butting contest concerning whose girl my mom was with Ernest. Again, my parents were never in a romantic relationship; it was sexual only, but the territorial behavior of my father goes to show that the soul tie created by sex is real and more influential than we have given it credit. In Prophet Ed Citronnelli's Advanced Spiritual Warfare Training, he teaches about the spiritual impact of soul-ties. What are soul ties? A soul tie is when two souls are joined or knitted together to become one. A soul tie is a connection with someone deeply embedded into your soul. This can happen in multiple ways, but it usually needs agreement. One thing to remember is that there are good soul-ties, and there are negative soul-ties. Soul-ties formed through sexual relations are the most common, and this is one Satan likes to use as a weapon, when it is performed outside of God's law, to bind people's lives and destinies.

My mother and father conceived and birthed me outside of God's law, negatively binding my mother and father together spiritually, which manifested in my father's ultimate jealousy over my mom's ex-boyfriend Ernest and triggering his anxious-avoidant attachment style, in which he rejected me again after I was born. As a result, my mom's anxious, ambivalent attachment style was triggered, and she then called my grandma Broadus, my dad's mom, and told her that my dad said that I was not his child. My grandma Broadus then gave my mom my dad's social so she could put him on child support. Insecure attachment history plays a significant role in how a person responds and recovers from trauma. Secure attachment is how the mind develops in an individual. The attachment styles that I've pointed out in my parents are Anxious-Ambivalent, and Anxious-Avoidant.

My mother, as an anxious ambivalent attachment style, masked her negative-self-image through dismissiveness, avoidance, and anger, though she generally had a positive image of others, meaning that she had a sense of unworthiness but generally evaluated others positively with the exception of this story being my father who became an unsafe person to her emotionally and psychologically.[22] Children who have an anxious-ambivalent attachment style are described as being distressed when their caregiver leaves them but are then inconsolable on their return. Anxious-ambivalent children fear abandonment but cannot trust their caregiver to be consistent. My mom had a rough early childhood with a harsh transition that occurred in her early adolescent years leading up to her participation in conceiving me with my father.

Reginald Wright, a little George Jefferson look-alike man who was a soldier who fought in the Vietnam War, is the earliest memory my mom had of her stepfather when she was four or five years old and her biological mother Linda Faye, who was her primary caregiver. It was at this time the foundation for my anxious, ambivalent attachment style began to take root in the psyche of my mother. My uncle Kirk was about eight or nine when Reggie romantically connected with my grammy, Linda Faye, revealed to my mother years later in adulthood, when my mom was forty-two, that he knew that Reggie had a serious drug

SURVIVING A CHEATING MAN'S HEART

problem and was on cocaine. Uncle Kirk saw signs that things were dangerous with this relationship at the age of eight or nine.

My mom didn't have any awareness of anything being wrong until one night when she woke up in the night to my grammy screaming because Reggie had flipped her over the coffee table like a Marvel superhero and landed on her, choking the life out of her. She was desperately screaming for help, and my Uncle Kirk and Mom came out of the room to see what was going on. Upon coming closer to the scene of the crime, it appeared that Reggie was in a sleepwalking state, meaning he had the appearance of not being fully conscious or awake or aware, though his eyes were open, and his body was moving. Registering what was happening and the urgency of the situation, my uncle Kirk then rushed up behind Reggie when he saw his mom being strangled to death by her husband. My uncle Kirk shoved Reggie with all the force he had in his husky body, doing what any young boy would do. The impact of the force of the collision between Uncle Kirk and Reggie resulted in a startle-like response in which Reggie seemed to wake up or become aware of what he was doing or at least in a more conscious state of mind where he let go of my grammy's neck. She had Bart Simpson choke marks on her neck and Jesus-like bruise marks on her back from contacting the coffee table, which was a long old coffee table that was dark mahogany cherry wood and famous in the 70s.

My mom recalls standing there crying and screaming, "Get off of her, get off of her," after coming into the room and seeing her father figure ram strangling her mother. Again, my mother was only 4 or 5 years old, and this core wound ingrained itself into her psyche, creating big T trauma in her memory and contributing to her anxious, ambivalent attachment style. Big T trauma is life-threatening events such as combat from being at war, child abuse, natural disasters, accidents, violent crimes, mass shootings, domestic violence, and the like. It is the OMG, I think I'm going to die trauma in which a person feels helpless, powerless, and paralyzed with terror.[23] It is important to note that trauma was not talked about until the 1980's.

Origins of trauma-informed care:

Understanding trauma and its impacts on people is a fairly recent development. In the 1960s, when Civil War veterans returned home showing signs of great emotional and physical stress, the literature of the day attributed their suffering to moral weakness and fatigue. This was an unkind and unhelpful interpretation. After World War I, there was a name for it (shell shock), but the moral assessment and lack of care remained. Again, it was not until 1980, after the Vietnam War, that the American Psychiatric Association added what is now called post-traumatic stress disorder (PTSD) to their diagnostic manual (DSM-III). This action was part of a growing awareness that different types of devastating events- not just war-based trauma- could lead to impaired functioning. Over time, a growing body of research showed that trauma symptoms were present in people who experienced child abuse, rape, and other forms of interpersonal violence and abuse.[24]

Connections were also made in the medical field. A significant correlation was found between people who experienced traumatic stress during childhood and adults who were exhibiting a significant health crisis[25].Various other disciplines (e.g., substance abuse workers, child welfare agencies, teachers, Christian counselors, and mental health professionals) also began to notice both the short and long-term impact of trauma on individuals including depression, anxiety, trouble concentrating, disturbances in sleep, withdrawal from relationships, substance abuse, and flashbacks. Over time, as various professions came to understand how trauma presented in their context, more appropriate interventions were developed[26].

Are you beginning to see the severity and complexity that trauma has on people and how it is displayed differently in each individual person? Many of you reading laughed, judged, mocked, slandered, devalued, and discredited the amount of trauma that I experienced in my marriage that was exacerbated through public humiliation. You had little regard, compassion, care, or concern for the deep roots of trauma that had plagued my life and Derricks and the intense spiritual component that is not talked about or acknowledged even amongst those in the church. Many of you even dared to diagnose me and tell me about trauma in my life when you had no authority or foreknowledge of how I was coping with and processing it. The suggestion of these unprofessional meta-verse diagnoses from many of you who are ignorant of the natural and spiritual impact of trauma was that I needed intense therapy for alleged mental and emotional health issues. And I say to you that therapy without God is dead!

Trauma goes to the core of the person and who they are, and the message is the opposite of a person who is created in the image of God and who is of value and worth. Who they are is someone to consume, use, and feed off; therefore, what God tells us about Himself makes no sense. He says I love you (Jn 3:16), I am a Refuge (Psa 46:1), I am your Shepherd (Jn 10:11), you are made in Our image (Gen 1:16). A traumatized person cannot process those concepts when they have experienced the life-threatening events mentally, emotionally, physically, and spiritually.[27] Often, the severely wounded undergo particular damage to their personhood day after day, year after year, that they do not accurately express.

Biblical counselors and ordained ministers often mistake the wounded's inaccurate portrayal of their life issues as being the marks of sin or faith struggles. Many ministers who know about my story and marriage made this fatal mistake when observing my spiritual remarks on the internet in response to the global dragging of my entire being. Furthermore, they did not see or care about my reality inside my video response behaviors and expressions of thought because I did not share what was happening due to my own confusion, shame, and fear. So, even the professional biblical counselor and clinical psychologists watching my life unfold in the public eye wrongly identified my wounds as problems to be addressed rather than wounds of oppression because of trauma. Instead of attributing the damage to the traumatic events of adultery, high profile marriage under public scrutiny, and active pregnancy with my third child, they provided incorrect, unprofessional, and spiritually illiterate assessments of my actions while providing inadequate counsel and public discussion posts on major media outlets.[28]

The fact that I can articulate and interweave these concepts into my life story is a miracle and testament to the divine healing power of God the Father, Son, and Holy Spirit. It is also the reason why I must continue to peel back the layers of the bitter roots that engraved itself in me well before I entered a 14-year entanglement with Derrick Jaxn. You are not getting the details of my life without the hard lessons learned the way out through the woundedness of Christ Jesus, correction, and rebuke. What you should be taking away at this point is that my marriage and its very public death was not and is not a laughing matter and is presented as being more complex than the surface-level commentaries spread by gossipers, slanders, liars, and mockers of God over the metaverse.

Recall my father's attachment style of an anxious-avoidant. Remember, attachment style describes how people relate to others based on how secure they feel. Anxious avoidant, also called fearful avoidant attachment style, is thought to be the rarest attachment type. Ironic or not that I was a fearful, avoidant attachment in my entire relationship with the self-love guru. Fearful-avoidant attachment is a complex pattern of behavior characterized by both high levels of anxiety and avoidance in relationships. People with fearful-avoidant attachments often crave intimacy and connection but are simultaneously afraid of getting too close to anyone due to past traumas or negative experiences.[29] Unfortunately, I cannot give a whole lot of context to my father's childhood trauma and parental upbringing because he has been dead for 22 years. On top of that, I was 12 years old when he died, and though I was around him at times, I really didn't know him like that since he was not my primary caregiver. My grandma Broadus, his mother, lived in Montebello on Eagle Street in Denver, Colorado, all my life until she passed away in 2005.

I recall being at Grandma Broadus's house more than being at my dad's to spend time with him. The house was the house of houses to be at for all things Broadus/Roberts family. My grandmother's house was full of pictures of her children and grandchildren, which was the focal point of the entire 3bd 2 bath 1,392 sq ft house. Leslie, my dad, was one of 10 kids that Grandma Broadus gave birth to and the fifth boy of her seven sons. It's hard to believe that my grandmother had the mental and emotional capacity to be fully engaged and present with each of her ten kids. The little that I do know suggests that some of her 10 kids felt abandoned. I know this because Barbara Lynn, my aunt, one of three girls birthed to my grandmother, commented on this on one of my social media posts. I never met my aunt Barbra Lynn, but I was very well aware of who she was as her picture was one of what seemed to be hundreds of pictures that lined the walls of her mother's house.

Aunt Barbara Lynn's comment on my post about her brothers and mother read, "You don't know me, but I am related. I always felt abandoned but learned that all things work for good. God has a plan for me. I just want to say that my daughter found you on social media, and I have been watching you. For what it's worth, I am so proud of you." I replied, "Thank you, auntie. Yes, all things work for good to GOD be all the glory." If one of the ten children of Emma Jean felt abandoned, the likelihood of some, if not all of her children having a similar feeling is highly possible. Understanding this splice of information from my father's early life and family dynamic makes the fearful, avoidant attachment style make sense in his short-lived life. Children who are raised to develop a fearful-avoidant attachment style often come from unpredictable environments filled with abuse, neglect, or abandonment. In these situations, a child can become conditioned to "chase" after their caregiver for the love and safety they seek while also running from and fearing this person as someone who is inconsistent and often abusive.[30] It's important to note that a person with a fearful-avoidant attachment style is often at an increased risk for unhealthy relationships.

Since I had a fearful-avoidant attachment style in my relationship and marriage, it makes more sense as to why we lasted as long as we did. I speak in the past tense of "was," a fearful avoidant because that version of me and everything that goes with it is dead. I am now securely attached to my personal Lord and Savior, Jesus Christ of Nazareth, and bound with a threefold cord (Ecc 4:12) with God the Father through the power of the Holy Spirit. My disagreement and renunciation of the fearful-avoidant attachment style at this stage in my life is the practical and tangible way I am living out the scripture of Colossians 3:9-10 in which I have put off the old woman with her deeds and have put on the new woman who is renewed in knowledge according to the image of Him who created me.

How did I inherit the fearful-avoidant attachment style like the father I did not know well? Remember what Frank and Ida Mae Hammond said in their book *A Manual for Children Deliverance.* Children can be born with anywhere from a few to many curses due to "the iniquities of the fathers (Exo20:5). In my family tree, from my mother and fathers' iniquities, I inherited the demons of fornication, illegitimacy, adultery, rejection, abortion, fear, avoidant, dismissiveness and abandonment which I did not begin getting cast out of me in the name of Jesus until I was separated in my marriage and through the first year of the two-year attempt to reconcile. The founding work of Frank and Ida Mae on the unsafe womb shores up the growing conviction that a baby still in the womb is not in a state of oblivion. That the little embryonic person can be spiritually influenced in either positive or negative ways. If a baby, still in the amniotic fluid, can be wounded by rejection, he can also be nurtured by love.

When should parents begin to love a child? Parents should begin openly confessing love for their child from the moment of conception. It is good to speak tender words of love and acceptance to a child throughout his or her nine months of development. It is indeed a mystery of God, but that little baby receives spoken love and feels wanted and secure.[31] Secure attachment refers to a bond where individuals feel safe, supported, and connected, enabling them to express emotions freely, seek comfort, and confidently explore their environment, knowing they have a reliable base to return to. An individual with a secure attachment style exhibits a consistent, interdependent, and confident relationship-related style. Children who are securely attached feel safe and supported by their caregivers. Securely attached adults are capable of forming lasting relationships.[32]

The attachment style you develop in early childhood is thought to have a lifelong influence on your ability to communicate your emotions and needs, respond to conflict, and form expectations about your relationships. Although the attachment style you were raised with does not explain everything about your relationships and who you become as an adult, understanding your style may help explain patterns you notice in relationships. Secure attachments with caregivers are believed to be essential for healthy development. It is considered that about 50% of the population has a secure attachment, while the rest fall into one of the insecure categories (anxious, avoidant, and disorganized). I fell into the category of anxious (fearful) avoidant influenced by my teen parents' trauma responses while I was in the womb. [33]

The overall emotional environment impacts the developing child within the womb. Evil spirits are given ready access to a yet-to-be-born child through many kinds of negative factors in his outside environment. Many would deny that such influences are possible, but deliverance ministers Frank and Ida Mae's documented experience has proven otherwise. In cases where the concept is illegitimate, like mine, as in many teenage pregnancies, there are usually many negative forces at work. For example, the unborn child is usually rejected by both the father and mother. Remember, my father came into agreement with this rejection upon receiving notification of my conception when he asked my mom, "Is it mine?"

In like manner, my dad:

1. Denied that I was his child after head-butting with my mother's ex-boyfriend Ernest.

2. Pressed my mom for an abortion and offered to pay for it.

3. Had no plan to marry her.

Denying all responsibility for emotionally supporting my mother after finding out that I was growing in the womb. In other scenarios, the young woman and her family deny the father access to his child. They are in a state of humiliation and want to punish the young man in every possible way.[34] My mother's family had no say so in the matter of my father's access to me. A level of humiliation was dished out when my father pretended as if my mom did not exist, which was also a denial of my existence in the womb that he paid dearly for through my mom's irritability. All such factors send tremors through the womb that foster insecurity and rejection.[35]

Recollect the words of Torace D. Solomon: "When the root is cut out, the bad fruit has to dry up! The process that I have laid out for you using the historical context of my parents, their parents, and their upbringing is the deep psychological work that needs to be done to be healed in mind, body, soul, and spirit. What I am doing is illustrating to you in story form and spiritual autopsy how to identify the root of your core and fresh wounds through the lens of the great physician (Mk 2:17). Psychology without God is dead, which is why a spiritual autopsy must be performed. An autopsy in the natural world in which we live is a medical examination of a body after death to find the cause- and sometimes manner- of death. A pathologist trained to perform autopsies thoroughly examines the inside and outside of the body.[36] Since God tells us not to look at things that we can see with our natural eyes but at things that we cannot see (2 Cor 4:18) we must pull the plank out of our own eye to see clearly (Matt 7:3-5). The system that I am drawing the blueprint for in this book is the practical way of living out that scripture.

I cannot shed light on the darkness of Derrick's cheating heart without thoroughly examining mine inside and outside from a natural and spiritual perspective. I've broken the mask of my own self-righteousness, pride, ego, and image by being raw, real, and honest about the stalk from which I came. Healing and Deliverance through the Art of Spiritual Warfare[37] goes beyond the shallow ideas of what you know about a situation based on what you can tangibly see. Now, I know a great deal of you reading this are hearing the terms healing, deliverance, and spiritual warfare for the first time with questions on the relevance it has to *Surviving a Cheating Man's Heart*. The other group of you reading have some knowledge about these concepts and are beginning to see that you need to go deeper into your history from the time of birth to receive the next level of your healing in mind, body, soul, and spirit.[38]

In my book *Healing God's Way: The Art of Spiritual Warfare, Deliverance and Healing*, I introduce the reader to The Physician. Mark 2:17 (AMP) says *When Jesus heard it, He said to them, those who are healthy have no need of a physician, but [only] those who are sick, I did not come to call the righteous, but sinners, to repentance.* The Great Physician is described even further in Mark 13-17, Matt 9.9-13, and Luke 5:27-32 when it says, *Then He went out again by the sea; and all the multitude came to Him, and He taught them. As He passed by, He saw Levi, the son of Alphaeus, sitting at the tax office. And He said to him, Follow Me, so he arose and followed him. Now it happened as He was dining in Levi's house that many tax collectors and sinners also sat together with Jesus and His disciples, for there were many, and they followed Him. And when the scribes and Pharisees saw Him eating with the tax collectors and sinners, they asked His disciples, how is He eating and drinking with tax collectors and sinners?*

A specialist called a pathologist performs autopsies. Pathology is the branch of medicine that involves the laboratory examination of samples of body tissues for diagnostic or forensic purposes. Pathologists who perform autopsies are medical doctors. They have expansive knowledge and specific training on the human body. [39] While it usually takes 11 to 13 years for someone to become a pathologist, it takes the Holy Spirit a millisecond as His expansive knowledge and wisdom on the human mind, body, soul, and spirit comes from Him being one of the triune beings that created it in His image (Gen 1:26). It is impossible to navigate the chambers of *A Cheating Man's Heart* and the crafty hoe that married him without being led by the Holy Spirit. It's critical that you identify that the Spirit of the Lord imparts wisdom and understanding, and He is doing that through a spiritual autopsy throughout this book as the divine pathologist who teaches, comforts and helps us through the treachery of adultery (Isa 11:2).

Life lessons involving events, people, and circumstances, timestamp God's sovereignty in producing "ideas, values, and principles" that comprise my ministry philosophy's spiritual DNA, which is being used as a guiding tool for the spiritual autopsy of my marriage to Derrick Jaxn. Statements of truth discovered from family, crisis, negative preparation, leadership backlash, and training have led me to identify eight values of personal philosophy, which you will see throughout this book series.[40]

Ministry Philosophy: - Da'Naia's Eight Spiritual DNA Values

Value 1: I must always have an intimate relationship with the Father, Son, and Holy Spirit
Value 2: I must feed my inner man to feed other people's, inner man
Value 3: I must believe that the Lord is the stronghold of my life
Value 4: I must be equal and show no partiality
Value 5: I must be responsible for all care and offenses connected to the sheep of my ministry
Value 6: I must know that I can do nothing without Jesus of Nazareth, Holy Spirit, and Father God
Value 7: I must know who I am in Christ
Value 8: I must know that I have not attained perfection[41]

I have personally learned and committed to these values during my tumultuous marriage, and negative backlash concerning my ministry delivery. A more detailed look at the process involving events, people in my life and marriage formed the foundations of the eight philosophical values. Several of the events and people in this book have been a part of helping me learn these statements of truth through negative experiences that are now *working "together for good"* (Rom8:28) to free millions of women from the snare of *A Cheating Man's Heart.*[42] An accumulation these experiences produced patterns of deep character development that has cut off the rotten fruit and pruned the excellent fruit for "mature ministry" to flow from new "mature character.[43] Evangelism as a "major role" functions as my role in telling how I survived 14 years *of A Cheating Mans Heart.* [44] Positive responses to the circumstances in my life are critical to your understanding of how I stayed in my toxic relationship as long as I did.

The sting of rejection filled my inner being from birth, producing an identity crisis, idolization, fear of men, and a lying tongue that contributed to the death of my marriage and the lack of respect I held for Derrick. In the short window of time, I had to experience my father while he was in life, an involuntary and automatic desire to chase after and transform into someone he could love and engage with emotionally plagued my thought life. from unpredictable environments filled with abuse, neglect, or abandonment. In these situations, a child can become conditioned to "chase" after their caregiver for the love and safety they seek while also running from and fearing this person as someone who is inconsistent and often abusive.[45] As early as the age of two years old I can remember identifying as tomboy which consumed my being as a young girl who desperately sought to become more lovable in the sight of my father, who appeared to love my brothers more.

Roughly fifteen years of my early life before Derrick was spent building this identity, feeding the fear of men and deception, and intertwining these beliefs into my spiritual DNA. This dark road of destruction allowed years of *"practicing unrighteousness* (1 Jn 5:17)" to become the stronghold keeping me bound to unworthiness, fear, and torment. [46] A stronghold is where a particular perspective or belief is vigorously defended or upheld; they are mentalities used to manifest unseen assignments into reality. The way Satan asserts his influence is by seducing you to create mentalities, perspectives, and ideologies that oppose the will of God for your life. Strongholds are built to defend the ground demons, who win by gaining your agreement. Demons need human agreement to do their work. We have been taught that strongholds are spiritual structures and that we can pull them down with physical gestures. That's cute, but the truth is that every spiritual stronghold is rooted in thought. That's the way Satan attacks! [47]

At twelve years old, this dark road became a valley of death (Psa 23:4); when my father passed away at 30 years old, shortly after, I gave him a piece of my mind concerning the rejection I believed he inflicted on me unfairly. Fragmented by his death, my eyes became full of darkness, blinding me spiritually, though I could see physically. Bitter roots sprang up in every area of my life for the next eighteen years after this life-changing event. After being healed by the Holy Spirit through the blood of Jesus, I know now that I was "chasing" my father and "transforming" myself into something I perceived he would love, care for, and choose, and that behavior did not die when he did.

In fact, it went through a metamorphosis process after his death through the biological process of dating in middle school, high school, being raped at 19, and meeting Derrick Jaxn three weeks after that rape which led to a 14-year entanglement. The anxious-avoidant (fearful) 'chase' (trap or cycle) gets triggered because the anxious person is wanting a close and intimate connection with their partner and is always looking to close down the gap and space between them and their partner so that the anxious partner has reached their optimum level of closeness in the relationship, which is very little space or gap between them and their partner..[48] While I was an anxious-avoidant, Derrick is a dismissive avoidant attachment style. People with a dismissive, avoidant attachment style tend to emotionally distance themselves from others, particularly in close relationships. These individuals often deny the importance of closeness and intimacy, maintain high self-reliance, and disregard or suppress emotional connections due to their defensive dismissal of attachment needs. The dismissive, avoidant attachment style describes a way of relating to other people that are distant, self-reliant, and distrusting. Individuals with a dismissive avoidant attachment style often value their independence and autonomy above emotional intimacy and connection.

This is often because these individuals were emotionally deprived in childhood and grew up with parents who did not provide enough emotional support or warmth. [49] Remember the bitter roots from which Derrick came in the "unsafe womb" of his mother Martha from conception to birth as she used cocaine until the very day he was born. Again, Frank and Ida Mae Hammond describe the spiritual impact of the mother's addictions in their book *Children's Deliverance Manual*, saying, it is well known that children can be harmed physically from the addictive habits of the mother, and children may even be born with addictions. Infants- of drug-using mothers go through painful withdrawal symptoms when the umbilical cord is severed, and the drug stimulus no longer passes from mother to child. Throughout the Hammonds Ministry, they discovered some people who later in life became enslaved to alcohol, nicotine, and other drugs due to the prenatal influence of their mother's addictions. While addiction did not show up with a consistent and persistent use of drugs and alcohol in Derrick's life, though he used these forms at times, addiction did show up in his life in the form of insatiable sexual encounters with women.

I point your attention back to the biblical reference of Abraham, Isaac, and Jacob, who were all oppressed by the demonic spirit of lying that was allowed to pass from generation to generation. Abraham and Isaac used the same exact lie. Jacob's lie took on a different form, though it did not change the fact that he lied just like his father and grandfather. In like manner, Derrick's mother's demon of addiction did not leave the family bloodline when she became sober after his birth. The demon of addiction took on another form within him, adding a sexual component. Derrick's inherited demons from the womb are no different than my inherited demons from the womb that influenced our early lives, our meeting each other, and our chase-and-trap relationship turned into marriage.

There are many signs of demonic influence. Remember, demons are ancient intelligent personalities, so boxing them into one definition is dangerous.[50] The manifestations listed below are just some of the ways you can identify demonic influence in Derrick and my life from our bitter roots.

Oppression
Mark 9:20-23 (AMP)

[20] *They brought the boy to Him. When the [demonic] spirit saw Him, it immediately threw the boy into a convulsion, and falling to the ground, he began rolling around and foaming at the mouth. 21 Jesus asked his father, "How long has this been happening to him?" And he answered, "Since childhood.* [22] *The demon has often thrown him both into the fire and into the water, intending to kill him. But if You can do anything, take pity on us, and help us!"* [23] *Jesus said to him, "[You say to Me,] 'If You can?' All things are possible for the one who believes and trusts [in Me]!"*

In this scripture, we see an example of oppression. The boy's father told Jesus that the demon who had influence over the child would compel [influence] him to commit suicidal acts. Any time a person is experiencing any type of oppression, there is a demonic spirit at work. Oppression doesn't have to bring the person any pleasure at all. If there is something that he/she wants to stop doing and can't, it should be dealt with through deliverance. Oppression manifests in many compulsive disorders: shopping, hoarding, eating, gambling, sex, exercise, etc. When a person is dealing with oppression, he/she is trapped in a pattern of repetitive and senseless thinking. These thought processes can prove difficult to overcome without the Ministry of Deliverance followed by therapy to help retrain thought life. And this is why I scream from the mountain tops that THERAPY WITHOUT GOD IS DEAD! [51]

The on-and-off pattern, followed by the 'chase and trap' pattern in my marriage with Derrick, plainly identifies the signs of demonic influence through oppression. Oppression walked through the door of our lives through the transgressions and iniquities of our parents. It's through our parents that we developed our attachment styles according to the secular psychology attachment theory. Since children develop their attachment styles from their primary caregiver, I must go back and revisit my mother, who was my primary caregiver, to bridge the gap between my development of the anxious-avoidant attachment style, which is identical to my fathers, though I did not have any close or emotional connection to him. My fearful or anxious-avoidant attachment style developed from being raised in an unpredictable environment when it came to my mom's mood or personality at the time. I say personality because she identified with having multiple personalities, which is a clinical mental health issue. My mother's identification with these personalities comes from a history of her father, Larry, being clinically diagnosed with Schizophrenia.

Schizophrenia is a severe mental illness that affects how a person thinks, feels, and behaves. People with Schizophrenia may seem like they have lost touch with reality, which can be distressing for them and for their family and friends. The symptoms of Schizophrenia can make it difficult to participate in usual, everyday activities, but effective treatments are available. The most effective treatment is deliverance by the power of the Holy Spirit.[52] In my book, *Traumatized: Is God a Monster or a Healer? In a Trauma-Informed Guide for Ministers to Understand the Mind of the Wounded*, I speak about the four failures that undermine healing the traumatized. Peter Scazzero addresses at least four fundamental failures hindering the believer's spiritual maturity and personal relationships today in his book *Emotionally Healthy Discipleship*, which I used as a framework for my book.

Scazzero released this book in 2021, reflecting the last twenty-five years of his ministry experience with churches worldwide concerning discipleship systems that have kept people immature. Scazzero goes on to say that he has discerned these failures as a lead pastor for a local church and his work around the world with different denominations and movements in urban, suburban, and rural areas and across racial, cultural, and economic divides. The absence of trauma-informed care coincides with the fundamental failures identified by Scazzero, though they are not limited to these specific failures.

1. We Tolerate Emotional Immaturity

2. We Emphasize Doing for God over Being with God

3. We Ignore the Treasures of Church & Psychological History

4. We Define Success Wrongly [53]

Let's begin with the same roots Scazzero uses, which I will use as a framework for examining the bitter roots in the lives of Derrick and me. The roots of healing the traumatized today too often result in people who are less whole, less human, and less like Jesus. Rather than more whole, more human, and more like Jesus. [54] The church is responsible for this as they have relied on systems and functions of referring traumatized individuals to outside professional help in the world of psychology. However, most psychologists and professionals in the field of assisting the traumatized learn and practice psychology as if God does not exist. Leading to our first failure.

Failure 1: We Tolerate Emotional Immaturity

Over time, our expectations of what it means to be "spiritually healed" have blurred to the point that we have grown blind to many glaring inconsistencies. For example, we have learned to accept that:

- God can heal all things, yet we rely on a psychological model practiced without the existence of God to invoke healing in the minds and emotions of the traumatized.

- You can function as a leader yet be unteachable, insecure, and defensive (Scazzero 6).

- You can quote the Bible with ease yet be unaware of untimely truths spoken to the traumatized, which result in wounding them further.

- You can lead people "for God" when, in reality, you refer them away from God when their sickness in mind and emotions prove to be beyond your skillset or too time-consuming.

- You can be hurt by unkind comments and behavior while justifying saying nothing to avoid conflict.

- You can serve tirelessly in multiple ministries and yet have little time to sit with the traumatized through the excruciatingly long process of recovering the whole person in Christ.

- You can lead a large ministry with little transparency, rarely sharing struggles, weakness, or lamenting with the brokenhearted in the long-term healing and recovery process.[55]

These are examples of emotional immaturity in action, yet we do not see them as the glaring contradictions they are. Why? Because we have disconnected emotional health from spiritual health. Where did we get the idea that it is possible to be spiritually mature while remaining emotionally immature?[56] The answer is multifaceted but let me focus on two significant reasons.

Reason 1: We No Longer Believe God is the Source of All Things, and without Him, we can Do Nothing.

In John 15, Jesus reveals the fullness of His divine power and authority when He says,[1] *I am the true vine, and my Father is the Gardner.* [2] *He cuts off every branch in Me that bears no fruit, while every branch that does bear fruit, He prunes so that it will be even fruitful.* [3] *You are already clean because of the words I have spoken to you.* [4] *Remain in me, as I also remain in you. No branch can bear fruit by itself; it must remain in the vine. Neither can you bear fruit unless you remain in Me.* Jesus states in Matthew 15:13 *that every plant which My heavenly Father has not planted will be uprooted,* Seeds planted in the mind of a traumatized believer through modern professional psychology will be uprooted because there is no life-giving anchor (Jn 15:1-4) needed for sustained long-term change rooted in the care plan.[57]

When we understand this failure, we can understand the failure of the church to connect mental health disorders and issues to the Source of Healing in all things. My grandpa, Larry's battle with schizophrenia, was influenced by demons, and the onset of this happened in his childhood, much like the boy I referenced earlier in the oppression section from Mark 9:20-23. I knew my grandfather Larry and was blessed to have spent a significant amount of time with him in the summer of 2010, which was one of my worst summer experiences with Derrick. I never personally experienced a psychosis episode with grandpa Larry, but I have heard about them and how it affected the families he created with his wives grammy Linda Faye and Grandma Gertha Lee. Psychosis refers to a collection of symptoms that affect the mind, where there has been some loss of contact with reality. During an episode of psychosis, a person's thoughts and perceptions are disrupted, and they may have difficulty recognizing what is real and what is not.

Psychosis often begins in young adulthood when a person is in their late teens to mid-20s. However, people can experience a psychotic episode at younger and older ages and as a part of many disorders and illnesses.[58]

As I understand my grandfather's mental health history, he showed signs of this in his late teens. Following the same spiritual law of Deuteronomy 5:9 and Exodus 20:5, my mother was 15 years old when she began to identify with being bipolar based on a description she was given in class. Ironically, this was around the same time I was conceived in her womb. Fast forward to my first public appearance as affair partners began blabbing at the mouth. Don't you recall several media outlets and professing Christians from the pulpit proclaiming that I was mentally ill for my behaviors and responses using biblical references, which include the imprecatory curses of the Bible? Do you think it's by accident that 99% of those who have knowledge about the scandal in my marriage came into agreement with this belief that I was suffering from a mental disorder, which was also instigated by my very loving and kind husband to those who actually know us in person?

Romans 6:16 (AMP) says, *[16] Do you not know that when you continually offer yourselves to someone to do his will, you are the slaves of the one whom you obey, either [slaves] of sin, which leads to death, or of obedience, which leads to righteousness (right standing with God)?*

In other words, no it was not by accident, that my mental health became a topic of mockery, debate, and discussion through the metaverse. This is why we need to understand how Satan attacks and why I am emphasizing the demonic elements in my very public marriage. We are all born into sin because of Adam and Eve's mistakes. To sin means to miss the mark or to trespass, but the type of sin that causes enslavement is more significant than just missing the mark. Sin cycles are categorized as iniquity.[59] Again, iniquity is when you know that what you are doing is sin, but you won't or can't stop it. Iniquity is the spiritual component as to why women like me stay bound in relationships and marriages to men who are slaves to sexual sin, which I call *A Cheating Man's Heart.*

Iniquity and sin cycles can be inherited from your parents and cause generational bondage. Derrick and I inherited our sin cycle patterns from our parents, which created the destructive pattern of the 'chase and trap' dynamic in the 14 years of active relationship and marriage. Many Christians confess their belief in Jesus Christ and strive to follow Him, but they are still enslaved to sin cycles. When Christ died on the cross, He eliminated the power that sin had over us. Any time you find a believer who has fasted, prayed, and cried out to God but can't seem to be separated from a particular sin, you will find a demon at work. There is an open door to his or her soul that has to be shut. They must allow the Lordship of Christ to reign in that area. Many times, people like me stay in sin cycles because of shame. [60] When you add emotional and psychological abuse to the mix, the shame is amplified and debilitating, creating a paralyzing effect known in the secular psychology world as the freeze response.

Freeze is one of the three most commonly recognized reactions of the stress response, and the initial response to danger in which a fight, or flight response is temporarily put on hold. The freeze response involves an immediate stilling of movement, with vigilance to the threat, and in preparation for an active fight or flight response.[61] The flight or fight response is an automatic psychological reaction to an event perceived as stressful or frightening. The perception of threat activates the sympathetic nervous system and triggers an acute stress response that prepares the body to fight or flee. Jesus in His humanity, was in this psychological state of being from the time of birth, having to flee as a fugitive and refugee to Egypt for some time (Matthew 2:12-23) to the time of his death (Mark 14:37-42).[62]

How do these things affect the mind and body? The mind or body is immediately triggered into a fight or flight as a biological reaction, where the sympathetic nervous system engages the body, similar to putting your foot on the gas of a car. The heart will race, hands will shake, and the body will begin to sweat. On the other hand, the freeze response is like putting your foot on the gas and breaking a car at the same time. The body becomes immobile (paralyzed), and depending on the risk factors of the person, the mind fractures or dissociates. All the behaviors a person normally engages in will be locked in a part of their brain. The closest illustration to this is the concept of locking a part of the brain away in a closet. All emotions, sensations, and physical senses are locked away in a closet within the brain. Likewise, the knowledge or data of the traumatic event is locked and stored in another area of the brain for the duration of the trauma. Depending on how long the trauma lasts, the individual will be dissociated until it's over. This means they will not have any emotions, they will feel numb, and often will not feel pain or not know what happened because they are still in a dissociated state.[63]

Compound trauma happens when you add physical or psychological abuse to this dissociated state. The National Center for Injury Prevention Controls Division of Violence and Prevention shows that 1 in 4 women experience severe physical violence from an intimate partner. Physical abuse is not more than psychological abuse. In fact, in most cases psychological abuse creates such deep-seated issues in the mind and thought life of a person, creating increased avenues for mental health disorders. Unfortunately, these statistics do not change inside the church. Psychological abuse seems to be a favorite form of abuse for oppressors who claim to believe in Jesus Christ of Nazareth because it's hard to prove, and there are little to no consequences established in our legal system to protect the mind and mental health of someone who is being psychologically abused. Someone married to an oppressor does not have a marriage characterized by trust, care, or honesty. It is enslavement. Oppressed wives become isolated and dominated over time. In order to survive, they must placate the endless demands and wishes of their oppressor.[64] My marriage meets this criterion.

According to Darby Strickland, clinical psychologist, and biblical counselor, women often do not reveal abuse. In fact, when asked directly about it by a counselor, 95% of women who have been abused deny that they have been abused. Shame is a contributing factor to this, but victims also often experience confusion about what is or has happened to them. Women entangled in the snare of *A Cheating Man's Heart* know something is wrong, but they do not know what it is or what to call it whether they are married or not. Going beyond the shallow concept of 'cheating is wrong,' those of you who have ears to hear and eyes to see will have the revelation that the root of this dynamic has everything to do with sin cycles. Since psychology without God is dead, it is important to note that shame is generally defined as strong negative emotions characterized by perceptions of the global devaluation of oneself.[65]

Shame is a self-evaluative emotion that invokes concern and attention about oneself. Since we are born into sinful nature, we are prone to shame as our eyes (Gen 3:7) have been open to aspects of ourselves, our behavior, the characteristics of our body, and our identity. Leading us to perform masking techniques to fit in. Shame distorts our identity by reflecting to us our perceived flaws, worth, and sense of belonging. Dyer et al (2017) conducted research comparing (dissociative identity disorder [dd] to Complex Trauma and General Mental Health with a healthy volunteer control group and found the trauma and mental health clinical groups exhibited significantly greater shame than those of the non-clinical sample.[66] God wants His people to be free from shame. It's my job as a deliverance minister to make sure that I expose, uproot, and tear down the secular mindset that reinforces shame in people who find themselves caught in the heart chambers of a man who is a slave to cheating. I'm doing that by publicly confessing my sin in the pages of this book series.

I cannot express the urgency of shifting your mindsets to be sensitive to trauma as a believer in Christ. Cheating and abuse scandals are not laughing matters to be discussed, mocked, and fed to slaves of gossip, slander, and lies on major news media outlets. Being informed about trauma helps you to refrain from reaffirming the shame that the people involved already feel and gives you an opportunity to encourage and affirm that it is okay to disclose the hidden abuse that comes along with cycles of cheating. The Holy Spirit cannot extract out of you what is not there. This means if you remain ignorant about trauma and its spiritual impact with a basic understanding of how it displays itself in the behavior of a person, you are no better than the cheating man and his heart in the eyes of God, which is a problem that you will account for with your ignorant commentary about issues of the heart in the marriages and relationships of other people that you do not know personally.

Psychology is viewed in many ways. Some Christians believe that it is all bad, and some don't believe it's bad but practice it as the secular world does. When my story hit the headlines, this discrepancy among professing Christians became evident as many Christians weighed in, saying that I needed to be in therapy that aligned with that of the secular world in order to be healed. Modern psychology produced a profound scientific account of human beings and developed complex ways of dealing with psychological problems without God. And this is one of the reasons so many of you have difficulty reconciling that God is the Source of healing, not years of therapy with a psychologist. This problem was created in the Church, which has resulted in different understandings of how to resolve it. Roughly 140 years of knowledge has been collected to better understand the Church's responses to trauma crises without the leadership of the Holy Spirit. Creating a problem that needs to be addressed.[67]

Psychology is in the Bible. Erick Johnson describes it as a beautiful, rich psychology that is written at the lay level; it is not written at a scientific level. It is written at an everyday level so that everyday people can understand it. So, when modern-day psychology developed in the early 1800s and developed this new approach where there is no God, it created a crisis in the Church. Evidence of this crisis has bubbled to the surface with my approach to healing out loud as I lead in my ministry from a place of weakness and vulnerability. Henrie Nouwen's video teaching *The Vulnerable Journey Chapter 2* lays the foundations for trauma-informed care that corrects the four failures that undermine the healing of the severely wounded, like myself. The way of Jesus binds the wounds of those experiencing extreme suffering in the way of vulnerability. Vulnerability comes from a Latin word (vulns) that means wound. Jesus's way is the way of woundedness. Jesus's wounds from being beaten beyond recognition forced Him to be completely co-dependent on other people to complete His finished work on the cross.

Wounded people are at the core of my ministry work and are my teachers. Traumatized people are the place where God comes to meet us and show us the fullness of His healing power because his strength is made perfect in our weakness. So, the solution is not asking how we, as believers and ministers, help more traumatized people. The more critical resolution comes from asking, how do we allow people who are traumatized to share their gifts with us? And call us to conversion, call us to wholeness, call us to love, that's the question, that's the healed process.[68]

Creating a timeline of events is the best way to navigate through the healing process to identify how God works throughout your life while shaping and creating a unique assignment for your life that glorifies His kingdom. Ephesians 2:10 says, *"For we are God's workmanship, created in Christ Jesus to do good works, which God prepared in advance for us to do."* The work that I've done so far in this book with digging into the bitterroots of Derrick and I, which was a factor in the death of our marriage, gives you a taste of what I do with the H.E.A.L.E.D school members. In this process, I have them identify their core and fresh wounds. Core wounds are things or people that have hurt, harmed, or impacted their lives from the age of birth to 18 years old. In T-chart form, members write down key people, events, and circumstances that shaped their lives from birth to the current point of their lives. On the other side of the chart, I have them write down their fresh wounds. Fresh wounds are things or people that have hurt, harmed, or impacted their lives from the age of 19 to their current age.

What we discover as they go through the process, and we talk it out is that there is a lot of childhood trauma and family influences that have impacted each person in ways they didn't realize. Healing is like an onion; many layers of an onion need to be peeled to get to the core or root of the onion. What happens when you don't peel the onion of your trauma is you begin to suppress and mask minor and major events, circumstances, or people who have hurt you, which leads to being overwhelmed and possibly results in dissociation. Masking (sometimes referred to as camouflaging) involves suppressing or hiding one's behaviors or traits to appear in a certain way. Emotional masking specifically refers to hiding or holding back on how one truly feels and presenting a different emotional state to the outside world.[69]

People can hide their emotions by altering their facial expressions, body language, or words, often as a way to adapt to the situation they are in because it may not feel appropriate to show how they really feel. Masking can be a conscious choice for many, but at times it can become an automatic reaction or a conscious choice that the person is unaware of. Sometimes, people may mask more because they receive negative feedback when they show their authentic selves.[70] In March of 2021, when I sat in front of the camera with my dear husband live in front of millions, I made a conscious choice not to mask. I literally showed up not hiding my emotions, which can be seen in the viral side-eye image of me floating around the internet. I was experiencing my authentic self without altering my facial expressions, body language or words. I was FREE from comparison and low esteem.

However, viewers around the world, most of which have hearts full of murder, attributed this to coercion and abuse. While there is some truth to that, it is also true that I was practicing self-care from a mental and emotional standpoint by experiencing my authentic self, authentic emotions, and, more importantly, authentic faith when it would have been much easier for me to mask by presenting a different emotional state to the outside world. An accumulation of traumatic experiences, with my public debut being the cherry on top, set in motion patterns of deep character development that cut off the rotten fruit and pruned the excellent fruit for "mature ministry" to flow from "mature character," which produced mature testimony of God saving me from the snare of *A Cheating Man's Heart*.[71] Positive responses to the circumstances in my life have been critical to the evangelistic work I have put together in this book for you to understand how I stayed so long in a toxic marriage and more importantly how other women who relate to my story stay in their toxic marriages or relationships.

I want to reiterate the spiritual impact of the trauma I'm laying out in this book goes to the core of a person because it attacks the identity of who they are and distorts the image of God. I describe this distortion of God as a "Monster" through the shattered lens of a traumatized mind that is trying to make sense of who God is and why He would allow such tragic events to play out in the lives of people like me. God is not a monster but a healer who loves, cares, and protects us. However, the messages a person receives and what I received amid extreme suffering are the opposite and must be addressed to recover the whole person's mind, body, soul, and spirit.[72] This is why I must continue exposing the bitterness of my childhood that I used to create toxicity in my marriage, which contributed to the overall death.

One of my mothers' personalities in my childhood was "that bitch" which I will refer to as the "anger demon" moving forward. The anger demon manifested just about any time my mother faced any situation in which she needed to be tough or protect herself. The earliest memory I have of the anger demon is when I was about five years old, waking up in the middle of the night, going to my doorway, and seeing my mom throw a chopping knife with accuracy and precision at my brother's dad, Big Drew. Culinary trained, my mom knew her way around a knife, and with her Compton, California upbringing, she knew how to use that knife, which I saw caress the left cheek and ear of Big Drew as I stood in the doorway that blessed night. I call it a blessed night because my standing in the doorway literally prompted my mom to shift her aim enough to intentionally miss shish kabobbing Big Drew and traumatizing me with blood that would have surely splatted all over me.

Anger was not the only demon or personality present during this situation; it was accompanied by murder. It should be obvious at this point that I received the demon of murder through the womb of my mother. It's important to know that I received a double portion of murder from my mother and father, however, since my mother was my primary caregiver, it is fair to say that the unclean spirit of murder was nurtured by my mother and her murderous behavior at times. Anger manifested itself in many ways in my mother throughout my childhood, earning her a reputation in our family that she does not play and will beat you down. I am grateful that my mother has received some deliverance since then and is still seeking deliverance in other ways. However, I have to acknowledge that her multiple personality outbursts had an effect and influenced me in ways that I did not realize.

I was a murderer in thought, speech, and character from the day Derrick met me to the final days of our active marriage. I murdered myself, and I murdered Derrick with my speech to make myself feel and appear better than I actually was. I cannot count how many times I called him an f-boy, a narc, and questioned if he was an Ahab. Self-righteousness was my weapon of choice before and in the early years of our marriage. I had no awareness, no care, and no ability to hear the subtle abuse that was in my speech when I had reached my boiling point with Derrick. While I was not popping off at the mouth every day, the times I did were significant and impacted Derrick. Most people could not tell based on how I presented myself at that time because I practiced cleaning the outside of my cup (Lk 11:39) instead of focusing on the inside and letting the outside follow. In other words, I practiced masking.

Unfortunately, I was not aware of all the psychological terms and nuances of how I was behaving until a marital counseling session we had with an established psychologist named Angela from the U.K. In her brief observation and studying the dynamic between Derrick and me, she said that both of you are psychologically and emotionally abusive to each other in different ways. I was stunned and silenced by this statement, and my mind began to wonder in what way I was psychologically and emotionally abusive. It was at that point I began to study and become informed about psychological and emotional abuse and how I acted on that in my marriage. My discoveries were shocking yet liberating at the same time. I learned that emotional and psychological abuse may not leave physical marks, but it can be just as destructive as physical abuse, leading to anxiety, depression, and addiction. Like physical abuse, they are primarily a means of control and a way for the abuser to feel superior.[73]

Remember, I developed a superiority complex with my thoughts that said, 'at least I am not the one who cheats.' This belief was a stronghold in my life and in my behavior in my relationship with Derrick from day until midway through our marriage. Again, a stronghold is a place where a particular perspective or belief is strongly defended or upheld; it is a mentality used to manifest unseen assignments into reality. As I began examining myself, the Lord began to show me how I would sit in closets crying, waiting for Derrick to come back from wherever he was to catch me to elicit an emotional and caring response from him that was caring. Usually, this behavior was triggered by me going through his phone and seeing pictures or videos of him having sex with other chicks. Instead of confronting him about it, I would resort to crying in the closet or sitting beside dressers and crying until he found me, then lying about the reason I was crying. My go-to lie to conceal the heartbreak from watching him balls-deep in another chick was, "I miss my dad." I'm just so upset I'll never get to know him.

Writing it out just makes me cringe as I recount that season of my life, but it is also a testament to the faithfulness of God to deliver me from being a murderer and abuser. The behavior that I described was psychological and emotional abuse. My primary goal was to gain control over Derrick's emotions so that he could respond and comfort me in the way I needed him to, through deception, by lying about why I was upset. Looking back on that time in my life, I truly felt and knew without a shadow of a doubt that my lying and deception to receive the level of comfort I needed after watching him smash other chicks was the only way I could ever receive what seemed like genuine care for my pain. After practicing this for nine years before we walked down the aisle, it became a way of everyday life; I was addicted to manipulating and deceiving to gain control and elicit an emotional response from Derrick that would console me after being crushed by his cheating.

The manipulation, psychological abuse, and emotionally abusive behavior that I participated in was witchcraft. At the time, I was actively behaving this way. I did not know that, but knowing what I know now, it was a thousand percent just that. Manipulation is treating, managing, or utilizing skillfully to control or play upon by artful or insidious means, especially to one's advantage. I was doing that with my response to seeing home porn that was not starring me. I was addicted to this means of getting attention or getting Derrick to see me, choose me, and pick me. Through sex, I inherited the demon of addiction from Derrick. As believers in Christ, we must understand why a soul-tie is formed and its spiritual impact on a person. Sex is not only physical; sex is also emotional and spiritual. This means that every part of you is involved when you are having intercourse with someone. Since we are a spirit that has a soul that lives in a body, our spirit, soul (mind, will, emotions), and body are all involved when we are having sex. [74]

In toxic and abusive marriages and relationships, this soul tie is called a trauma bond, which makes it difficult to see clearly and leave their toxic or abusive situation. Soul-tie is the spiritual component, while trauma bond is the natural and psychological component that must be addressed for whole-person healing and recovery. It is during sex that the knitting of two souls and spirits takes place, as your body is connected to the person with whom you are having sex. You become one with the person you sleep with. It was during my first sexual experience with Derrick two weeks after we met that I was infected with the demon spirit of addiction, which was only one of many that I inherited from the union. Our biblical reference to this is 1 Corinthians 6:16 *Or do you not know that he who is joined to a harlot is one body with her? For the two, He says, shall become one flesh.* So, let's explore addiction.

Addiction

Proverbs 25:28 (AMP)

[28]Like a city that is broken down and without walls [leaving it unprotected] is a man who has no self-control over his spirit [and sets himself up for trouble].

When you combine oppression and sin cycles, you get an addiction. I repeat, any form of addiction is tied to a powerful demonic influence. [75] The demon of addiction that I inherited through my soul-tie with Derrick presented itself in the form of compulsive physical and mental need to have an experience of being consoled, cared for, and protected. The addiction also characterizes my behavior of sitting in closets and other behaviors as a response to oppression. Identifying the spiritual component of my behavior and decisions does not justify or make my manipulative and abusive tendencies okay under any circumstance. In fact, it is something that I am not thrilled to be sharing with you and that I felt great shame for because, there was a very real natural and spiritual impact that it had on Derrick that I personally feel drove him further away from God.

I do not take credit for his personal decisions and choices that was not in alignment with the standards of God, but I do take responsibility and accountability for my role in not creating a space where the Holy Spirit could do what only He could do the help Derrick make wiser personal choices and decisions. This leads me to another silent killer that contributed to my thinking there was hope for my marriage. Guilt. Guilt is a feeling of worry or unhappiness because you have done something wrong, such as causing harm to another person, according to the Cambridge Dictionary. People often use the words guilt and shame interchangeably, but the two emotions affect us in different ways. June Tangney, PhD, of George Mason University, talks about the difference between shame and guilt, their role in our mental health, and how they affect our behavior. Along with why some people are especially prone to shame or guild, and what you can do when guilt or shame is harming your mental health, especially when you feel guilty over something that is not your fault or that you cannot change.[76]

So, what is the difference between shame and guilt? What role do these emotions play in our mental health? Are they useful tools of persuasion? Does trying to guilt or shame someone into changing their behavior usually work? How early in life do these emotions appear?[77] According to Dr. Tangney, in a nutshell, when we feel shame, we feel bad about ourselves. We are fundamentally flawed because we did something. It reflects who we are as a person. I'm a bad person for having done that. Guilt, in contrast, focuses on a behavior somewhat separate from the self. You can be a good person but do a bad thing. And so, when people feel guilt, they typically feel bad about something they've done, something specific, or not done that they should have. So how then does guilt and shame affect people's mental health? Are people who are prone to feeling shame more susceptible to some mental health disorders? Dr Tangney answers saying, yes, actually, Freud was wrong on one point. Well, he's quoted as saying guilt is the cause of neurosis. And actually, it seems to be more shame, that people are prone to feeling bad about themselves because they failed or transgressed. People who are prone to shame about the self, are more susceptible to a range of different psychological and behavioral problems. Since psychology without God is dead, we must look at the spiritual component that goes along with guilt and shame.

Mental Torment
Matthew 18:34-55 (AMP)

[35]*And in wrath his master turned him over to the tortures (jailers) until he paid all that he owed.* [35]*My heavenly Father will also do the same*

to [every one of] you, if each of you does not forgive his brother from your heart.

One of the most common signs of demonic influence is mental torment. One of the major open doors to mental torment is unforgiveness. In the scripture above, Christ teaches us about a person who was turned over to tormentors because he refused to forgive. Torace D. Soloman defines mental torment as a lack of peace. People who are constantly afraid, worried, angry, anxious, or sad are people who likely have come under some form of demonic oppression. God's word tells us how to think and overcome mental warfare, but when we don't submit to that word, we open ourselves up to attack. Are you beginning to see the significance of the spiritual component that makes leaving an abusive and toxic marriage more complex than just leaving?

We need to realize that not only is psychology not a substitute for spirituality, but spirituality is not a substitute for psychology.[78] This leads me to the second reason we have the idea that it is possible to be spiritually mature while remaining emotionally immature.

Reason 2: We have Little Faith and Deny His Power

Mark six tells us about Jesus' visit to His hometown and that He could not do any miracles there except lay hands on a few sick people and heal them. In verse six, we learn that Jesus was amazed at their lack of faith. Faith is required to tend to those who have experienced severe Trauma in their lives to give them hope for the future [79]. However, because of the complexity of Trauma, the church has developed systems and functions that have created unhealthy developments in our spiritual and emotional lives. In fact, to be emotional is, if not sinful, at least less than spiritual.[80] Trauma is an emotional response to a terrible event impacting the spiritual and physical components of a person, overwhelming them with extreme suffering. As a result, the relationship and view of God are distorted along with the relationships of others, which are significantly impacted because of what has happened. When this occurs, God becomes a monster in the mind of the trauma victim. I was no exception to this effect, even as I ministered the word of God to others.

Most Christians value the spiritual over every other aspect of our God-given humanity; the physical, emotional, social, and intellectual. This prioritizing of the spiritual can be traced back to the influence of a Greek philosopher, Plato, who lived several centuries before Christ. His influence on various leaders in church history continues to impact us today. [81] is message, which later became part of the thinking of those in the early church, was essentially, "The body is bad. The spirit is good."[82] In other words, any aspect of our humanity that is not spiritual is suspect at best, including emotions. This limits the acceptable sphere of our life in God to certain spiritual activities, such as praying, reading Scripture, serving others, or attending worship. The problem is that it does not challenge us to think critically and expand our faith to believe or minister wholeness to the parts of people that are human, which include the physical, emotional, social, and intellectual dimensions.[83]

Mental torment is a major factor at play in the minds of women who are caught in the chambers of *A Cheating Man's Heart*. Mental torment includes, but is not limited to, hearing voices, fears and phobias, suicidal tendencies, anger and violence, self-condemnation, and depression. Fear can also manifest as dark shadows following you.[84] Don't these descriptions sound eerily close to secular mental health disorders? Demonic influence is not the same as demonic possession. Possession is a poor translation. The original wording in the Scripture for possession should have been translated as demonized. The KJV incorrectly translates it to be "possessed with devils". Nothing in the original Greek supports the word possessed, which is completely misleading. Possession suggests ownership, and we cannot be owned by demons. However,

Christians with unsubmitted areas in their heart can be influenced and oppressed by the kingdom of darkness.[85]

I was born demonized or oppressed by demons with the dynamic that took place between my teen parents. As I began to grow older in age and experience life, those inherited demons became stronger, more mature, and more active members of my life, and I had no awareness of their existence or influence on my life. Derrick is in the same boat as me, and you are too. The ministry of deliverance is one of the most misrepresented ministries in the modern church. Most churches today view this ministry as dramatic and unnecessary. They try to numb the symptoms of demonic oppression with exciting sermons and declarations of financial turnaround. They have replaced the need for radical spiritual encounters with never-ending praise breaks. While praise is a powerful tool for breakthrough, it should never be confused with or replace the ministry of deliverance. On the other hand, we have churches that operate in deliverance to some extent, but they are so judgmental and religious that it makes people ashamed to need freedom.[86]

Joel 2:32 (NIV)

[32]And everyone who calls on the name of the LORD will be saved; for Mount Zion and in Jerusalem there will be deliverance, as the LORD has said, even among the survivors who the LORD calls.

Deliverance is for EVERYONE who chooses to call upon the name of the LORD! The church is the only entity in the world that has been given authority over the kingdom of darkness, and that authority came directly from the Head of the Church, our Lord, and Savior Jesus Christ.

Luke 4:28 (NIV)

[28]The Spirit of the Lord is on me, because he has anointed me to proclaim good news to the poor. He has sent me to proclaim freedom for the prisoners and recovery of sight for the blind to set the oppressed free

The reason that deliverance ministry hasn't been embraced by many churches is because people have stopped following Jesus practices. They have stopped using the authority that Jesus gave and try to cast out demons by their own intelligence.[87]In other words, they try to cast out demons using secular therapy which is learned and practiced as if God does not exist. And if God does not exist then the demons that people have are not being cast out in intense years of therapy, they are being multiplied. Deliverance is a ministry of grace, meaning that it can only happen through divine intervention. Human intellect is not enough to get people to breakthrough. We must cast out demons with the authority of heaven.[88] Demons cannot be counseled out; they have to be cast out by the power of the Holy Spirit and in the name of Jesus. There is no other way!

Romans 14:17 (AMP)

[17]For the kingdom of God is not a matter of eating and drinking [what one likes], but of righteousness and peace and joy in the Holy Spirit.

Deliverance brings people into righteousness, peace, and joy. Demonic influences come to keep people from righteousness because they want us to live shameful and unclean lives.[89] Since deliverance is for everyone, this means that those called to the pulpit are no exception to receiving freedom from demonic oppression in the name of Jesus. As I mentioned before, I was preaching the word of God; I was also being affected by trauma and the oppression that goes with it. Humility is required in order to receive this deliverance, whether you're in the pulpit or the pews of the church. The Apostle Paul said it best in Philippians 3:12, saying, *not that I have already obtained all this or have already arrived at my goal, but I press on to take hold of that for which Christ Jesus took hold of me.* Jesus also teaches us the humility required as ministers of God through the story of the Apostle Peter when Jesus predicts His death in Matthew 16.

The scripture *says that from that time on, Jesus began to explain to his disciples that he must go to Jerusalem and suffer many things at the hands of the elders, the chief priests, and the teachers of the law and that he must be killed and on the third day be raised to life. Scripture then says that Peter took him aside and began to rebuke him. "Never, Lord!" he said. "This shall never happen to you!" Jesus turned and said to Peter, "Get behind me, Satan! You are a stumbling block to me; you do not have in mind the concerns of God, but merely human concerns."* The aforementioned scriptures here serve as rock-solid evidence that Ministers of the Word of God have not arrived and are still in need of DELIVERANCE by the power of the Holy Spirit and in the name of Jesus.

I cannot tell you how many times I stood or was pulled out from the crowd by catchers to receive deliverance over the last four years in the freedom arena of Ed Citronnelli Ministries. Since we cannot be owned by demons, it was easy for me to identify an area of my life where I was oppressed by a demon as I did the hard and excruciatingly painful work of examining myself to get to the next level of my healing in mind, body, soul, and spirit. Confronting the trauma in my life forced me to wrestle with the complexity of my own brokenness partially caused by unfaithfulness in my 14-year stint with Derrick. So, let's talk about trauma.

Trauma

Isaiah 41:10 (NIV)

[10]So do not fear, For I am with you; do not be dismayed, for I am your God. I will strengthen you and help you; I will uphold you with my righteous right hand.

I did not become a survivor of *A Cheating Man's Heart* because I have arrived or have everything figured out. I became a survivor because I've made a choice to remain in a place of being brokenhearted and contrite spirit in the presence of the Lord, whose strength is made strong within me in my weakness. The final common sign of demonic influence in my toxic relationship is unaddressed trauma. What I am articulating to you through the pages of this book about my trauma, Derrick's trauma, and the trauma we created with our toxic traits was not in my vocabulary or reach of wisdom or understanding. All the things, nuances, and details of the toxicity that infected my marriage and led to its death have come 100% from the wisdom of the Holy Spirit.

Since I was experiencing traumatic experiences every day, physically, mentally, and emotionally, I was severely affected by trauma in my soul in a number of different ways. Trauma often needs to be addressed by a seasoned deliverance minister and a therapist, echoing my stance that therapy without God is dead. Some effects of trauma showed up in small ways, like how Derrick raised or shifted the tone in his voice. At other times, I would have a jumpy startle response when he would walk up behind me to simply hug and caress my backside. It also manifested in me imitating other women who Derrick had been cheating with in order to be and feel accepted by him, leading to competitions that I never won.

The effects of these behaviors and manifestations of demons were devastating. The enemy used the effects of these events to leave me paralyzed to the point I was stuck in a loop of my trauma. The enemy

91

then magnified this when adultery went public, and my own account of what I had experienced, written in the post, 'I knew her body, better than I knew my own', was twisted and manipulated. Which was orchestrated by Satan so he could infect me with more demons as I was experiencing active traumatic events in order to keep me from developing into what God designed me to be in this generation. But thank God for the helmet of salvation!

Earning the title "Miss Helmet of Salvation" after blurting out Ephesians 6:17 live in front of over four million viewers online worldwide is the only divine explanation for my mind not dissociating amid active big T trauma while carrying my third child in the womb. The whole armor of God is taught to us in Ephesians 6:10-18. Verse 12 says *for we do not wrestle against flesh and blood, but against principalities, against power, against the rulers of the darkness of this age, against spiritual hosts of wickedness in the heavenly places.* It goes on to say in verse thirteen, *Therefore take up the whole armor of God, that you may be able to withstand in the evil day, and having done all, to stand.* The evil day in my life came when TashaK partnered with her demons to expose Derrick's unfaithfulness. And doing everything I could do to stand, I relied on the only person who could save me. The Word of God, which is the Helmet of Salvation.

A smart soldier takes time to gather intel on his opponent before going into battle. I gathered intel through several deliverance ministers from 2019 until the day I made my public debut. The Holy Spirit guided and helped me gather this intel and personally prepared me by telling me multiple times in 2020 that the affair partners would go public. The first time God spoke to me about the affair partners going public was in March of 2020 when Derrick was confessing to another six women besides the two Ashely and Autumn who he was in full-blown relationships. According to Derrick's confession via text message, "Aston, Makayla, LaNai, Kirsten, Porscha and resurface of Dunnie and

Shatera came in the picture. However, the latter two he claimed that "no line was blurred in even the slightest as it relates to flirtation or telling anything about our marital details."

In the middle of Derrick crushing my heart with the sludge hammer of his uncontrolled private organ, God spoke in a still, small voice. The married one's husband will find out about this. Mid-text conversation as Derrick was explaining how he fell into such a dark place and felt so bad for his infidelity, I interrupted and told him that the Lord said the one who is married husband will find out. I told him I don't know how, or when but he will find out. Two months later, on one of Derrick's popup visits to Denver, he tells me that the one who is married has been "very loose-lipped" about their sexual relationship. Since she went to Tuskegee, Porcsha's notoriety and adultery in her own marriage around Skegee circles was bound to be a topic of discussion among the masses. When he told me, I just pursed my lips and shook my head.

Leviticus 20:10 (NIV)

[10]If a man commits adultery with another man's wife- with the wife of his neighbor; both adulterer and the adulteress are to be put to death.

When sin is committed by any person, community, or nation, the law of the Spirit of Life must carry out judgment based on the particular unrepentant sin committed. Since Derrick has proclaimed to be a Christian as of February 4th, 2020, and was still in a relationship with Autum and another woman who is in a 10-year-plus abusive relationship while trying to win me back, the unsubmitted areas of his heart, was influenced and oppressed by the kingdom of darkness. Due to this, the law of the Spirit of Life had to carry out judgment based on the sin that was committed by the adulterer and the adulteress because he (they) did not receive through Christ Jesus the law of the Spirit who gives life and sets them free from the law of sin and death (Rom 8:2).

Shortly after Derrick's departure from Denver, the Lord came to me in a dream, showing me a house that I was in, which appeared to be my house; everything was fine, and then all of a sudden, a gigantic elephant came stampeding through the house destroying everything, but me and my children were unharmed. After waking from the dream, I received the interpretation, and the Lord confirmed to me again that the affair partners would go public. Again, I wasted no time in texting Derrick; the Lord said the affair partners will go public; I do not know when or who, but it will happen. He also said, "What are you going to do now that you are John Gray?"

Romans 14:4 (NIV)

⁴Who are you to judge someone else's servant? To their own master, servants stand or fall. And they will stand, for the Lord is able to make them stand.

In the 2018-to-2019-time frame when John Gray's infidelity was going viral on the internet, Derrick made a series of videos on the topic addressing John Gray's unfaithfulness. Ironically, he was personally being unfaithful in our marriage with Ashton and cousin Tiffany, while hiding "business only relationships with Dunnie and Shatera" while "turning down" romantic relationship inquiries from singers Jazmin S. and Keri H. in his DM's from me, but speaking to his predominantly female audience about how to protect themselves against *A Cheating Man's Heart*, even if he is "in the church". The video sparked outrage from the Gray camp, and Derrick, John Gray and his wife Aventer, hopped on an IG live. The live did not go well, in fact it exploded, like the atom bomb when it hit Hiroshima, when Aventer and Derrick got into a quarreling match while Pastor Gray, put his hood on his head, and sat back while his wife defended him. It is not my job to say whether, she was right or wrong, but it is my job to point out that when God has called a person, especially one who is to minister His word, He is very clear that you shall touch not, His, anointed and do His prophets no harm.

Since Derrick was not a believing man at this time, this spiritual law and principle meant nothing to him, after the verbal boxing match between Derrick and Aventer, he went on to make two more videos which he later took down. What he failed to realize is that when he put his mouth on a man of God, regardless of his blatant sin of adultery, he was attacking the image of God and his bride, the church, on the public platform that God gave him. Again, since the law of the Spirit of Life must carry out judgement based on the sin committed, the Lord boomeranged Derricks transgressions against John Gray, back to him, since he was actively committing the same sin.

Matthew 7:3-5 (NIV)

³Why do you look at the speck of sawdust in your brother's eye and pay no attention to the plank in your own eye? ⁴How can you say to your brother, let me take the speck out of your eye, when all the time there is a plank in your own eye? ⁵You hypocrite, first take the plank out of your own eye, and then you will see clearly to remove the speck from your brother's eye.

The above Scripture is why I have spent so much time digging deep into my bitter roots, combined with those of my parents, Derrick's, and his parents. It is impossible for me to share this story without thoroughly exposing and examining the demons, and toxicity that I brought into the marriage that contributed to the overall death. Now that you have a solid foundational understanding of the bitter roots in my marriage, we can examine the ignored red flags.

The Ignored Red Flags

Remember, In the beginning, "Shawn" met "Danielle" according to the original novel *A Cheating Man's Heart* by my soon-to-be ex-husband Derrick Jaxn. Since the Cheating Man's Heart Series is not "a work of fiction, names, characters, places, and incidents" as claimed in the publisher's notes, it is clear that Shawns' character, actions, and behaviors are a cover for the identity of Derrick Jaxn the man and the brand. The books are his confessions in story form! "Likewise, Danielle's character, actions, and behaviors are a cover of the identity of me, Da'Naia Jackson, formerly known as Da'Naia Broadus, at the time these events and incidents took place in the first book of the trilogy. As I move you forward in the story of the early days of my toxic relationship, you will have a more well-rounded view and understanding of the bitterroots that displayed themselves through actions, behaviors, and belief systems, which were red flags that I ignored. Healing God's way requires a thorough examination of the identity, mentality, emotions, physical, and spiritual components of a person when they die in all those areas, leaving them stuck in mentally abusive and manipulative relationships, like mine. Resulting in the feeling of being connected to that person and allowing the truth of their abuse to be irrationally rationalized. So, let's go deeper into the days of my life.[90]

As the story goes in the *Family Matters* section of *A Cheating Mans Heart*, it was about 5 a.m. on a Thursday morning. The sun was still asleep and Shawn, I mean, Derrick Jaxn wasn't. He had an appointment with a therapist in two hours, that he had been waiting for all week.[91] It's not by accident that the covert character Shawn, begins his journey with anticipating a very much needed therapy session. The missing component in this story is that God was not present, and since God was not present, the therapy sessions were dead. Shawns therapist, Jesica, who's character was inspired by a fellow Tuskegee Alum, Jesica Holley, was completely caught off guard, when Shawn shows up for his therapy appointment. She says, "Wow, I had no idea you were coming. The appointment was under a completely different name, a female's name if I'm not mistaken."

In the same way that the therapist in the book expressed, she was not expecting Shawn to show up; since the appointment was under a different name, I was not expecting to come to the harsh reality that Derrick Jaxn never genuinely loved me. Let's go back to the masking concept we discussed in the *Two Sides to Every Coin* section. Do you remember what masking is? Masking (sometimes referred to as camouflaging) involves suppressing or hiding one's behaviors or traits to appear a certain way.[92] The persona Derrick Jaxn was birthed through the toxic dysfunction of my 'chase' and 'trap' relationship with the self-love ambassador who's known as your internet big brother. In its infancy, the persona of the Derrick Jaxn brand was called the Jaxn Files.

The Jaxn files was a blog that Derrick created in which he would give his perspective on topics, mainly concerning relationships, to those in his sphere of influence who would ask him. It was 2012 when the Jaxn Files was birthed and received large amounts of attention. But what inspired the Jaxn files? Let's go back to the summer of 2010 when I was blessed to spend a significant amount of time with my grandfather Larry while also experiencing one of the worst summers with Derrick. Since I entered into the relationship with an insecure attachment style on January 13th, 2009, it was normal for me to be in a mental space of feeling insecure, being dismissive, avoiding things that needed to be confronted, manipulating and relying on psychological abusive tactics to elicit a "caring and loving" response from Derrick to meet my emotional needs.

Dunnie, Mesha, Mookie, Jazmine, Dascha, Iman H., bad girls club Natalie, along with a host of others, became the triggers that fueled my manipulative and psychological tactics to 'keep Derrick' the summer of 2010. Dunnie, who is also an alum from Tuskegee, was instrumental in helping Derrick form his Team Jaxn organization on campus, which led up to the conception of the Jaxn files. She wrote his bios on his social media, connected him with people, and she directed him in areas of truly developing a business model that he could build on while at the same time being his lover. I cannot tell you how many videos I watched of Derrick smashing Dunnie in our shared apartment at the Reserves at Auburn. Or the countless recordings I watched of her getting dressed after he nutted in her and singing the love songs of Beyonce as she grabbed her bra, after what I could only perceive as pure ecstasy at that time.

But Dunnie wasn't the only one! In one of my manipulating Derrick into consoling me for his blatant cheating moments, I remember taking his phone while he was sleeping, sitting in the bathroom, and watching Mookie ride him like a horse. Mookie was one of the ratchets that worked with us at IHOP in Auburn. The woman was harsh and combative with me every time we worked the same shift, and I never understood why until I saw their video in the archives. Can you say traumatized? While that was traumatic to watch, I came to the realization that the real damage had been done to my soul. It was in this summer that I was in rotation as an unaware and unwilling participant, that I began the process of masking and trying to imitate these women's porn videos with Derrick. It was the summer that I came to accept that all men cheat and that this was the normal, acceptable way to do a relationship. It was reinforced by my conversations with Derrick that these relationship dynamics are normal, but it gets worse than that with some guys, so at least he's not like those niggas, who really dog their girls out.

Again, in the early days of our relationship, I had no concept or awareness of mental, emotional, or psychological abuse. I also had no awareness of narcissistic or psychopathic characteristics or traits. It's only by the power of the Holy Spirit that I am able to make sense of the situations, events, and conversations that took place between Derrick and me early on, which were screaming RED FLAGS, that I ignored. But I must go deeper in order to pinpoint earlier signs of toxicity that contributed to the birth of the Jaxn Files. Rewinding back to the beginning, Derrick and I met on January 13th, 2009, in business calc at the prestigious Tuskegee University in Tuskegee, Alabama. Three weeks before we met, I was raped, and I never told a soul. Rape is a trauma with spiritual consequences. Sex is spiritual whether consent is given, or it is taken by force. In either case, a soul tie is created, and the two become one flesh. The soul is comprised of three distinct attributes; the mind, will, and emotions. Understanding each part of the soul will allow us to see where and why ties happen.[93] A soul tie is a linkage in the soulish realm between an individual, an idea, and organization, or another person.[94] This can happen in multiple ways, but it usually needs agreement. Remember that there are good soul ties and negative soul ties.[95] When it comes to rape or any other non-consented sexual experience, a negative soul tie is created. Since sex is the most common soul tie, Satan likes to use it as a weapon when sex outside of God's law is performed, which includes non-consensual sexual contact, violating God's law. Satan then uses this violation to bind people's lives and destroy their destinies.

The soul tie is a connection between the human spirit and another person's personality, soul, will, mind, emotions, heart, and consciousness. Since I was raped, I was soul-tied to my offender, Brian. Brian was someone that I knew; it was during the first winter break of 2008 of my freshman year at Tuskegee when I went to a party against my mother's warning. Since I was living in her house that summer, and she was taking care of all my needs, especially financially, it was expected that I would follow the rules of her house. The rules where I needed to be in the house before 11 p.m., make sure I cleaned up after myself and do my part for the daily maintenance of the house. Well, one night, I decided I was going to go to a party that would violate the return before 11 p.m. rule. I went to the house party, which was thrown by an individual who invited a mixture of guests. Upstairs, there was loud secular music playing, along with bottles of alcohol being passed around by the guests.

In sequence with everyone else, I grabbed a cup and filled it with drink. Since I was not a seasoned alcohol drinker, it took me a while to get through the Smirnoff apple drink of my choice. I remember I was wearing a brown, white, and golden sweater dress with white pants under it. As the alcohol began to take its course through my body, I remember feeling really good and relaxed. Since I knew a lot of people there, including Brian, I had no need to be alarmed about my surroundings or concerned that anyone there would hurt me. After some time of conversing with people and sipping my drink, I decided to go to the basement level, which was filled with about 5 people. Again, I knew these people, so I was not concerned. Music was also playing down there, but it was more of a chill and chat vibe going on between those who were there.

Not too long after being downstairs, Brian comes down with a drink in hand, walking in close proximity to me. To this day, I cannot remember the exact words that we exchanged, but I can speak to the perceived feeling, I had was that there was some flirtation that he was doing with me. Again, I did not think anything of it because we were not the only one's downstairs, and I did not perceive him as a threat to me. After about 15 minutes, the other people began their accents upstairs. Directly across from the stairs was a black futon couch bed that I was sitting on. As I was watching people go upstairs, one by one, I stood up, with the intent of going upstairs as well. However, Brian had other plans. Immediately upon standing up, he stood up and stepped in front of me and leaned in to try and kiss me. I pushed him off and attempted to go up the stairs. I have no memory of a verbal exchange during that interaction, but I do remember feeling that I was now in danger.

Upset that I pushed him off, Brian grabbed my arms from the backside and pushed me down on the futon bed. At this point, I wanted to fight and flee, but I ultimately lay there frozen, inebriated, and trying to convince myself that this was not really about to happen. Brian was holding me down with one arm and upper body while reaching down to pull his penis out and remove my pants, creating the negative soul tie and rape trauma that influenced the way I viewed my relationship with Derrick.

In order to fully understand the rape and soul-tie dynamic we must define force. According to RAINN.ORG, force doesn't always refer to physical pressure. Perpetrators may use emotional coercion, psychological force, or manipulation to coerce a victim into non-consensual sex. Some perpetrators will use threats to force a victim to comply, such as threatening to hurt the victim or their family or other intimidation tactics.

2 Samuel 13:11 (NIV)

[11] But when she took it to him to eat, he grabbed her and said, Come to bed with me my, sister."

King David's son Amnon rapes his half-sister Tamar using a manipulation tactic of pretending to be ill (verse 5) and then blatantly ignores her pleas for him not to force her. Prior to this, we see Dinah, daughter of Jacob and Leah, who was forced to have intercourse with Shechem the Hivite. Since sex is a spiritual act, a soul tie was created, which is noted in Genesis 34:4 when it says, *"his soul was strongly attracted to Dinah."*

So, what is God's view on Rape? The term sexual assault refers to sexual control or behavior that occurs without the explicit consent of the victim. When I pushed Brian away from me during his attempt to kiss me, I was communicating that I was not mutually in agreement with his pass at me. Some forms of sexual assault include attempted rape, fondling or unwanted touching, forcing a victim to perform sexual acts, such as oral sex, penetration to the perpetrator's body, or penetration to the victim's body, also known as rape. The FBI defines rape as penetration, no matter how slight of the vagina or anus with any body part or object, or oral penetration of a sex organ of another person, without consent of the victim.

Now what does the Bible say about this? Rape is addressed directly and depicts a gross violation of God's design. The laws of Deuteronomy 22:13-29 are related to offenses involving women. Verses 13-22 deal with crimes involving married women and verses 23-29 deal with crimes involving unmarried women. Skipping to verses 28-29, rape is clearly addressed. The law specifies that in a sexual assault, the woman was responsible for actively resisting (Deut22:24). Going back to verses 25-27, case law statements are provided which define the penalty for rape, which was death or tribute to the woman, which includes marrying her without the option to divorce. In either scenario, wherever it is mentioned, the Bible condemns rape based on the level of resistance. Since we perish for a lack of knowledge, we do not know the procedures and protocols to care for the wounded soul of the traumatized mind. I was traumatized after my encounter with Brian, and my response to that Trauma was dismissal, denial, and avoidance that the situation ever happened. Does that sound familiar? Do you remember the toxic pattern of behavior from my generational bloodline? Didn't my mother dismiss and deny that she was pregnant with me, though she received very clear positive results from a home EPT? Now connect that to what we know about Trauma. Again, Trauma is an overwhelming experience or event that exceeds the capacity of a person to cope. Once that threshold is exceeded, the mind of the person dissociates.

During the first 5 years of my relationship with Derrick, I was silent on the matter of rape because my mind was still in a dissociated state in which my mind had locked up the experience and separated my normal mental process, causing a lack of connection in my thoughts, memory, and sense of identity.[96] My identity had already been attacked, broken, and shattered before I even met or willingly engaged in a relationship with Derrick. Merriam-Webster Dictionary defines identity as the distinguishing character or personality of an individual; the relations established by psychological identification; the condition of being the same with something described or asserted; sameness in essential or generic character in different instances, sameness in all that constitutes the objective reality of a thing and oneness.

The theological profundity in the Fourth Gospel gives foresight and insight into Jesus' time horizon through the themes of oneness, love, and friendship.[97] Oneness language is identity, an identity, in God. Life [Zoi] begins at conception (Jer. 1:5), creating instant oneness that generates agape [ἀγάπη] love (John 15:9). The one [εἷς hies] whom Jesus loved [agapaó] (Jn 13:23) is a nurturing language that is best related to a woman (Matt 12:48) who learns she is with child. The two become one (Gal 3:23) instantly as the mother prepares for the nine-month gestational period in which the being that will be birthed matures to full term. Once the mother's hour has come (Jn 16:21), pain comes as she begins the three stages of giving birth. Enlightened scholars and believers in Christ should ask how God took a four-thousand-year gestational period to birth the Anastasi [Resurrection]. Creating Zoi [Life] (Jn 11:25). While reducing the gestational period from thousands of years into a nine-month process. This wisdom embedded in "the Oneness Motif in the Fourth Gospel that Mark L. Appold (1976) argues, plays a significant role in understanding the theology of the Gospel". Which is the genetic makeup of our identity.[98]

Unpacking the rape here is important because it exposes the broken consciousness that Bishop R.C Blakes teaches with hopes of transforming broken-conscious women into queens through the process he calls Queen-ology. Unfortunately, I did not heal God's way, which tainted my lens of what a healthy, loving, caring, and honest relationship looked like. If you think that this is deep, let us peel back another layer of bitterness and bondage that fought against me in the early days of my relationship with Derrick. Rape is a demon that I inherited through my generational bloodline. The demon of rape is an attack of sexual violence on the physical, psychological, and emotional parts of a human being. It partners with the demons of hurt, shame, humiliation, molestation, torment, suicide, and insanity.[99]

Since spiritual law says that whatever demon, the father does not repent, renounce, and announce, the son will have to battle, it is not a shocker that I was defeated by the demon of rape that had attacked my mother. At 7 years old, my mom was raped by two teenage boys, who were around the age of 17 years old, who had befriended my uncle Kirk, who was 11 at that time. During a conversation between Uncle Kirk and my mom in their adult years, it was revealed that it's possible the teenage boys, motivation for befriending an 11-year-old was for the sole purpose of having their way with the little sister. My mom. If you think that is traumatic, it gets worse! On the horrible day, this event took place, Uncle Kirk was present, and not only present, but he held one side of my mom's arm and leg down while one of the boys held the other side of her arm and leg down while the other teenage boy proceeded to pull out his penis to penetrate her underdeveloped vital organs.

Full penetration did not happen since my mother screamed and cried with a combination of a trickle of blood, which knocked some sense into my uncle Kirk, who intervened by yelling at the boy to stop.

Again, according to the FBI, rape is penetration, no matter how slight of the vagina or anus with any body part or object, or oral penetration of a sex organ of another person, without consent of the victim. Remember that sex is spiritual. Therefore, a negative soul tie was also created in this overwhelming event that my mom experienced. On top of that, she also experienced betrayal trauma when her big brother, who should have been more of a protector, participated in her sexual assault. As a result, another set of negative soul-ties was created with her brother and the other teenage boy, who was waiting to have his turn as he held her down.

Since my mom did not have any connections with anyone who was knowledgeable about the spiritual impact of sexual abuse, she never fought that demon. As a result, that demon came my way and whipped me up from 19-32 years old until I received deliverance in the freedom arena of Ed Citronnelli Ministries. Let's dive deeper. Since the demon of rape is also abuse, the demon of abuse was another inherited generational bloodline curse. However, the demon of abuse did not start with my mother, but with my grammy, Linda Faye. Do you recall the traumatic event my mom experienced when she was 4 or 5 years old when her stepfather was ram-strangling her mother? If your answer is yes, then you realize my mom witnessed domestic abuse. Apparently, that was not the last time abuse was witnessed by my mother, indicating that my grammy never defeated that demon. Therefore, the demons of rape and abuse gained the legal grounds to run through the bloodline.

Even after receiving deliverance from rape and abuse, I did not know anything about going to the courts of heaven to bring the alter and spirits of abuse and rape up on charges, to issue a divine restraining order and permanent injunction so that they could no longer have a legal claim to my bloodline. My ignorance of this had me perish mentally and emotionally when my oldest daughter, Marlee, told her dad that Cousin Carter touched her privates. Marlee was five years old at the time she disclosed this information to her father, and I was roughly a week away from being nine months pregnant with our third child Eliy'Sha. Let me remind you that the first wave of affair partners went public in March of 2021, and I found out two days before my marriage became a public spectacle that we were expecting our third child. Every day of those nine months, I was experiencing reoccurring trauma. The impact was that I could barely get out of bed; most days, I was withdrawn from everyone, my body was in severe pain daily, and I just could not think properly.

Adding to this state of being overwhelmed, Derrick brings me the news that Marlee has said that Cousin Carter has touched her privates. Derrick then proceeded to ask me how we should handle this, and I said, "Well, I think we need to investigate this, and restrict unsupervised interactions until we can figure out what happened." Derrick then asked me, do you want to take the lead on that, or do you want me to?" my reply was, "I need you too because I do not have the mental or emotional capacity to deal with this." Now Carter is Derrick's nephew and youngest son of one of his older sisters, Yida. It's hard for me to navigate this particular detail because Marlee did not come to me directly and tell me this, and after being out of the relationship with Derrick and sitting with this situation and how it played out with the investigation, it has created questions within me as the whether he made this story up, to see how I would respond, but also to support his bashing me to his family, to support his premeditated discard of me.

Since I cannot be certain as to whether he made it up, the whole family goes through a very tough process to figure out what happened. I can only share the facts of what I know to be true as far as coming to a resolution. Yida was notified of the accusation, and you can hear the heartbreak and confusion in her voice while at the same time saying that she understands that we have to have it investigated. After that dreadful call, Derrick was responsible for seeing the investigation to completion since I was not in any healthy place mentally or emotionally to cope with the possibility of my daughter being molested. The local authorities were called, and a report was filed to start the investigation process. Since Carter lives in Alabama, and the incident was said to have happened during a trip to Alabama, the local authorities had to contact the local department in Alabama to move the case along.

While we were waiting to hear back about the next steps in investigating Marlee's statement, I told Derrick that we needed to get Marlee checked out by a doctor so they could tell us if they noticed or saw anything alarming that would support this claim. Derrick's response was that if I wanted to have it done, then I needed to be the one to set that up. After a few weeks, the Alabama officials sent out their professionals to Yida's house to speak to Carter, who was also a minor, who was roughly 12 years old at that time. What I was told by Derrick is that the professional investigators did not perceive or see indications within Carter's responses that led them to believe that inappropriate touch was at play. Months went by with no additional updates on the Alabama department investigation. At that point, I had already given birth to our third child and was better mentally and emotionally than I was in the last month of my pregnancy.

Still not settled with having no full resolution to Marlee's claim, I began asking Derrick for updates. My asking agitated him, and his response every time I inquired about it was if you want to know, then you need to be the one to call them. He texted me the number, and I started calling. Every time I called; I would get voicemail. Then, one day, I received a call back from the sheriff's office, and he pulled up Marlee's case, but there were no notes or updates on the case that were noted in her file. Unsettled, I asked him if he knew when there would be updates, and he told me that he would need to reach out to the case manager. I never heard back, and I always got voicemail when I continued to call for an update. To this day, the case is still unresolved as far as I know. But God knows all things.

The most significant thing to note about this situation is that the demons of rape and abuse appear to have had access to another generation, which was my child. Again, it highlights the spiritual law that if the father does not repent, renounce, and announce an agreement with a demon, the son will battle the same demon. As far as I know and understand the situation, my daughter had to battle the same demons that my grandmother had to battle because I failed to see the full process of deliverance to completion. I did not renounce and announce, followed by taking those spirits and alters to the courts of heaven. Robert Henderson teaches on the courts of heaven in his book Operating in the Courts of Heaven. The court of heaven is not a way that we pray, it's a dimension that we step into the presence of God as the righteous Judge according to the prophet Daniel's vision in Daniel 7:9-10.

It's important that I thoroughly examine the impact that rape had in my life, not only to show the level of broken consciousness that I had before I met Derrick but to show the spiritual impact it had during our relationship, which opened the door for attacks on our children. I reference Clinical Psychologist Diane Langberg again, who explains the spiritual impact of such experiences on a person as being so significant because the messages received through the trauma are about the identity of the person who has experienced the life-threatening event and, therefore, the identity of God, whom the offender(s) represent to the victim. "Stealing someone's freedom or self-respect by ill-treatment is just as serious and threatening as stealing one's possessions. Deuteronomy 19-21,22:1-23:14 and 23:15-24:7 emphasize how the victim of such ill-treatment that has created trauma in their life puts the dignity of the individual at stake.[100]

Human dignity is addressed on three fronts: the dignity of existence, the dignity derived from the homogeneity of a corporate group, and the dignity of personhood.[101] In this section, I will address the dignity of personhood and the dignity of existence. Jesus was traumatized so that we may live and have life and life more abundantly (Jn 10:10). However, when the dignity of existence and the dignity of personhood is violated, it is common that people who have experienced adultery, rape, and other forms of abuse or trauma, to express the feeling that they have been violated and their privacy invaded. Reflecting on my life thus far has exposed grief and unimaginable suffering after adultery, rape, child birthing amid trauma, and public humiliation attacking the dignity of my personhood. It is clear then that the prohibition of commandment eight "you shall not steal" is not intended to be limited to taking something that belongs to another but is viewed in the larger context of any invasion of privacy. Such actions have the effect of dehumanizing and threatening the dignity of personhood.[102]

In brief, the details I have disclosed about my life as it relates to the invasion of a confession of at least 11 women in my marriage (though that number is higher), unhealed rape trauma, and the public invasion of intimate details concerning the turbulence in my marriage when the affair partners went public created a deep spiritual wound within me that's impact distorted the image of God as I desperately sought to understand who He is and why He allowed these things to happen to me.[103]

The complex trauma that I have revealed so far illustrates how easy it is for someone to struggle with seeing God clearly as healer who is close to them and cares about them when they are broken and in contrite spirit, instead of a monster who leaves them hanging in the balance to figure it out with the limited resources that are currently available in the body of Christ today as a whole. In December of 2008, when Brian raped me, God became a monster to me, and what do you do when you see a monster? You run, and that's exactly what I did, which led me to negative co-dependency. Secular psychology defines co-dependency as a learned behavior that can be passed down from one generation to another. It is an emotional and behavioral condition that affects an individual's ability to have a healthy, mutually satisfying relationship. People with negative co-dependency often form relationships that are one-sided, emotionally destructive, and/or abusive.[104]

However, co-dependency is not inherently bad as the secular psychology world has defined it. In fact, God created co-dependency, and He intentionally created human beings to be co-dependent on Him. Holy Spirit-led biblical psychology teaches you were created to be co-dependent on One person, God the Father, Son, and Holy Spirit, which is a consistent command throughout scripture from Genesis to Revelation. When God said, Let *Us make man in Our image, according to Our likeness* in Genesis 1:26, He created our identity and innate co-dependency on Him as the creator of all life. The Holy Spirit then inspires the writer of John to repeat and agree with Himself when it is written, *I am the vine, you are the branches. If you remain in Me and I in you, you will bear much fruit; apart from Me, you can do nothing* (Jn 15:5).

Identity then has everything to do with who we are in God, and Satan's job is to attack that identity and distort it using people, circumstances, and events so that we become negatively co-dependent on people or world value systems and beliefs, which is idolatry. As I naturally ran from God, who had become a monster, I naturally attracted a negative co-dependency with Derrick three weeks after the assault. Do not discredit the impact of the bitter roots from which I came, where my mother and grandmother encountered the demons of abuse and rape that they never dealt with because God had become a monster to them, too, though they were not consciously aware of their distorted view. I'll ask again, what do you do when you see a monster? The answer is you run, which was the learned behavior passed down from my Grammy's generation to my mom's generation, to my generation. Unfortunately, I am seeing signs of that in my children's generation.

Moving forward, while I was sitting in business calc, front row, listening to Dr. Kim, a strong medium voice from my right said, hey, are you a model? I turned and looked at Derrick and then looked down, wondering what gave him that impression. Before I could lift my eyes from my binder on the floor, I heard, are you a model? Again. In a soft and timid voice, I replied, yes, I used to model, followed by a soft smile stretching across my face. Let's pause here and get a director's view of the same scene. According to *A Cheating Man's Heart* by Derrick Jaxn, Shawn Fletcher, a student at Tuskegee University, has just postponed his "sex-only relationship" with Jazmine. The sexuationship was coming to a halt because Jaz hit him with the "we gotta talk" line. In short, she had taken an interest in "Lewis" and needed to end the placeholder pussy position she was in for Shawn. Shawn responds by saying "I had a feeling this all was just a cry for attention anyway. Yeah, I was that narcissistic. As far as my sex life was concerned, the show must go on."[105]

As the story goes, according to Derrick's novel, Shawn got in his first class of the spring semester, and all of his classmates came back looking fresh, wearing everything on their Christmas list. Interestingly, January 13th, 2009, was the first spring semester class in business calc. But I digress. Shawn then sits in his usual seat towards the back with the rest of the in-class text Messager's and exam, whispers, prowling for new talent to add to the team. As Shawn looks to the door, he sees a prospect walking in. Her stride was a little awkward, almost dorky, but she was cute. Hair was naturally textured into a neat bun, and she had slanted eyes.[106] I am going to interject here, one of the things Derrick has told me from day one, is that he loved my slanted eyes, but let's move on to see what *ACMH* has to say.

Danielle was a little on the classy side with her attire, but Shawn never shied away from a challenge. Inviting you deeper into his thought process, Shawn says in his mind, "Sometimes, girls will try to throw you off by not showing cleavage or calling attention to themselves, but he was no rookie. He knew the game and he knew it well." The novel goes on to say that Shawn ran a full background check on her by the time she sat down, and he liked what he saw. [107] Here's were *Surviving a Cheating Man's Heart* and *A Cheating Man's Heart* crossroads. As Shawn looked at the front of her binder, there were some professional photos of her; one had a saxophone, and the others were more along the lines of Walmart catalog ads with her smiling on a swing set and whatnot. Pause. Do you see the similarity between Derrick and my first interaction in business calc and "Shawn's first interaction with Danielle"?

Intrigued by this binder and photos, Shawn says, "Hey, what's good, ma." He said it with that look in his eye and a half grin. She paused long enough to give Shawn the who the hell you talking to face and proceeded to pack her books. But he couldn't be defeated that easily. He had a work ethic. "I'm sorry, that came out wrong," he said. I meant to say, hello, how are you, Danielle?"[108] Creepy, yet eerily identical to our true identities as Derrick and Da'Naia. Second to me entering into this relationship with Derrick, with unhealed rape trauma, which was a red flag ignored, comes the *ACMH*. Now, *ACMH* was written four years after our first meeting on January 13th, 2009, and of course, there were many red flags between day one and the birth of *ACMH*. However, *ACMH* is a complete, 99% accurate account of real-life events and incidents that transpired between Derrick and I, and Derrick and other women. He is literally confessing his heart condition in the pages of all three books in the trilogy.

Whether you have read the trilogy or not, you can tell from the excerpts that I've shared that Shawn, Fletcher, never looked at Danielle as a person who is deserving of love and respect, nor had any value outside of what he could get from between her legs, to replace Jaz's, temporarily out of order, placeholder pussy. In the words of Shawn

SURVIVING A CHEATING MAN'S HEART

Fletcher, he was on the prowl looking for new talent to add to the team. Does this behavior sound like a biblical character that you know?

1 Peter 5:8-9 (NKJV)

⁸Be sober, be vigilant; because your adversary the devil walks about like a roaring lion, seeking whom he may devour. ⁹Resist him, steadfast in the faith, knowing that the same sufferings are experienced by your brotherhood in the world.

If it was not for the blood of Jesus, who has washed away the shame and guilt from my heart from ignoring this red flag, I would not be able to share this in great detail because it is just too plain that something greater than toxic entitlement is at play. I know you're asking yourself; how did you not say anything about this blatant confession and mirror image of your life story being written and sold to the world? I was a broken, conscious, and psychologically abused woman, who did not have God, nor could I trust Him, since He was a monster to me from the rape. I can say that I read *ACMH* from its beginning stages to its final draft, and I initially thought that this sounded so much like our story, but I ignored that gut feeling. Derrick added to my dismissal of it by commenting, "It's crazy, this sounds similar to us, doesn't it?", I would always say "yes", and he would reply, "yeah, but it's not".

Again, to a person who does not understand trauma and its various impacts on a person, they would begin to victim blame here. The reality is that I was not thinking properly! I had a soul tie, otherwise known as a trauma bond. Remember that psychological abuse causes such deep-seated issues in a person. I was plagued with deep-seated issues that qualified me for real mental illness, which has everything to do with demonic oppression. My mind was fragmented due to the four-year 'chase' and 'trap' cycle of psychological abuse, which made my mind the perfect playground for the one who was on the prowl from day one. This fragmented state made me the better candidate for wife over the other 100 or so women, which is the only reason he selected me as wife. But when the Lord healed my mind, I became nothing more than a used condom thrown on the ground beside the trash can. I was not even worth being put in the trash can during my public and premeditated public discard. It wasn't shocking, but it was clear that my role from the beginning was to be a part of a team that I did not know I was signed up for since day one.

I want to be clear that the trauma I experienced is not an adequate justification for not healing, seeking help sooner or leaving the relationship before we went to the altar. I simply use it as a teaching point that brings understanding to why people like me stay in mentally and emotionally abusive relationships. It's just not that simple. Going back to the terrible, horrible, no good, very bad summer of 2010, the summer I began learning other girls' bodies better than I knew my own. It started when I began seeing video after video of Dunnie, Mookie, Mesha, and many others, home porn videos filmed by Derrick. After watching those in silence for a period of time, without disclosing what I was seeing to Derrick, I began the toxic behavior of trying to trap him into confessing without me having to be forthcoming about going through his phone. Another toxic trait I developed and normalized until we sat down for the first five days of pre-marital counseling sessions with Dr. Turpeau.

My toxic behavior was me setting Derrick up through the honesty box by pretending to be another girl who he had been cheating with, when I knew he was literally out with another girl at the time. The plan backfired miserably since he simply asked the girl why she was tripping; she said she didn't know what he was talking about, which meant I was the culprit. He wasted no time confronting me on the issue, replying back to the honesty box thread, Da'Naia, I know this is you. Panicked, I

SURVIVING A CHEATING MAN'S HEART

stopped replying, and fear filled me up as I anxiously waited for him to return to our shared apartment at the Reserve at Auburn. It was close to midnight when he finally arrived, and I was shaking because I didn't know how I was going to explain this. Derrick's face was covered in disdain and discussion as he came in and said the dreadful words I was fearfully anticipating for four hours before he walked through the door, "I can't do this relationship anymore because I can't trust you." I burst into tears and began begging and pleading with him to give me another chance, but he was adamant that he could not trust me and that it was over.

I was crushed beyond words; I felt like I was physically sick and that my heart could give out at any second. He didn't say another word to me before going to our shared room to lay down. After a few minutes, I walked back into the bedroom and climbed into the same bed, but this time, there was a large gap between us, which was opposite from the spooning position we had been accustomed to doing that usually put us both to sleep. It was this summer when I knew something was wrong, but I didn't know what to call it, and at the same time, I didn't want it to stop. I was addicted.

I want to take the time now to highlight the toxic traits and behavior I was displaying in the early days that carried over to the engagement period before a layer was peeled off in the first couple of sessions with Dr. Turpeau. The first red flag that indicates that I was not in any position to be in a relationship with anyone, let alone Derrick, was that I remained silent after being sexually abused. Every sexual assault survivor's story is different, and how each survivor deals with their experience are incredibly personal. Sadly, there are too many reasons why survivors like me keep their sexual assault a secret. The burden of holding such a traumatic event in silence can pose a lifetime of emotional turbulence as well as physical complications.[109] It's actually not abnormal for a sexual assault survivor to remain silent as many concerns and challenges plague the person's mind when it comes to speaking out against their perpetrators. Here are some common fears and reasons why survivors keep silent:

- Fear of retaliation or punishment from their perpetrator
- Fear of victim-blaming
- Fear that they won't be believed.
- Fear they will have no support or a place to turn for help.
- Fear of being shunned.
- Being conditioned by the perpetrator to keep silent.
- Blaming themselves for the sexual assault[110]

I remained silent because I feared being blamed for the rape, considering I was drinking when it occurred. Unfortunately, in marriage, as I was unpacking active betrayal trauma with public humiliation, I was simultaneously unpacking rape trauma. In my conversations with Derrick, he cast doubt on my being raped because I was drinking, and based on his knowledge of women, it's more likely that I invited that energy, which is victim blaming. Another reason I remained silent is because I feared not being believed. After Brian raped me, I did not go home that night, I stayed in the same house until the sun raised. I was not the only one from the party who crashed at the host's house, and though I was not in close proximity to my abuser for the remainder of the night, I sincerely felt like no one would believe me. Next, I blamed myself because I was drinking and not as alert as I had been groomed to be by my mother.

Remember, my mother had been raped, and though she had not dealt with all the layers of her own rape trauma, she was very vocal to me about her experience as I was growing up. After I was raped, I felt like I had let her down and dishonored her. Logically, this was far from the truth, but in my traumatized mind, it was 100% truth. While all these things reinforced my silence, there is one that trumps all of them and really delivered a fatal blow to my overwhelming guilt and shame, I had broken my vow before God and a host of witnesses to remain a virgin until marriage. Leading me to expose another layer of bitter roots that contributed to my toxic behavior and ignoring of red flags.

Ecclesiastes 5:5 (NIV)

⁵It is better not to make a vow than to make one and not fulfill it.

Breaking the vow I made on July 20th, 2007. Before I continue, let me point out that Derrick's birthday is July 20th. Isn't that ironic? Moving forward, I made a vow to God before witnesses that I would not have sex until marriage. Little did I know that vow would be broken by a forced sexual experience I denied happening for 5 years after the incident. Add on meeting Derrick three weeks later and voluntarily giving it up to him two weeks after that, totaling 5 weeks post-rape trauma. Yes, I got myself into a whole mess. The word vow is defined as:

To give, consecrate, or dedicate to God by a solemn promise. When Jacob went to Mesopotamia, he vowed to God a tenth of his substance and his own future devotion to his service (Gen 28)

To Devote: to make vows or solemn promises, he that vows must be careful to perform (Ecc 5:5)

The vow that I made before God July 20th, 2007, was no small thing. However, I didn't know how big of a thing it was until I hit ministry school. If you are counting, that is 15 years in between making the vow and understanding what a vow to God really means. God expressly commands that anyone who vows to him must fulfill their oath, or the consequences of Deuteronomy 28 are sure to be their portion. Today's world in which we live has normalized breaking vows as standard practice, but before God, it is simply sin. It is the belief system that says, If I'm not happy in my marriage, it's okay to leave based on lack of happiness alone. Again, this highlights the emotional immaturity that we tolerate in the body of Christ. I am no exception to falling prey to this immaturity before I was forced to go deeper into the things of God to become an emotionally healthy disciple as outlined in Peter Scazzero's book.

In these pages I will pick apart the price I paid for not paying what I vowed. I want to stop here to be very clear that the act of being forced into a sexual encounter was not my fault. I refuse to take responsibility or accountability for the actions of someone else's poor decision-making. I will and am taking responsibility for the actions and decisions that I made leading up to a situation in which I could be taken advantage of sexually. This level of acknowledgment and confession is needed for the Holy Spirit to heal deep and debilitating soul pain within us. Acknowledging my rebellion against the rules of my mother's house comes from mature self-evaluation.

Exodus 20:12 (NIV)

12Honor your father and your mother, so that you may live long in the land the LORD your God is giving you.

I did not honor my mother's house when I decided I wanted to go to a party that I knew would break her home before the 11 p.m. rule. Again, I want to reiterate that the act of rape itself was not my fault, so do not hear what I am not saying. Honor means high esteem; adherence to what is right or to a conventional standard of conduct according to Oxford languages. While it seems miniscule to look at this detail and find fault, it is a critical component when it comes to plucking out demonic roots that have given legal rights to demons to access your life. I was operating in sin since I was still under my mother's roof, and I was unmarried at this time. Since all sin is the same weight in the eyes of God, this seemingly small sin opened the door for Satan to attack, and he did. Of course, at the time, and for the next twelve years thereafter, I did not view this detail as a sin that I needed to repent for. It came after peeling back layer after layer of hatred, anger and bitterness towards Derrick and my sexual abuser that this revelation struck me in the heart.

Leading me to yet another missed red flag within my sexuationship with Derrick. Not too long after our first sexual encounter in the dorm room of Russel Hall, Derrick and I were chatting, and he said, "I had a dream; God told me to stop messing with you and leave you alone". I have to pause writing here, cover my face, and shake my head on this one in disbelief that I missed God's warning. However, the reality is that I did because my thoughts when Derrick shared with me his dreams were, "Why would God tell him to leave me alone? What's wrong with me?" While that is not necessarily a bad thought to have, I should have been asking what is wrong with Derrick, that God would tell him to tell me, Derrick needed to leave me alone. The lesson here is that though I viewed myself as a Christian and thought I was saved, I did not know how to hear the still, small voice of God[111]. Let alone have a close enough relationship with Him to go directly to Him about what that statement meant.

Knowing what I know now, makes me think, ugh, how could I have been so naïve, God was literally trying to save me from 14 years of heartbreak, humiliation and abuse. Yet, I ignored the message and proceeded to do what I wanted to do. At this point, doing what I wanted to do began to highlight that my behavior and decision-making were not just a sin but it was iniquity. Remember iniquity is when you know what you are doing is wrong, but you can't or won't stop. Looking back, I also have to acknowledge the demon transfers that I inherited from Brian during the rape. Unfortunately, I did not know Brians background enough to identify which demons I inherited from him, but I can point out the obvious ones of rape, anger, torment, perversion, arrogance, the spirit of error, shame, corruption, and lust.[112]

Just when you thought I was done listing my demons, my decision to rebel and go to the party also opened the door for the demons of rebellion to have access to my life, and those demons partner with defiance, seduction, hatred, suspicion, distrust, confrontation, and control[113].Naturally the secular law of attraction became the demonic highway that connected my rape trauma mind to the predator mind of Derrick Jaxn. I say predator mind based on the text in *A Cheating Man's Heart* that describes Shawn a.k.a Derrick, who was on the "prowl looking for new talent" [114] Rape opened the door for all the dangers that come with negative soul ties, which are:

1. A soul tie that makes a person easily influenced, manipulated or even worse, abused, even if they are unaware, they are being so.
2. Leads to serious injury or even death of someone if it is an ongoing abusive relationship.
3. It can sabotage your future relationships, like future marriage.
4. It can bring curses and problems that can affect your personal success.
5. It can affect your progress in life.
6. It can affect your God-given purpose and destiny on the earth.
7. It can rob you of mental and emotional peace.

8. It can have long-lasting psychological effects.

9. It can affect future libido and sexual drive with your future husband (wife)

10. It can cause barrenness in women[115]

I want to add that if you move on, you will not want to leave them hanging around. Let me give you an example. Have you ever met someone who's in an abusive relationship in which maybe their partner beats them every day or perhaps even tried to kill them a couple times? Yet instead of leaving that person, it seems like they can't; it's like an invisible force that keeps on drawing the person back to their abusive partners, or even if they finally leave them, they can't seem to stay away very long, even if it means their abuser may kill them? Do you want to know why that is? The answer is a negative soul-tie.[116] In my case, unhealed trauma attracted unhealed trauma, which led to a 14-year negative soul-tie. Follow me deeper into how a negative soul-tie is created.

Deuteronomy 7:26 (NIV)

[26]Do not bring a detestable thing into your house or you, like it, will be set apart for destruction. Regard it as vile and utterly detest it, for it is set apart for destruction.

Often, we take the word house in the bible as a literal structure in which we live and call home. However, we suffer from a lack of knowledge and fail to see all the ways in which a house is used as a symbol for a deeper spiritual revelation of God. We know this because 2 Corinthians 5:1 (AMP) says, our body is the house in which our spirit lives here on earth. When that house is destroyed, then God will give us another house. That house is not made by man's hand. But God made it. It will last forever in heaven. Think about that for a moment, if our physical bodies are the house in which our spirit lives, and our bodies are also the temple of the Holy Spirit (1 Cor 6:19-20) then it's safe to say that we should not be bringing any detestable thing into it according to Deuteronomy 7:26 which is not limited to a physical habitat in which we reside.

Now, let's connect that to my life and what you can take away from your life. I willingly engaged in a relationship with Derrick three weeks after being raped. Two weeks after meeting Derrick, I willingly had sex with him, which continued throughout our entire pre-marriage relationship. Not only did my unhealed rape trauma influence my decision to bring detestable things into my physical body, but so did my willingness to participate in pre-marital sex. Again, the bitter roots of my life had more influence than I knew or ever gave them credit for when I was in the middle of my sin. Both of my parents engaged in pre-marital sex in order to conceive me, and both of them continued having pre-marital sex after I was born. God, however, is very clear in his thoughts on pre-marital sex; he literally says those who practice this will not inherit the kingdom of God (Gal 5:21).

Since God's word is not partial to any man or woman, my decision to engage in consensual pre-marital sex with Derrick meant that I was on the highway to hell. Aborting three children during that process earned me an express lane pass straight to the fiery pit to burn for eternity. Thank God for Deliverance, mercy, and forgiveness! Unfortunately, I did not start receiving deliverance until year 11 of being with Derrick, but ironically enough, it was my generational inheritance to be rescued by God before I drowned in the trauma of the relationship. It's important to note that if there are generational curses, then there are generational blessings. The generational blessing working in my favor came from my great- Grandmother Eva Mae Buchanan who was an evangelist of her generation. Eva, whom I will refer to as Mother moving forward, founded the church where I made my vow to remain a virgin until marriage. Disciples of Christ New Testament church in Denver was the blessed inheritance link working in my favor when I was living my life of sin with my boyfriend.

Right here is another opportunity for me to acknowledge that God's word will not return to Him void. Mother prayed some prayers for the generations after her and instilled some basics of the solid foundation in Christ in her daughter Linda Faye and her granddaughter A'Nedria, whom I call mom. Proverbs 22:6 says *to start children off on the way they should go, and even when they are old, they will not turn from it.* I am grateful to God that He put this in the bible because I needed it. After being raped, everything I knew and desired to know about God vanished as shame, guilt, and worthlessness overcame me. Through this lens, I encountered a man with no spiritual anchor working in his favor that would reel him back in when temptation presented a buffet full of women who had an express pass into the marriage.

I did not understand how much this impacted my relationship and marriage until I read *A Cheating Man's Heart* in the process of getting divorced when I saw clearly that Derrick's heart was never in alignment to do things God's way from day one, according to the text. In the *Me, Myself, and ...Damn Who Is That?* Section of Derrick's novel, Shawn's first step on the campus of Tuskegee University changed the game for him. As it is written, Shawns first mission was to get to know him first, so he decided to become spiritually in tune with himself.[117] Huge red flag, how does one become spiritually in tune with oneself? If anyone is a believer in Christ Jesus, then they are to die to themselves and become one with the Father, Son, and Holy Spirit, who supplies all strength and directs your paths. The text then goes on to say, "I always had a relationship with God, but I could never quite get a handle on

Christianity."[118] Before we move forward, let's get an understanding of what relationship means. Relationship is defined as:

The state of being related or interrelated.

1. The relation connecting or binding participants in a relationship: such as:

    (a) Kinship

    (b) A specific instance or type of kinship

2. A state of affairs existing between those having relations of dealings

    (c) A romantic or passionate attachment[119]

Now that we have the relationship defined, how is it that Shawn, a.k.a Derrick, had a relationship with God but did not acknowledge Christ Jesus of Nazareth, on which our Judeo-Christian faith is built? Let's explore this more in the text of *ACMH* that reads, no matter how many times Shawn fasted, sat on the front row at church, sang along with the choir, abbreviated cuss words, and repented when they slipped, something about him never quite got it right, and he got tired of asking questions no one had answers to. I have no doubt that there was a concentrated effort put in for Shawn to know God. However, it is a screaming red flag that Shawn knew of God but did not know Him as in having a connecting or binding relationship. How do I know this?

John 17:12 (NIV)

[12]while I was with them, I protected them and kept them safe by that name you gave me. No one has been lost except the one doomed to destruction so that Scripture would be fulfilled.

Jesus, in this verse, is speaking this as a part of His prayer to our Heavenly Father, declaring that no disciple of the One true and living God was lost. Meaning that even in a backsliding state, a person would still have a level of conviction, which leads to true repentance. Repentance means a change of direction in your mind or thinking and can only be executed by the power of the Holy Spirit. Furthermore, Godly sorrow brings repentance that leads to salvation and leaves no regret, but worldly sorrow brings death according to 2 Corinthians 7:10. In order to see more clearly the heart condition of Derrick, who uses the character of Shawn Fletcher to express his authentic emotions we must continue to analyze the text. Unanswered to Shawns questions left him wondering who King James was and why we should trust his version of the Bible. From Shawns' perspective, it was fair to know a little about Mr. James' biography. [120]

After asking so many questions and getting the same answer, "Pray about it." Shawn decided he could do that from his dorm room with Joel Osteen smiling on his TV. *ACMH* then goes on to say, besides, the guilt of giving into my flesh did more to distract him than help him find himself. So, he made peace by agreeing that if God gave it to him, then there must've been a reason for it. He figured it'd be better to find out the reason the hard way than to die and never know at all. Finally, Shawn proclaims, so it was time for my hormones to experience emancipation at its finest.[121]

Ask yourself if this agrees with the truth of God's word. Do these streams of thought written in the pages of *ACMH* align with Godly sorrow and repentance, even for that of a backslider? Furthermore, in Jesus' prayer, when He says no one has been lost, combined with the 2 Corinthians 7:10 statement godly sorrow brings repentance, leading to salvation and leaves no regrets, clearly highlights that false repentance was the only thing Shawn ever achieved because true repentance leads to salvation and no regrets. Since God is not a man that He should lie, there

125

is no one past, present or future who truly desired Him and truly regretted the sin in their life who could conclude, even in a backsliding state, that God gave them over to experience the desires of their flesh. In fact, when we do see God giving someone over to the desires of their flesh, He has turned them over to a debased mind in which they are free to live and act how they want to without any correction from the Holy Spirit (Rom 1). Bringing worldly sorrow, which leads to death. God's wrath against sinful humanity is clearly stated in:

Romans 1:18-32 (NIV)

[18] *The wrath of God is being revealed from heaven against all the godlessness and wickedness of people, who suppress the truth by their wickedness,* [19] *since what may be know about God is plain to them, because God has made it plain to them.* [20] *For since the creation of the world God's invisible qualities- His eternal power and divine nature- have been clearly seen, being understood from what has been made, so that people are without excuse.*

What this means is that God very clearly states that those who walk by the flesh will not inherit the kingdom of God (Gal 5:19-21). He also clearly states as written in Romans 1:18-20 that He (God) makes it plain to them. The bitter reality is that God made it very clear to Derrick in a dream that he needed to leave me alone. It was clear enough that something in Derrick remembered to tell me this, though I, too, blatantly sinned against God as a backslider. Four years before *ACMH* was written God already revealed that Derrick's heart condition in hopes of saving me from years of humiliation and heartbreak. Ignoring this warning led to the written confessions and true desires of Derrick's heart in his three-book series, which reveal a commitment to what he calls "the Single Man's Code of Conduct (SMCC)."

A Cheating Man's Heart spells out the SMCC as 10 rules as follows:

1. Never have unprotected sex. Wrap it up, strap twice, pull out early, morning after pill, water hose it down afterwards. You can never be too safe.

2. Never tell any secrets of your past. That's when you're forced to trust.

3. Never go out on dates that are in broad daylight, nor show you were thinking about her. A completely generic dinner and movie dates are allowed but that's it.

4. Never give or accept gifts from the heart. Those are tiny investments of love that you never notice until everything's ended and it's time to get rid of them.

5. Never answer calls before booty call hours. Otherwise, you'll position yourself as someone who's there when needed.

6. Never allow tagged photos on Facebook. If this rule is broken, they must be blocked and ignored for some other unforeseen reason you're too emotional to discuss.

7. Never use words like "beautiful," "amazing," or "special" to describe what you think of them. Those are danger words when it comes to the heart.

8. Never tell the truth about what's on your mind. You'll indirectly rely on them to care and if they do, you're screwed.

9. Never meet her friends. They will catch you doing something. You can't avoid that. When they do, you need to be able to say they don't know you.

10. Never allow feelings room to grow. If for whatever reason they slip in, you must cut it off.[122]

Does this sound like a man who is qualified to consider a woman as someone he could date or later marry? Is this line of thinking reflective of a man who is in relationship with God or even concerned with what God wants? The answer is no it's not, and though *ACMH* was not written at the time Derrick, and I first met, the SMCC was very evident in our early dating life. One thing I can appreciate about Derrick's writing in *ACMH* is that he was honest about having a red flag that was waving for him in the relationship, which was, "the closer we got, the more he realized that I was way out of his league".[123] Yet, at the same time, I too missed that same red flag as I believed that he was out of my league and that I was fortunate to be with a jock who had morals and values.

Yes, I said morals and values because three days after the meeting, we spent every second and hour outside of class, not working, texting, and talking on the phone. Sleep was not even a good reason for us to break from our conversations so we did would every typical romance movie depicts when a couple is falling in love, we fell asleep on the phone and woke up with the other person still one the other side of the phone. Love was in the air and hormones were raging, I was in love and so was he after 3 days. Major red flag here because three days is not enough to know anything of substance about a person. I also know it seems like I am dramatizing the sensation of feeling in love so quickly, but it is the whole truth and literally happed in three days. On day four, we found ourselves at Tuskegee Lake in his '99 Grand AM, which became one of our go-to spots for all things: love and romance. It was at this lake that he played several songs from his hometown of Enterprise, Alabama, for me. Tuskegee Lake was also the place where we developed our relationship theme song, *"Kiss Me Through the Phone"* by Soulja Boy.

If only I had known, then what I know now about soul ties when it comes to music and objects and how they work together to keep you bound mentally and emotionally to a person. Since I did not know the power and influence of secular music and my unhealed trauma, it was easy for me to bust it wide open for Derrick on day 12 of getting to know him. Yes, that made me a hoe under every definition. It's also the reason why he thought I was a hoe, treated me like a hoe in our on-and-off-again relationship, and continued to treat me like a hoe even in marriage. And I am not mad at that because I was being just that, a whore. It sounds harsh, but there comes a time when you have to be raw, real, and honest with yourself and then God about your whorish ways. Whoring comes in many forms, just like abuse, and we must take that into consideration when examining ourselves because all of us have whored at some point, and some still do, though it may look different. I know you're wondering what I mean by that, right?

Jeremiah 31:31-33

[31] "The days are coming," declares the LORD, when I will make a new covenant with the people of Israel and with the people of Judah. [32] It will not be like the covenant I made with their ancestors when I took them by the hand to lead them out of Egypt, because they broke my covenant, though I was a husband to them declares the Lord.

As believers in Christ, we make up the body of Christ, and the body of Christ is the bride of Christ. Meaning you, as a believer, are the bride of Christ, whether you are male or female. Due to this, you have accepted Jesus Christ of Nazareth as your groom, otherwise known as the bridegroom in the Bible. Therefore, when you sin according to the obvious acts of the flesh, which are, *sexual immorality, impurity, and debauchery; idolatry and witchcraft; hatred, discord, jealousy, fits of rage, selfish ambition, dissensions, factions, and envy; drunkenness, orgies and the like* (Gal 5:19-21), you are acting like a hoe and committing adultery against the LORD who is your husband. If there is anything in you that truly desires the Lord, then the Holy Spirit should be hitting you right in the heart with conviction because all of us have sinned and fall short of the glory of God. Clearly, I have since I am telling you my story in which I was committing the acts of the flesh of sexual immorality, fits of rage, hatred, murder with my speech, idolatry, witchcraft (zodiac, horoscopes, BeyHive), jealousy, selfish ambition, envy, drunkenness and revelries and many more. No, at the time I was participating in these things, I did not see, think, or know these were sins that were jeopardizing my inheritance of the kingdom of God.

Ultimately, as someone who professed to believe that Jesus Christ was real and Lord, I failed to realize the spiritual impact of my decisions and actions that contributed to a 14-year bad marriage. I'm counting all 14 years because the word of God tells us that *the two shall become one flesh*, and when you have sex with someone spiritually, you have entered marriage with them, though you may not be legally married to them in the natural world. Remember, a soul tie is a connection with someone deeply embedded into your soul, and because sex is not only physical but emotional and spiritual, so we are either creating our own marriages outside of the will of God with fornication or repenting, renouncing, announcing and practicing abstaining from sexual immorality until God highlights the person who He has for us in His perfect will.

The death of my marriage with Derrick was a result of my decision to be with Derrick without consulting God and creating the relationship on my own terms against God's warning that He gave to Derrick. And that was the red flag of red flags that I missed, which is my contribution to the total annihilation of the entire relationship, leaving me with a crushed and broken heart, while also crushing and breaking the hearts of my children. And this is why God hates divorce because it jeopardizes the offspring, which are our children who suffer from the violence that comes when two people have torn away from each other in mind, body, soul, and spirit. Now let's explore the most amazing days of my life with Derrick collided with the most horrendous days of my life with Derrick through the lens of lust of my eyes as the Holy Spirit continues His spiritual autopsy on the cause of death of the union of Da'Naia and Derrick Jackson.

Discussion Questions and Topics:

How does trauma impact the mind, body, soul and spirit of a person?

_____

_____

_____

In what ways can you identify with my story?

_____

_____

_____

List out three patterns and behaviors that you have noticed in your bloodline that seems to be repeating in each generation.

_____

_____

_____

Chapter Summary/Key Takeaways

1. Soul-tie: when two souls are joined together or knitted to become one.

2. Sex: sex is not just physical, it's emotional and spiritual.

3. Trauma: an overwhelming experience or event that exceeds the person's ability to cope.

4. Generational Curses: sin or iniquity passed down through the bloodline.

5. Iniquity: when you know what you are doing is wrong, but you can't or won't stop.

6. Abuse: goes to the core of a person and the messages they receive are that they are someone to use, consume and feed off.

7. Rape: a soul-tie is formed in all forms of sex whether consent is given or not (yes, even in cases of children sexual assault).

8. Deliverance: is the ministry of love.

9. Soul pain: can only be healed by God, that is why psychology without God is dead.

Chapter Two:
I'm in Love! Or is it Lust?

⧞⧞⧞

Day seven, after meeting Derrick, we found ourselves at a party thrown by some of his Auburn University friends. The party was like any other college house party, with music, drinks, and finger foods. I had never been to Auburn, so it was an exciting and scary experience for me. I was texting my mom from the time we left the Tuskegee campus until we arrived at our destination in Auburn. Derrick was no threat to me from what I perceived at that time, and even if he was, most likely, I would have ignored it since I was only a few weeks past having a rape experience. I realized after being healed from sexual assault and many unfortunate events that occurred between Derrick and me that I was triggered going to the house party. The last time I had been to any house party was when I was raped, resulting in me pretending like it never even happened. However, my body's muscle memory did not forget, so I was very closed, timid, and reserved when we walked into the noisy house full of drunk college students.

As we walked through the house, I remember feeling a lot of anxiety, and I could feel my body temperature rising, I was getting hot, and I'm not talking about hot girl summer hot. Derrick led the way as he began greeting his hometown friends Pervis, Jon, and Ryan, who he also introduced me to, as his girl, though we had not yet made anything official. I relished him being bold enough to claim me as his without us having an official conversation because, to me, it meant that he was thinking long-term about our future. I have no logical, rational explanation as to why I felt him proclaiming me as his girl before we even had a conversation, indicated that he had a vision for a future, but it did, and I loved it, though I did not wear my heart on my sleeve. In the living room of the house was a gray couch that had a few people sitting on it, Derrick escorted me to that area, and I sat down. He proceeded to the kitchen to grab us a few drinks, which were non-alcoholic for me. As he was walking back from the kitchen, I stood up to greet him while grabbing my drink, then he plopped down where I was sitting.

The expectation was that I was going to sit on his lap, but I ended up sitting on the arm of the couch right beside him. Honestly, the thought of sitting on his lap didn't even cross my mind, but why would it? Considering no parts of my sexual organs had been in close contact with a mans since the sexual assault. It felt like only seconds after my tush hit the arm of the couch that Derrick's medium deep voice said, "why don't you sit on my lap"? I gave him a half smile and hesitantly stood, walked in front of him and sat on his lap, like I was sitting in a built-in chair at a desk. Yes, that's how awkward I am. I sat straight up, looking straight ahead at the people dancing and having a good time in the living room. Basically, there was nothing intimate about the way I was positioned on his lap. It took Derrick saying, "why are you sitting like that? Turn towards me", for me to loosen up and take a more intimate and close seated position on his lap. So, I turned slightly to the left and placed my arm around his neck.

Suddenly, one of Derrick's arms slipped under my legs and the other around my waist as he briefly hoisted me up and shifted me in a way that was more comfortable for his manhood but also placed our faces in close proximity, which was the game changer. The music was playing, yet it seemed like there was complete silence in the room as I gazed into his eyes, and he gazed into my eyes. I was in love, and I could feel the love radiating from him, then the inevitable happened. We had our first kiss, which was a peck with no tongue. My heart was melting in my chest and beginning to pick up speed. After the first peck, we stayed locked in, looking into the depths of each other's souls; we never spoke a word, and went in for the second peck on the lips, which was five seconds longer than the first, followed by another peck and another peck until we pecked enough to part our lips and let our tongues slide into each other's mouths. Everything about the kiss was right; the best way I can describe it is to bring to your remembrance the Love and Basketball scene when Monica and Quincy were about to have sex for the first time after prom.

The remainder of the night, it was almost like Derrick, and I were the only ones at the party; we got up, walked around a bit, and talked with some folks but found ourselves pressed against each other with my back facing the wall and gazing into each other's eyes once again. No words were spoken, but it was definitely a dialogue of I love you, I love you, too, being exchanged through our unbroken eye contact. Of course, the attraction was so strong that Derrick leaned in for another kiss, and I willingly met him halfway. The wall kiss stopped everything in the room; it was like everyone vanished, the room was filled with the brightest light that there is, and it was just Derrick and I in that moment. Honestly, it was the wall kiss that made me ready to bend over and let him hit from the back in the middle of the party. As our lips parted and we exchanged tongues, I remember feeling like we were moving in slow motion, like the kissing scene in Drumline between Devon and Laila.

My view and perception of what love and relationships should be like mostly came from movies and television, though the real-life model home of my parents' dynamic was hovering in the background. Therefore, on a subconscious and unconscious level, everything that transpired in the first seven days of my knowing Derrick was connected to a scene from one of my favorite movies and tv shows. Love and Basketball was one of my all-time favorite movies, and I watched it frequently during my last year in high school and through the first semester at Tuskegee. I longed for that type of relationship dynamic that Monica and Qunicy had pre-college and the first part of college, and I wanted to avoid the turbulence that hit their relationship when Quincy started cheating and their relationship ultimately ended. I just knew that the horrible part of their relationship in the movie would never be my portion. Boy, oh boy, was I wrong!

Let me take a moment and highlight some red flags, naivete, and straight-up immaturity that indicated I was not qualified to be anyone's girlfriend or hold a position on anyone's roster, especially Derrick's. As discussed in the red flags section, my silence on the sexual assault did more damage to me than the 'chase & trap" dynamic that took place between Derrick and me over the years, which was a red flag that I was not eligible to be in any romantic relationship. At the same time, there was a lack of wisdom, understanding, and knowledge about the impact of sexual assault, and my understanding was that you survive and keep going on with your life like my mom did. In other words, sexual assault was normal in that it occurs, but I had no awareness of the brokenness that it leaves behind because I did not see any emotional side effects in my mom when she told me her stories of rape from her childhood. So, I did not take into consideration trauma and its impact being different on each individual and that the model of how my mom handled her rape, which was void of emotion, was not strength and survival; it was dissociation and fight survival response.

My mom was callous from her brutal upbringing with witnessing abuse, being raped and betrayal trauma from her brother along with that rejection from my father when she disclosed her carrying me in her womb to him. Due to this, she earned a reputation and took on the persona of "the anger demon" because she did not display any soft side of herself to anyone. All of this was lying dormant in my heart during this experience with Derrick at the house party. Additionally, my compare and contrast movie and TV relationships to real life illuminate my immaturity and broken conscious mentality, which made me a fresh prime choice for someone "prowling for new talent to add to their team"[124]. My unhealed trauma, naivete and immaturity contributed to years of pain that could have been avoided if only I could have resisted the urge to follow my flesh after the wall kiss. And that is 100% on me and not on Derrick, nor is it a pass for Derrick's failures and shortcomings that contributed to the death of our relationship.

I am giving you these details because they are the bricks that created the foundation that later birthed the Jaxn Files. It's the detail that highlights the strength of the soul tie that was created before we experienced the turbulence that would come in the summer of 2010. It was the glue that projected this image of real love and ecstasy, which romanticized the faulty, crooked, and lethal foundation upon which we built a family that was obliterated when the media became a factor. Remember that Derrick also had his own unhealed trauma, immaturity, and toxicity that was running in the background during this phase of our blooming relationship. Of course, at the time these events occurred, I had no awareness of these factors having an impact, nor can I definitively say that Derrick had an awareness of these factors and the impact that they would have on our souls.

Leading me to expose the dysfunctional family unit that was modeled for many of us who grew up in broken model homes. Dysfunctional families sweep things under the rug and choose to keep things hush, hush in the family. Complete resolve to issues is never accomplished in these family dynamics, and unfortunately, black families are masters of dysfunction and sweeping things under the rug. We model and teach what secular psychology calls masking. Again, masking is the process in which an individual camouflages their natural personality or behavior to conform to social pressures, abuse, or harassment. Camouflage is also a demon spirit of deception that tries to conceal motives. It partners with the demon of deception.[125] In his sermon series entitled Model Homes, Bishop T.D. Jakes provides context into dysfunction and differences that each person who enters into marriage brings based on their family dynamic. Jakes goes on to say, "There's a difference between mentoring and modeling; you can be mentored by a lot of people, but what often prevails over mentoring is what was modeled in front of you."

I modeled what I saw my parents do with each other and what they did in their relationships outside of each other, and Derrick did the same thing. Emphasizing that broken black families are dysfunctional in various ways, and no, this is not an all-or-nothing saying. Clearly, some functional black families teach and model healthy relationship dynamics, communication, and emotional regulation. However, the majority of black families experience dysfunction at higher rates. Dysfunction is also not limited to black families, families from all nationalities and backgrounds experience dysfunction in various ways that also affect their romantic relationship dynamics. The difference is that they have more exposure and education when it comes to the psychology of people and the psychological impact that happens when various types of trauma and unforeseen events occur.

Due to this lack of knowledge, black families and relationships perish at much higher rates than those of other nationalities. Simply put, we do not teach mental, emotional, and psychological health to our children because we are not mentally, emotionally, and psychologically healthy, yet we pride ourselves on pulling up our bootstraps and doing what needs to be done, giving us the sensation that we have accomplished success. The reality is that though we may have accomplished some things that disprove racial statistics, we have failed miserably in the area of training our kids in the way that they should go so that when they get old, they will not depart. We have modeled emotional immaturity for them, which impacts every area of their lives, including love and relationships. Furthermore, we fail to connect and acknowledge the spiritual impact of dysfunction which is backed by the demonic spirit called marriage breakers.

Now let's connect the pieces of the model home from which I came:

1. Premarital Sex led to my conception.

2. Aborting me was considered, resulting in the creation of a wound of rejection in the womb.

3. My father rejected me initially after birth.

4. My parents had a sexuationship relationship which was considered normal.

5. I was raised by a single mother.

6. I became a tomboy in hopes to gain my dad's attention and affection.

7. My father died when I was 12 years old.

8. I made a vow to God to remain a virgin until marriage.

9. I was raped at 19.

10. My vow to God was broken in the rape and when I willingly had sex with Derrick.

11. No emotional response was displayed in my mom's telling of her sexual assaults.

The summary of all these things comprises the genetic makeup of my character and integrity as a person and potential relationship partner. According to Oxford Languages, character is defined as the mental and moral qualities distinctive to an individual. Meaning my attitude, morals, and ethics were developed based on these significant events and circumstances, which influenced how I viewed life and how I made decisions. Examining oneself based on 2 Corinthians 13:5 requires you to dig deep and analyze every person, circumstance, or event that has occurred in your life so you can get to the root cause of your toxic behavior in order to change through the power of the Holy Spirit. Understanding the complexity of these bitter roots does not grant permission to justify bad actions or poor decisions; what it does is help us see how we became that way. Digging into these details is not only healing God's way but also the necessary work needed to identify negative strongholds in our beliefs that are leasing mental and emotional space, ultimately keeping us bound to our sinful nature and emotional immaturity.

Remember a stronghold is a place where a particular perspective or belief is strongly defended or upheld. The eleven items that I identified from the model home I came from developed my perspective and beliefs that:

1. It's okay to have pre-marital sex and serve the one true and living God.

2. It's okay to abort a baby and still believe that I am saved by the blood of Jesus.

3. Rape happens but as long as you keep achieving it will heal that gross violation of personhood.

4. Sexuationships are normal relationship dynamics.

SURVIVING A CHEATING MAN'S HEART

5. My father's rejection and lack of emotional connection with me in life had no significant impact on my view on men and relationships.

6. God is a Monster; I mean why else would he allow me to be raped?

7. Showing your emotions on your sleeve makes you week.

8. If I have a child, I have everything I need to take care of them on my own, should the father not want to be involved. Many women in my family have done it "successfully."

9. Changing something about myself will bring the love, acceptance and validation I desire from a man.

All of these are examples of emotional and spiritual immaturity that created a thought pattern that agreed with the ideologies of Satan and his kingdom. Essentially, these nine beliefs were fact-based lies that acted as the glue to string these thoughts together as the truth and normal behavior, leaving me blind to my sin. Why is this significant? Satan asserts his influence by seducing us to create mentalities, perspectives, and ideologies that oppose the will of God for our lives.[126] The battleground for spiritual warfare is in the mind and my agreement with these twisted truths defended the legal rights demons had to occupy mental and emotional space in my thought life. Secular psychology's term dissociation is the same thing as a negative stronghold in which the mind copes with stress by disconnecting things usually associated with each other. So, when I was having pre-marital sex after sexual trauma the guilt of my sin and my view of God as a monster disconnected me from my identity in Christ. Leaving room for the demons I acquired to present the lie that I can have pre-marital sex and serve the one true and living God as truth. Consequently, I stayed blind to my sin because I didn't view it as sin, I viewed it as normal behavior that was covered by the blood simply because I believed that Jesus Christ is Lord.

The impact of the immaturity and naivete resulted in me blindly falling in love with Derrick in three days, though it felt like I had known him my whole life based on the over-investment of time we spent having conversations on politics, religion, and family. My romanticized perception of this storybook love story of having found true love in three days was fueled by what I was letting enter my eye gates.

Matthew 6:22 (AMP)

[22] The eye is the lamp of the body, so then if your eye is clear [spiritually perceptive], your whole body will be full of light [benefiting from God's precepts]

Have you ever heard the phrase "the eyes are the window to the soul"? Well, that statement was developed from Matthew 6:22. Our eyes are the window into our body and are one-way demons that can enter us and/or deceive us. The eyes are also the way we can see if someone is filled with the Holy Spirit or oppressed by demons. The lust of my eyes was fed through my love for Disney channel relationships and secular romance flicks. Every time I watched Love and Basketball, Drumline, Dirty Dancing, and Dirty Dancing Havana Nights, my eyes became an open window for the demon of lust to enter my body. I lusted after a "love at first sight" experience. Little did I know that was a spiritual law that Satan perverted to bring into reality with my love in three days' connection with Derrick.

Mark 11:24 (KJV)

²⁴Therefore, I say unto ye, what things soever ye desire, when ye pray, believe that ye receive them, and ye shall have them.

According to Hebrews 4:12, the word of God is active and alive. Therefore, when we are in obedience or disobedience, the word of God is active and living, carrying out various results that bring the things of God to our lives or give room for Satan to destroy our lives. Since I was in rebellion against God's word and following the lust of my eyes based off T.V love, I believed and received the lustful desire of my flesh and not the perfect will of God, which was the perversion of Mark 11:24. Anything that God does, Satan perverts, with our disobedience against God's word. Once I met Derrick, we spent every waking and sleeping moment meeting up and talking on the phone. I believed the lie that I had a fairy tale love-at-first-sight experience with Derrick. As a result, my heart was opened, and shortly after, my legs opened, too.

The phrase lust of the eyes is found in 1 John 2:15-17,*¹⁵ do not love the world or anything in the world. If anyone loves the world, love for the Father is not in him. ¹⁶For everything in the world- the lust of the flesh, the lust of the eyes, and the pride of life- come not from the Father but from the world. ¹⁷The world and its desires pass away, but whoever does the will of God lives forever.* So what is the lust of the eyes? Simply put, the lust of the eyes is the sinful desire to possess what we see or to have those things which have visual appeal. This coveting of money, possessions or physical things is not from God, but from the world around us. John emphasizes that these physical things do not last; they will pass away. In contrast, the child of God is guaranteed eternity.[127]

I coveted the world's idea of love and I received just that which was confirmed when Derrick and I were gazing into each other's eyes at the party. My eyes were unhealthy, and my *body was full of darkness* (Matt 6:23). Not only were my eyes unhealthy, but they were weak like the eyes of Leah. Genesis 29 introduces us to Leah, Rachel's older sister, the wife that Jacob, their husband, loved. It's important to note that every time we see a man who has more than one wife in the Bible, there is a consistent theme of rivalry between the women in which one is loved, and the other is unloved by the husband. Analyzing the text further, you see a jealousy or competitive nature between the women. Jealousy is a spirit rooted in insecurity and aims to destroy relationships. It partners with envy, suspicion, and spite.[128] I knew her body better than I knew my own because of this spirit and relationship dynamic with the legion of women romantically involved with Derrick from the time I met him until the day the statement of divorce hit the internet.

Ecclesiastes 1:9 (NIV)

What has been will be again, what has been done will be done again; there is nothing new under the sun.

Jacob, Leah, and Rachel's story is no different than that of Derrick, Me, and the legion of women who had inappropriate relationships with Derrick throughout our on/off relationship and our marriage. I know this to be true because the Bible literally declares that there is nothing new under the sun. Let me show you how our stories correlate. *Jacob laid eyes on Rachel, daughter of his uncle Laban*, as written in Genesis 29:10. According to Derrick's novel *ACMH*, Derrick "looked to the door and saw a prospect walking in" which I've disclosed is me under the name of Danielle in the book..[129] What does the Bible reference and Derricks book have in common? Both men were drawn to the women by laying eyes on them. What did we learn about eyes? The eyes are the lamps of our bodies and they're either healthy or unhealthy (Matt 6:22). Now let's look at the differences between Jacob's view of Rachel and Derrick's view of me written in the pages of his novel.

Genesis 29:16 says, *Now Laban had two daughters; the name of the older was Leah, and the name of the younger was Rachel.* Verse seventeen goes on to say *that Leah had weak eyes, but Rachel had a lovely figure and was beautiful.* The next verse tells us that Jacob was in love with Rachel and told Laban, *I'll work for seven years in return for your younger daughter, Rachel."* I want to stop and make a critical point here; Jacob was in love with Rachel at first sight. What this tells us is that love at first sight is not inherently bad. However, we get into error when we are looking through the lenses of unhealthy eyes because we have not developed an identity in Christ, who provides the light to our lamps. Jacob's view of Rachel was through healthy lenses, which can be identified by his actions in pursuing a relationship with Rachel. The action step was that he was willing to work for her father seven years to gain her hand in marriage.

In the ancient Near East, marriage was a contractual arrangement between the woman's father and the husband. She remained in her father's household until a suitor paid a bride price (Duet 22:28-29; Ex 22:15-16) to compensate the father for the reduction of the household. At that point, she became formally engaged and legally contracted for, although still living "under her father's authority" (v. 21; lit. "in her father's house). Later at the marriage feast, the union was consummated (Gen 29:22-25) and the woman took up residence in the household of her husband. The laws of Deuteronomy 22:13-23:1 require these contractual norms and terminology.[130]

In contrast, Derrick's gaze upon me as I walked through the door of Dr. Kim's' class was described as being awkward, almost dorky, but cute, according to *ACMH*. Additionally, Derrick adds to this in his Dear Future Wifey interview by saying, "she walked in, I think she had on a black colored button up with black slacks, pretty face slanted eyes, nice curves. He goes on to say, "honestly it was all physical when I first looked at her". Now let's look at Derrick's actions in pursuit of me, according to *ACMH*. Derrick writes I ran a full background check on her by the time she sat down, and I liked what I saw. On the front of her binder were some professional photos of her; one with a saxophone, the others more along the lines of Wal-Mart catalog ads with her smiling on the swing set and whatnot. "Moreover, he writes, this one was going to be interesting, and he couldn't wait for class to let out. When it did, he wasted no time."

"Hey, wha's good ma" he said, with that look in his eyes and a half grin. I paused long enough to give him the Who the hell you talking to face and proceeded to pack my books. The text ends with, But I (Derrick) wouldn't be defeated that easily. I had work ethic.[131] Do you see the difference between Jacob's and Derricks' work ethic? Jacob's code of ethics was to go to her father and work for a period of time to earn her hand in marriage because he was in love with Rachel. In other words, he followed the contractual agreement custom between Rachel's father, Laban, in accordance with God's perfect marriage design. In stark contrast, Derrick had no regard for God's perfect design for marriage because he was going off his self-developed ethical code of conduct, the *Single Man's Code of Conduct (SMCC)*. On his own admission, Derrick said when I looked at her, it was all physical, emphasizing my nice, curves and slanted eyes. Considering this evidence, it is safe to say that Derrick looked at me with lust and not with the love that Jacob had for Rachel, who is described as having a lovely figure and beauty.

What else sticks out to you when it comes the Jacob and Derrick's approach to pursuing a woman? One that sticks out to me is the emphasis on Rachel's beauty throughout the beginning stages of their blooming relationship. Proverbs 31:30 says, *charm is deceptive, and beauty is fleeting, but a woman who fears the LORD is to be praised*. I find it interesting that before Jacob mentions anything about Rachel's beauty, he sees her operating in an esteemed position as a *shepherdess who was tending her father's sheep* (Gen 29:9). Immediately, Jacob rushes to serve Rachel by *rolling the stone away from the mouth of the well and waters the sheep of his uncle Laban, whom Rachel had brought to the well to care for*, which was her established job in her father's house.

Devon Franklin, NY Times bestselling author, producer, and relationship advisor, discusses how you know a healthy man vs a toxic man in an IG Reel. Franklin goes on to say here's how you know the difference between a healthy man and a toxic man. The healthy man is looking to be of service; the man whose toxic is looking to be served. Devon then says, If I am a man that's only looking to be served, I'm not going to see you, because I'm only going to see you through the lens of how you service me. If I'm looking to serve and be of service, I will see you. What's your needs? What's your thoughts? What's your dreams? What are your hopes? What do you want to do? How do you want to do it? Why do you think that? Why do you feel that? So, I'm actually evaluating what is in front of me and identifying how I can make a benefit or contribution, verses looking at it like what's in it for me, what am I going to get out of it from her, what am I going to get out of this.[132]

Can you see the difference between Jacob's and Derricks' approach more clearly now? As Jacob laid eyes on Rachel for the first time, he went over and served her in her current job of shepherding her father's sheep (Gen 29:10), before he even made mention of her beauty or her lovely shape (Gen 29:16). Therefore, Jacob fits the description of the healthy man that Devon Franklin speaks about who is looking to serve and be of service, therefore he could see Rachel for who she was, and he was in love with her on first sight without ever having a first date or sexual encounter. On the contrary, Derrick was "prowling for new talent to add to his team," obviously fitting the description of the unhealthy man Devon Franklin described as a man only looking to be served; therefore, he could not see me, nor could he see me in marriage nine years after our meeting January 13th, 2009. Unfortunately, Derrick still cannot see me, nor does he have an ounce of respect or regard for me as the mother of our three children.

Placing me in the category of Leah the unloved wife of Jacob who was rejected by him the morning after their wedding, when Laban, her father deceived Jacob by giving Leah to Jacob first before giving him Rachel. Imagine having sex with a man and the next morning waking up to him, and he's acting like whatever happened never happened, and he's completely disgusted with you. Can you say dirty, worthless, and used? Better yet, can you see how traumatic that could be and how the impact could result in the feelings of being used, consumed, and fed off? Since sex is not just physical it's emotional and spiritual, the dynamic between Jacob and Leah resulted in a trauma bond that kept Leah hoping, wishing, and praying that Jacob would see her and love her.

The three days it took for Derrick and me to be in love, turned out to be a lie wrapped in a marriage of the love that Jacob had for Rachel. I've since learned being separated, waiting on the final divorce decree that the whole time, from start to finish, was a Jacob and Leah relationship where Jacob never loved or saw her, though she birthed 10 of his children. However, he did maintain the status quo of providing food, water, and shelter for her, which I guess she should have been grateful, but the question is, was she? Genesis 29:25-29 reveals to us *that after Laban's deception of giving Leah to Jacob and not the one whom he loved, Rachel. Another seven years of service was required for him to work for the hand of Rachel.* Further, he had to finish Leah's bridal week. Jacob finished the week with Leah, and then Laban gave him his daughter Rachel to be his wife. Jacob's commitment to Leah was transactional since he did not have a heart desire for her but was obligated to care for her after having sex with her, making them one flesh.

The transactional nature of their marriage was built on a negative soul-tie as the foundation for which their marriage was built. Remember

Laban deceived Jacob, who asked for Rachel, but instead gave Leah, as it was not their custom to give the younger daughter in marriage before the older one (Gen 29:26). Meaning the marriage of Jacob and Leah was built on a lie, there was nothing of substance connecting them nor was there any commitment, friendship or intimacy desired in Jacob's heart for Leah. All of this, however, did not stop Jacob from continuing to have sex with Leah or having children with her. You may be thinking, what in the world? Yes, this dynamic between Leah and Jacob shows you the power of a soul tie and how the two become one flesh according to the word in Genesis 2:24. It also highlights the nature of the curse that God decreed in the garden after the fall of Adam and Eve from grace.

Darby Strickland said it best in her book *Is It Abuse?* Stating oppressive husbands are like brambles. Jacob operated as an oppressive husband to Leah, while he was a loving and caring husband to Rachel. A bramble is a leafless and brittle shrub, and it cannot protect anything. We need to truly dissect and study in close proximity of the pure, unfiltered word of God what this means in oppressive marriages in the church. In order to do this, we must start with a basic foundation of understanding the curse that was given by God in the garden. Genesis 3:16 says, *and to the woman He says, I (God) will make most severe your pangs in childbearing; In pain shall you bear children*, which is the first consequence of rebellion after the fall in the garden. The text goes on to say, *yet your urge shall be for your husband, and He will rule over you*, which is the second consequence of rebellion after the fall in the garden.

The Nelson New King James Study Bible notates Genesis 3:16 by stating, your sorrow and your conception: These two words mean *"your sorrowful conception"*. Meaning, the woman's joy in conceiving and bearing children will be saddened by the pain of it. *"Your desire shall be for your husband"* is notated as, desire here can also mean "an attempt to usurp or control" as in Genesis 4:7. We can paraphrase the last two lines of this verse this way: *"You will now have a tendency to dominate your husband, and he will act as a tyrant over you.*" Initiating the battle of the sexes, each strives for control and neither live in the best interest of the other. The antidote is in the restoration of mutual respect and dignity through Jesus Christ.[133]

Consequence, then, is defined as a conclusion derived through logic, something produced by a cause or necessity following a set of conditions. As a result of the fall of Eve in the garden, all women are born under the curse from the fall in Genesis 3:16. Additionally, many women desire or have strong urges to have a husband or for their husband to be characterized by trust, care, and honesty. However, oppressive marriages are not characterized by trust, care, and honesty; they are characterized by domination and fear, which is enslavement. Oppressive marriages are not built on the fundamentals of healthy, mutual, and willing respect, love, care, trust, and honesty. Therefore, the oppressive husband becomes a ruler over his wife, which is why love, relationships, and marriage done outside the will of God is dangerous.

The Jewish Study Bible notates that after the fall of Adam and Eve in the garden, the knowledge came with the shame of nudity that they had lacked in their childlike innocence before the fall. Serving as a symbol of a much more encompassing sense of guilt and ominous estrangement between God and the primal couple. Oppressive marriages are a result of estrangement from God. Husbands with oppressive tendencies show they have no relationship with God. We see evidence of this with Adam after the fall when he lamely attempts to pass the blame on his wife & God for pulling her from his side. The wife, with more credibility, then blames the serpent. [134] In both cases, neither one took responsibility nor accountability for their part in the fall from grace. The same thing happened in the marriage of Jacob and Leah and Derrick, and I because *nothing is new under the sun*, according to Ecclesiastes 1:9.

Jacob made love to Rachel, and his love for Rachel was greater than his love for Leah (Gen 29:30). Love in this scripture is the Hebrew word 'Ahab,' phonetically spelled aw-hab' meaning to love according to the Strongs Concordance of the bible number 157. Additional context to the Hebrew word describes it as beloved, to dearly love, friend, friends, loved, showing love. What this shows us is that Jacobs's heart's desire was to have friendship, intimacy, commitment, care, love, and mutual willing respect with Rachel. On the other hand, he acquired Leah by means of deception. Therefore, the only connection he had to Leah was sexual, which drew him back because of the spiritual link we call the soul tie. Consequently, Jacob's treatment of Leah included a lack of engagement, care, friendship, intimacy, commitment, love, and mutual willing respect, leaving Leah mentally and emotionally in shambles.

Before we are introduced to the extreme anguish of Leah's heart crying out from her suffering in a loveless marriage, we see God the Father, Son, and Holy Spirit intervene and come close to her broken and contrite spirit. Genesis 29:31 states *that when the LORD saw that Leah was not loved, he enabled her to conceive, but Rachel remained childless.* Throughout Scripture, God is called by various names. People in the Bible gave some of these names to Him, while others are names that He calls Himself. Each name describes a part of His character. A woman named Hagar first used one of these names. When God met her in her distress, she said, *"You are the God who sees me. I have now seen the One who sees me"* (Gen 16:13). This phrase, "The God Who Sees Me"," is translated as "El Roi" in Hebrew.[135]

Educated with this background information, helps us to understand more deeply the Genesis 29:31 statement that the LORD saw, Leah. As in the case of Hagar, God shows compassion to the unfavored mate, thus partly equalizing the disparity between her and her co-wife. Barrenness, in some instances a punishment[136], serves in Rachel's case to place her in succession to Sarah and Rebekah[137]. El Roi is the God who numbers the hairs on our heads and counts our every tear.[138] Psalm 56:8 confirms this idea, saying, *you keep track of all my sorrows. You have collected all my tears in your bottle. You have recorded each one in your book.* He knows every detail of our circumstances. When we pray to El Roi, we are praying to the God who knows everything about us. Even the most attentive parent must sleep, but our Heavenly Father never closes His eyes to us. El Roi never misses details about what is happening. He sees everything.[139]

Again, before we hear Leah open her mouth to express her extreme suffering in her loveless marriage, we see El Roi come to her and bless her to equalize the disparity between her and her co-wife. *Now, with child Leah, she gives birth to a son named Rueben, for she said it's because the LORD has seen my misery. Surely my husband will love me now (Gen 29:32).* Pause here for a moment and think about Leah's response to El Roi. What stands out to you about Leahs thought pattern? After having given birth, she first recognizes that God has intervened. However, she believes that the LORDS blessing her with the child will translate into her husband seeing her worth and value. In the ancient Near East, a woman's value was determined by her ability to birth children, specifically male children who would be bloodline carriers for their father's house. In like manner I birthed my first child with Derrick, Marlee, during a time when his roster had 99 other women in rotation. Shortly before conceiving Marlee on January 1st, 2016, I was a willing participant in Derrick's rotation of whores. I knew he was smashing, Tristen, Makini, Jaleesa, Shatera, Dee NC, Chels, Desiree, Whitney, Erica, Candace S., Crystal, Milf, Cookie, our friend from Haute Geek Couture, Rochell, IG comedian LaLa, some chick named Pinky in his DM's along with a host of others who would fill the rest of this page if I kept listing names. During my pregnancy, he was still smashing these chicks, and I was still allowing him to smash me; however, I thought he was being more cautious and following rule 1 of his own ethical code of conduct:

Never have unprotected sex. Wrap it up, strap twice, pull out early, morning after pill, water hose it down afterwards. You can never be too safe.

Why would I think that is beyond me? I do not have a logical answer for it, but I thought he cared more for himself and me than that, but like always, I was wrong. It was in my 4th month of pregnancy with Marlee that I was doing some backend work for the Derrick Jaxn brand that I came across a video of Erica and Derrick having sex on what seemed to be a couch, a brownish-colored couch to be exact. Erica was bent over doggy style while Derrick was hammering her from the back; a white creamy substance was coming out of her onto his penis; she was moaning; he was talking; there was no condom, and I was traumatized. Devastated is an understatement, I still do not have adequate words to describe the type of pain I felt in watching that while I was 4 months pregnant with our first child. However, I can speak about what contributed to my devastation from my thought pattern at that time. I had believed the lie that God had blessed me, starting with giving me back the first child of three that I aborted with Derrick. Therefore, in my mind, Derrick's acceptance of that and what seemed like support from him translated into him being able to see me and my worth as the mother of his child. Do you see how my thought pattern aligned with that of Leah's after birthing Jacob's first child?

The reality is that it did not change a thing, nor did it kindle any ounce of genuine love in the hearts of Jacob for Leah or Derrick for me. In my case, Erica ended up getting pregnant by Derrick as well; at the same time, I was pregnant. Allegedly, she aborted the child, from what I was told by Derrick. It is possible she did abort as he is good at aiding a woman with that decision, like he did with me and a chick from Auburn named Latreece, who got pregnant by him that terrible summer of 2010.

After seeing a video of Derrick and Erica, I sent him a stream of video messages, bawling my eyes out and telling him exactly what I had seen and how hurt I was for him being so reckless. It's also when I began obsessing over the other chicks and stalking their pages, learning everything I could learn about them.

I learned that Erica is from Derrick's hometown area of Enterprise, Alabama. Surprising enough, on a trip to Enterprise, to reveal to Derrick's mom she was going to be a grandmother again. Derrick and I ran into Erica at the gas station. I was sitting in the car, a whole six months pregnant, while he was pumping gas, and guess who pulled up right next to us. Erica gets out of her car and goes into the store. Derrick goes into the store, and they both come out like nothing has ever happened. I was pissed off, but I held my peace, and Derrick got back in the car without any mention of the fact that he had clearly seen Erica after; I had just watched him smashing her in FB messenger two months prior. Fast forward to literally hours before I went into labor with Marlee, Derrick was driving me to Krispy Kreme in Marietta, Ga, at 11 p.m at night, Erica called, and he answered the phone, chatted for a bit, and got off like nothing ever happened. I snapped at him, and he responded that anytime she calls, he needs to answer the phone because he hurt her very badly. His response sent a dagger to my heart that paralyzed and stunned me to the point of silence and became a pillar of hatred stored in my heart toward him.

Let's revisit Devon Franklin's view on how to tell the difference between a healthy man and a toxic man. Are Derrick's actions and words displayed towards me while carrying our first child in alignment with that of a man who is looking to serve or be of service? The answer is no, and if Derrick was not looking at me through healthy eyes as I carried and birthed Marlee, why would I think that would change with the birth of our second child, Derrick Jr, four months after we walked down the aisle? According to Genesis 33, *Leah conceived again, and when she gave birth to a son she said, because the LORD heard that I am not loved, he gave me this one too. So, she named him Simeon.* Again, following Leah, I thought, I am having a boy, the first-born son of Derrick, and surely, he will desire me and love me. Sadly, that was not the case even in marriage after I made it very clear to him that in marriage, I had full expectations of monogamy. Of course, with no regard or care for my demand, Derrick rekindled a flame with cousin Tiff, who apparently is a family favorite, Dunnie, who was cloaked under the name of Teresa Langley in his phone and working in the Mentally Stimulate Me card game area of Derricks business, along with Makini, Nicole C., a high up person affiliated with The Main Choice haircare line, another person affiliated with Mielle hair care line. Honestly, there are many others, but for the sake of time, I will move forward with examining the root cause of death of my toxic marriage.

Genesis 34 says, *again Leah conceived, and when she gave birth to a son, she said, now at last my husband will become attached to me, because I have borne him three sons. So, she named him Levi.* Do I really have to say it? February 2021, I found out I was pregnant with our third child, Eliy'Sha; while I genuinely believed that Derrick was putting in an honest effort to pursue his personal relationship with the LORD with spiritual leadership, I was not hyper-focused on him seeing me and loving me, though the hope that he would still lingered in my heart. At this point in time, I had already left him for 8 months to sleep on my mom's couch with our two older kids after discovering the eleven women he confessed to had been having meetings in my room without me.

I was not only dealing with betrayal trauma from Derrick but also betrayal trauma from Autumn, who worked at the front desk of One Life gym in Cumming Ga in 2019. My spouse and I were regulars at One Life, and I finally felt like I was stepping into purpose. I started a fitness IG, so I regularly posted about the weight loss transformation I was going through. I went from 273lbs in January 2019 to 199lbs by April 2019. Quick weight loss was achieved through a combination of diet, nutrition, weightlifting, plyometrics, and CrossFit. Every day, I would come to the gym and be greeted by the girl at the front desk, Autumn. She would hype me up for my lifting session and even held my kids in her arms, helping me walk them to the kid's center. Every day, she smiled in my face. Turns out her belly was full of balls from one part of me joined to another. Imagine the impact on my self-esteem.

Complex betrayal trauma is what I was dealing with at this point. The National Library of Medicine defines betrayal as the sense of being harmed by a trusted person's intentional actions or omissions. The most common forms of betrayal are harmful disclosures of confidential information, disloyalty, infidelity, and dishonesty. They can be traumatic and cause considerable distress. The effects of betrayal include shock, loss and grief, morbid preoccupation, damaged self-esteem, self-doubting, and anger. Not infrequently do they produce life-altering changes. The effects of catastrophic betrayal are most relevant for anxiety disorders and OC D and PTSD in particular. Betrayal can cause mental contamination, and the betrayer commonly becomes a source of contamination. In a series of experiments, it was demonstrated that feelings of mental contamination can be aroused by imagining unacceptable, non-consensual acts. The magnitude of the mental contamination was boosted by the introduction of betrayal themes. Feelings of mental contamination can also be aroused in some perpetrators of non-consensual acts involving betrayal. The psychological significance is spiritual and lethal.[140]

The keywords in this abstract are betrayal themes. Theme is defined as a subject or topic of discourse or of artistic representation; a specific and distinctive quality, characteristic, or concern according to Merriam-Webster Dictionary. Can you identify the theme of my relationship with Derrick? Consistently, from the beginning, throughout the off times and the on times, and throughout what I desired, and thought was a monogamous marriage, betrayal has been at the foundation. Betrayal is a tool of dishonor that robs a person of his/her ability to trust. It partners with the demons of isolation, rejection, hurt, deep hurt, and anxiety[141]. Nearly all of the affair partners knew exactly who I was, talked to me to my face, smiled at my face, and some even held my kids. I found out in February 2020 that Autumn was still involved, providing words of comfort to calm the soul of my spouse for my sudden and unannounced departure to my momma's house. Literally, while trying to "get me back," Autumn was comforting him as a "friend." For some reason, to this day, there is confusion as to why I was not in a hurry to get back to GA or allow him access to our two kids. I told him some years before marriage and again in pre-marital counseling with Dr. Turpeau that we never finished, that I felt like he made it hard for me to have friends because I didn't know if I was going to be surrounded by people with sexual history with him. He told me I was tripping; if I didn't have friends, it had nothing to do with him. Turns out Autumn was a gym friend, and the reality was she wasn't the only one in my friend circle having meetings in my bedroom without me. Desiree is another Tuskegee grad who I stumbled across in Derricks' archive of sex videos of various ladies. I was actually pregnant with our first child, Marlee, when my eyes consumed the footage of Desiree in Derrick's house in Marietta, bent over doggy style in his bed. She had these circle-like tattoos that go up the spine of her back and connect in some weird way.

Apparently, they were a whole couple, and from her FB page, she thought she was the one and that he would be moving to take their relationship to the next level of commitment. Well, if I was unloved and carrying his child, she definitely was not in the running to be anything other than placeholder pussy, when one of the many of us was not acting right. I was roughly three months pregnant when Desiree was flown out by Derrick to ATL to spend a few days. Derrick had spent the night at my house, and of course, it was not void of sex. At sunrise, Derrick began getting his things together to go and prepare for his next round of booty with Desiree, whose flight was arriving within the hour. I knew she was flying in because I was handling his emails, and thousands of receipts in their various forms lie within his email.

Well, in my manipulation to control Derrick, so he can console me for his upcoming sexcapade, I asked him to take me to the mall. He obliged, took me to the mall, and bought me a shirt and another outfit. Right before leaving, we stopped by the food court and sat at a table while waiting for our order. I looked at Derrick and asked him what one thing was special between you and me that you did not do with anyone else? He replied, "I am only raw" with you.

And the Holy Ghost lie detector test determined that was a lie. Crushed, I determined in my mind that I was going to fuck him up!

On my next doctor's appointment to check on the growth of the baby, I asked Dr. Sermons to run another set of STD tests on me. He looked at me puzzled because they generally do not run another set of tests after your first visit, so of course, his first question was, is there a reason why? Derrick was sitting beside me on the visitor's chair while I was on the exam table; I kept my eyes focused on Dr. Sermons, and his eyes were toggling between me and Derrick, waiting for my reply to his question. "I have reason to believe that I have been exposed to STDs, and I want to make sure that me and the baby are okay. Dr. Sermons locked his eyes on Derrick, pursed his lips, and said OKAY, walked out, and let his nurse, who was in the room, start the process of drawing blood and swabbing my lower region so they could be tested. Derrick looked horrified, and he was humiliated, according to his words, when we walked out of the appointment. "Why didn't you come to me if you had any concerns about catching something?" I replied, "You're a liar; you said the one thing we did that you did not do with anyone else was being raw. I have seen the videos of you and Desiree, Shatera, Jaleesa. You're a straight fuck boy."

Apparently, I wounded him pretty well with my actions and words, which is what I wanted to do, because he dropped me off at my apartment in Dunwoody, GA, and went to his house in Marietta. By God's grace and mercy alone, my STD results came back negative for sickness, which meant Marlee was not in danger of catching something more in the womb than what she had already acquired. Remember that children can be infected with demons in the womb. A short recap through my entire pregnancy with Marlee, I was watching countless women have sex with Derrick; though we were not claiming boyfriend and girlfriend status, he was staying at my apartment, we spent time, we had sex, and did all the things that unsaved boyfriends and girlfriends do. Underneath that, I was seven years into watching other chicks from Tuskegee and others from our time living in North Carolina, sex videos with Derrick. Not to mention Alexandria, who sent me pictures and video of her and Derrick in what seemed to be like her dorm room, participating in sexual activities while we were actively in a relationship in 2015.

Deeper than that layer remained the unhealed rape trauma and daddy issue trauma from my father's sudden death when I was 12 years old that I had never healed from. What I have revealed and am describing is complex trauma (CT). CT surpasses PTSD, usually in symptom severity. It comprises of significant difficulty with emotional regulation, relationships, self-identity, and fragmentation of the self. Although the effects of trauma are not in the events themselves but in how the body and mind register the events, CT usually arises from traumatic events occurring in an extended and continuous fashion, usually early in life.[142] Examining my life to this point in the story, the trauma from my childhood concerning my father and mothers rejection of me in the womb, my father's death, rape trauma and the treachery of the cycle of abuse between Derrick and I, compounded with visual trauma from watching home porn videos, was an extended and continuous flow of traumatic events that never were addressed from a psychological or spiritual standpoint. The pain I was experiencing mentally, emotionally, physically, and spiritually was inflicted interpersonally by humans instead of natural disasters or car accidents. My caregivers, my mother, and father, formed my attachment style of fearful avoidant, and Derrick, becoming an attachment figure who was supposed to be supportive and protective, created a stronghold belief system that made it virtually impossible to escape.

The psychological impact of this trauma bubbled to the surface during my pregnancy with Marlee, in which I lacked connection, experienced intrusions, avoidance, had trouble concentrating, irregular sleep, and hypervigilance, which was so upsetting that these things created major social and emotional, and occupational impairment to my day-to-day life. All nine months that I carried Marlee, I was involuntarily re-experiencing the trauma, flashbacks, and intrusions of the sex tapes with other chicks looping in my mind, which was my mind's attempt to integrate and process the disturbing content toward a resolution that felt complete. Unfortunately, as my mind strived to resolve the traumatic events, its efforts became counterproductive and I developed a severe case of baby blues that turned into severe post-partum depression after birth, for which I received a clinical diagnosis.[143]

My mind was damaged, and while I was not clinically diagnosed with PTSD, I am confident that I had developed that from the continuous flow of trauma in the environment of just being in a relationship with Derrick. PTSD rewires the brain's information processing system to interpret unthreatening stimuli as threatening. PTSD makes it more difficult for sufferers to attend to new or essentially non-threatening information and regulate one's attention and concentration.[144] In other words, my brain had been rewired to focus on the negative traumatic events and graphic images of Derrick and his many wives. I lived day to day with him continuously in a threatened state as my mind could not differentiate between non-threatening and threatening events, interactions, and behaviors of Derrick, who claims to have had moments when he was doing "everything" right, yet still experienced rejection and lack of appreciation from me. Imagine waking up every day with graphic images of your spouse going to Pound Town with a million different chicks while you are carrying their child.

From a EMDR viewpoint, this is why traumatic memories are considered to be stored "dysfunctional," in a disjointed and disintegrated way, separate from adaptive information and other positive experiences or self-knowledge.[145] The disintegration of information is largely considered to be what prevents a given traumatic event from resolving naturally on its own, and what makes specific aspects of traumatic memories detached from the person's sense of self. In this sense, traumatic memories become essentially housed psychologically as "timeless emotion and bodily sensation".[146] Spiritually, this type of trauma, which I was experiencing through my carrying my first child, went to the core of who I was; the messages my brain was receiving were opposite of a person who was created in the image of God who is of worth and value. Who I was someone to use, consume, and feed off, so my decision to stay in communion with Derrick was because I did not see any value or worth in myself, nor did I believe that leaving him would open up an opportunity for me to be of value or worth to anyone else. The world value system of women with children is that if she has kids and is not married, she's used goods and is only worth long-term situations.

Therefore, even years after seeing the first sexual video of Derrick and other chicks from college, combined with that of those I saw in my first pregnancy and again in marriage, the traumatic events had a significant psychological and physiological impact on me. My trauma augmented a survival need for close attachment with people who were accessible, responsive, and emotionally engaged. However, PTSD eroded my development, and I felt a sense of safety and trust that promoted and maintained a secure attachment to those who could help in my family or therapists. I was in need of deep connection to help heal my trauma, and the continuous violation of Derrick's behavior, whether he was "having an inappropriate conversation" or smashing chicks, resulted in a gross violation of connection, which was a branch of the root of my trauma.[147] I had to learn that that deep connection could not be fulfilled by the average person, it had to be fulfilled by the person of God who is the source of all healing.

Relationships with my family and best friends Sydney and Jazmyn began to weaken, not only in an interaction sense but also in my subjective identity, the purpose of my relationships outside of Derrick, and the need for emotional intimacy. The toll of the untreated trauma took on my relationships was generalizing not only my immediate attachment relationships but also my relation to social networks and community. I didn't belong anywhere with anyone in my mind, resulting in me feeling discouraged, confused, hopeless, shameful, and guilty [148]. Let's pause here and examine the effects of all this distress on a baby in the womb of a mother experiencing re-occurring trauma untreated until after birth. Many prospective studies have shown that if a mother is depressed, anxious or stressed while pregnant, this increases the risk for the child having a wide range of adverse outcomes, including emotional problems, symptoms of attention deficit hyperactivity (ADHD), or impaired cognitive development.[149]

Although genetics and postnatal care clearly affect these outcomes, evidence for a prenatal causal component is also substantial. Prenatal anxiety/depression may contribute 10-15% of the attributable load for emotional/behavioral outcomes. The mechanisms underlying these changes are just starting to be explored.[150] But women's mental health is an integral part of her fetus environment, explains Catherine Monk, a medical psychologist at Columbia University in New York. And a burgeoning body of evidence shows that a pregnant woman's psychological health can influence that of her child. Monk began working with pregnant patients early in her clinical career, and she has spent more than 20 years researching the effects of maternal stress, depression, and anxiety on offspring.[151]

Recently, she co-authored a review in the Annual Review of Clinical Psychology describing the mechanisms by which a mother's mental state may shape her fetus' developing brain. In a lab group, Monk and her colleagues gathered information about how anxious expecting mothers were using a standard questionnaire. When they separated the data by low-anxious verse high-anxious groups, they saw that the fetuses of women who were not very anxious didn't show a heart rate change at all. But fetuses of women who were more anxious had an increased heart rate in response to the stressful task. So that suggested that these fetuses were responding differently despite receiving similar sounds and other stimuli from their mothers as the other group. If a fetus' heart rate changes more in response to cues from its mom, how does that correlate with a greater risk of anxiety and ADHD?[152]

In a subsequent study, they found that a reactive heart rate in fetuses of mothers with prenatal depression was associated with less connectivity between two regions in the brain known as the amygdala and prefrontal cortex. The amygdala is a part of the brain circuits involved in regulating emotion and detecting and experiencing stress responses. The prefrontal cortex is involved in the control of behavior, speech, and reasoning and can dampen the amygdala's reactivity to stimuli. So, the idea is that even early on, babies of more depressed mothers have less of a connection in their brain between the amygdala and the prefrontal cortex, which may be an early sign of less cognitive control over emotion. Other labs are showing similar links between these two parts of the brain. Additional studies suggest that something about maternal anxiety is associated with the placenta functioning differently, which can affect how much cortisol reaches the amniotic fluid. That's one of the challenges with this research: it may not matter exactly how much cortisol is in the woman's circulation, but what level the fetus is exposed to via the placenta and amniotic fluid.[153]

Marlee's developing brain in my womb, while I was experiencing re-occurring trauma, was affected in all these ways from a psychological and medical standpoint. Since psychology without God is dead, the spiritual impact must be examined as well. *A Manual for Children's Deliverance* by Frank and Ida Mae Hammond speaks to the spiritual impact on a baby in the womb based on the emotional environment. Hammonds writes that the overall emotional environment has an impact on the developing child within the womb. Evil spirits are given ready access to a yet-to-be-born child through many kinds of negative factors in his or her outside environment. Again, many would deny that such influences are possible. However, a mother-to-be's emotional condition will also influence the unborn child. In other words, the baby will be vulnerable to the same kinds of emotional spirits that the mother carries- such as fear, anger, and depression. Therefore, it is good for the mother to be happy, confident in the Lord, and healthy in her emotions. Such factors in the home environment, such as fighting, quarreling, and loud music, affect a child's emotional health. His or her nervous system can also be damaged. Ideally, the father should provide strong emotional support to the home environment through his love for both mother and child.[154]

Do you recall the working framework for telling the difference between a healthy man and a toxic man provided by Devon Franklin? A toxic man is looking to be served and evaluating what he can get from a woman or a relationship with a woman; therefore, he cannot see her. Derrick could not see me, nor could he make any correlations between his Single Man Code of Conduct behavior and the natural or spiritual impact it was having on me or our unborn child, in and out of relationship and marriage with him. However, El Roi, the most important man, saw me and my misery and carried me through the places of quicksand that I had been stepping into mentally, emotionally, physically, and spiritually in the entanglement with Derrick. A man who is committed to his flesh and experiencing it for all its worth is a dangerous man to any woman, but especially one who is carrying his child. Recklessness occurred on both of our parts, I had every opportunity to, at minimum, require that Derrick wear a condom the times we had sex, and I knew that he was engaged with other women. The only exception would be that I would say is in marriage because I did not expect or believe that he was having sexual encounters with women since I was very clear that I was not going to have a repeat of our pre-marriage days.

Is your mind blown yet? Follow me deeper into the life of Leah and her marriage to Jacob. Genesis 35 says, *she conceived again, and when she gave birth to a son she said, "This time I will praise the LORD." So, she named him Judah. Then, she stopped having children.* Can you identify what is different about Leah's response to God blessing her with her fourth child? No desire for her husband's love or attachment was present in her acknowledgment of God blessing her. Instead, she focused her attention on God by saying, *"This time I will praise the LORD."* And this is where my personal Lord and Savior, Jesus Christ of Nazareth, receives one of His names as the Lion of Judah, who is the fourth son of Leah. It took Leah, who had given birth to four children, to realize that she had to take her eyes off her husband Jacob and focus them on the LORD, who was looking at her suffering the whole time with a desire to do something about it.

I did not have a fourth child, but my third child was named Eliy'Sha because God is my salvation, and he turned the focus of my heart and eye desires towards Him. Again, what we consume with our eyes affects our mental, emotional, and spiritual state. Eyes were the gateways that connected Derrick and I at the party and led to our first sexual encounter after twelve days of knowing each other. What you need to understand about gates is that they are meant to keep what's inside, inside and keep what's outside, outside; that's why we have gates outside our houses so that everything that is not needed inside can remain outside according to a teaching on types of spiritual gates, by Apostle Miz Mzwakhe Tancredi. So, as much as we have gates in the natural realm, we have gates in the spiritual realm. That's why the Bible declares *that we are not fighting against flesh and blood but against principalities, wickedness, and rulers of the power of darkness.* It's critical to understand this because when Derrick and I locked eyes at the house party in Auburn, I was not being attracted to him through healthy eyes (Matt 6:22), I was being seduced by unhealthy eyes, empowered by demon spirits who were attracted to the demons' spirits inside my unhealthy eyes. The spiritual law is that whoever controls life in the spiritual control's life in the physical, and since Derrick and I were both giving in to the works of our flesh when we had our first kiss, which turned into cheek clapping, we were being influenced by wicked spirits in the spiritual realm that was manifesting in the natural world.

The devil is in trouble because I am revealing to you one of his strategies that he uses on people, which ensnared Derrick and me in a demonic marriage not ordained by God through the gates of prison. Prison gates are meant to lock you up; they are generational, and what locked up your parents and grandparents if they did not receive freedom by the power of the Holy Spirit and the blood of Jesus gives legal rights to lock you up. I've disclosed generational patterns in Derrick and myself through the pages of this book, noting patterns, and decisions that have been repeated from our parents and grandparents down to us, and we had no awareness that these things had any influence on our belief systems and oppression by demons. The lust of the eyes are prison gates that are meant to keep you inside, and these prison gates specialize in generational stuff. My mom and dad were enticed by the lust of the eye and ended up having sex when they were supposed to be playing video games, which conceived me. Derrick's mother and father were not married, and they had an attraction that came through the lust of the eyes that conceived him. Both of our parents had pre-marital sex, conceived outside of God's perfect design for marriage, and birthed children into sexuationships.

Following the same sequence in our generational bloodlines' connection to the prison gates of the lust of their eyes. Derrick and I locked eyes at the Auburn house party on day seven of knowing each other; at that party, we had the most amazing kiss that was like a romantic scene in a movie, and boom, five days after that, I found myself, doggy style in his Russel Hall dorm room having pre-marital sex. A year later, in 2010, we conceived 2 children back-to-back, which I aborted with him sleeping in the chair by my side in the clinic. Again, we conceived in 2012, when he once again was sleeping by my side in the clinic. Four years after that, we conceived again in the wee hours of New Year's Eve/ Day intoxicated, which I found out about three weeks later when my boobs were sore, prompting me to take a home EPT. It's not by accident that these patterns and behaviors are evident in me and my parents and again between me and Derrick in our failed relationship and marriage.

Apostle Miz Mzwakhe Tancredi goes deeper to say that prison gates look at what defeated the first-born at home; these gates do not just bring something new; they use the same strategy, which we see in the book of Acts and because of the power given to Peter, the gates of hell shall not prevail. However, we see that Peter was sleeping and the church was praying, and the Bible declares that as the church was praying, the prayers of the church released an angel, and the Bible says that an angel of the Lord appeared in the prison. One of the reasons I am telling the story in this book is because those who are in relationships and marriages like mine are in prison gates and need to be delivered by the power of the Holy Spirit. I do not care how many years you have been in the prison gates of your treacherous relationship, but I pray right now that the Holy Spirit releases angels on your behalf and that the prison that you are in gates begin to shake and collapse as the ground quakes to break the chains off your wrists, ankles, and neck in Jesus mighty name.

I'm in love! It was a sensation and feeling that sent warm fuzzies shooting through my body as I swapped spit and tongue with Derrick at the house party. His eyes said everything I needed to know that I was safe, wanted, and cared for, and my heart became his from that moment forward. I genuinely loved him, from the unhealthiest place within me, a broken conscious place, until 2017, when I began taking my eyes off him and focusing on my fitness journey. Unfortunately, at this point in the story, it has been revealed that from day one, Derrick looked at me with unhealthy eyes; based on various events discussed in this section, the evidence suggests that he did not have a heart desire for me, as he had his mind set on how he could be serviced by me and not to serve me or be of service. Therefore, as he looked back at me at the party, it was not with the love that Jacob had when he looked at Rachel; it was lust.

A Woman that Finds a Husband, Finds a Toxic Man

As the party was dying down and people were headed out to do whatever they were going to do the rest of the night/morning, Derrick asked me if I was down to go to IHOP with his friends who had hosted us at their house party. I agreed, and we headed out, hand in hand, to his 99 Grand AM. The car was beat up, but it worked, safely getting us to our destination. Upon arriving, we met up with Jon and his girlfriend, Teanna, Jermaine and his chick, Pervis, and his girlfriend, and Ryan, who was single in the group. The host sat us at our table and dished out menus. I began looking at the menu and deciding what I would get. Derrick looked very uncomfortable as I was deciding between the steak tips and eggs and the chicken fajita omelet. After giving us a few minutes to browse the menu, the waitress came to the table to get our drink orders, I ordered apple juice, and Derrick ordered water. Once the waitress left the table to fill out drink orders, Derrick leaned over and said, you might want to order water; I can't pay for that. I looked at him and said, "That's cool; I have my own money, and I'll pay for it; you should get something too; it doesn't make sense for you to sit here without food." When the waitress returned with our drinks, Derrick wasted no time choosing what he wanted and placed his order. During the remainder of the night, we chatted with his friends and enjoyed the rest of our night.

On the drive back to Tuskegee with full bellies, Derrick and I rode hand in hand all the way down the back road to campus. I remember Derrick expressing being taken aback by my gesture to pay for his food and drink at IHOP. The thing that captured his attention the most was that I slipped my debit card under the table when the waitress came back to collect payment for our order because I didn't want him to be embarrassed in front of his friends. After all, a girl, who is not technically his girlfriend, is paying for his food and drink on what was our first date. Ugh, my naivete just makes me want to vomit as I write this text, but the reality was that this was a red flag that I ignored. I had no dating etiquette, boundaries, barriers, or standards since my idea of relationships was based on what I had seen on Disney channel. All the experiences that I had prior to Derrick from my high school days were way less dramatic and more in tune with a Disney Channel original, as I went to a predominantly white high school.

While I was no longer in high school, the same behaviors, characteristics, and traits I had in my high school relationships carried over into my first date experience with Derrick. Go back with me to 9th grade at Smoky Hill High School so that you can clearly understand what toxic traits carried over into my college dating experience. Joseph was my first boyfriend in high school; he was pushing 6 ft tall in ninth grade, at least from my perspective since I was only a whopping 5'2 as a freshman. I was friends with Joseph's cousins Ashely and Darrin, a.k.a

DJ, who were brother and sister, though Ashley was older than Joseph, DJ, and myself as a junior upperclassman. I learned a lot from this group of people, as they were black Panamanians, which was a unique experience. Joseph asked me to be his girlfriend in Mr. Nelson's class one day, and I said yes, of course. Honestly, the whole relationship was like a scene from a high school musical, which is partly why I had this romanticized idea of how relationships should be carried out. Joe walked me to all my classes and carried my books for me, even when we didn't have the same class that period. He would also greet me after every class, and we spent as much time as we could during the school day.

The great thing about the whole relationship is that we lived in close proximity to each other, so we would meet up at Mission Viejo Park and hang out, kiss, and talk. At the time Joe and I were dating, sex was not a big topic of conversation, nor were we trying to escalate it to that level. In fact, I spent a lot of time hanging out with Joe's family, his mom and dad, and his older brother Jomar and cousins Ashley, and DJ. Panamanian families are kind of close-knit and do everything together. Joe's cousin group was called the Fab Five because there were five of them, cousins that were holding it down. When I say I was connected with the whole family, I was connected with the whole family because Ashely and DJ's mom, Dilma, and DJ's dad, Darrin Sr, knew who I was and had welcomed me while I was in a relationship with Joe, and even after Joe and I ended the relationship. In summary, Joe's family knew me well enough that his parents let us hang out in his room with full trust that nothing inappropriate would be going down. Joseph and I dated for a total of nine months before I had to break up with him, not because of anything he did wrong, but because of something I did wrong by violating my mom's curfew restrictions one night after being out with Joeseph, his brother, Ashlee, and DJ.

So, my mom allowed me to go to an event at Six Flags, which had a popular haunted house setup that everyone wanted to go to that year. I went under the instructions of having to be back at home at 10 p.m. Long story short, 10 p.m. came and went, and my mom was calling my phone; I was not answering intentionally because I was not ready to go since I was having so much fun. Well, when I arrived home at 11:30 p.m., my mom was waiting for me at the door. My mom had not yet been delivered by the power of the Holy Spirit, so I got slammed against the wall, and she started cussing and swinging; all I could do was cover my face and take the hits. When she was done, she grabbed her keys, drove me to Joseph's house, and said go to the door and break up with him. Tears filled my eyes as I opened the car door and took my walk of shame up the walkway to his house. I rang the doorbell, and his mom answered the door. My head hung low, and tears fell; with my voice cracking, I said, I must break up with Joseph. In her Spanglish accent, she called for Joseph to come downstairs. When he came to the door, I looked up again with eyes full of tears and said, "My mom said I have to break up with you." He said OKAY, and his mom closed the door. I was humiliated, and a pillar of hatred towards my mom was created in my heart.

Remember my act of rebellion when I went to the house party that winter break of my freshman year of college? Are you picking up on any similarities between my thought pattern and behavior from that time frame and my freshman year of high school? The glaring similarity should be that in both instances, I was in full-fledged rebellion against my mother, dishonoring and disobeying her. In both instances, I made a conscious decision to ignore the set curfew, which resulted in something traumatic happening for me each time, though I did not view my breakup with Joseph as traumatizing until 19 years after the event occurred.

1 Samuel 15:23 (AMP)

For rebellion is as [serious as] the sin of divination (fortune-telling), And disobedience is as [serios as] false religion and idolatry. Because you have rejected the word of the LORD, He also has rejected you as king.

My rebellion when I was 14/15 years old while hanging out with Joe and his family was the same as witchcraft, and since I was also attending a haunted house at that time, I openly invited additional demons to come to distort and destroy my life. The beat down I received from my mom after my act of rebellion, missing curfew with Joe, was not enough to change my behavior and thought pattern; it fueled the behavior and thought pattern because my mom had now become an enemy of my heart and soul, though I was not consciously aware of this at the time, nor was I a few short years after, when, I repeated the same offense by intentionally ignoring her 11 p.m. curfew, going to a party, that I was drinking at, which led to a gross violation of my personhood, rape.

Holding on to unforgiveness in my heart towards my mom reinforced the prison gates that pre-existed in my generational bloodline. Unforgiveness is addressed in the bible time and time again, throughout the scriptures, with a strong warning that anyone who holds unforgiveness towards another has not been forgiven by the Father, resulting in being released to the tormentors and forfeiting the kingdom of God if this heart issue is not addressed before their last breath. Matthew 18:21-35 introduces us to this concept with the parable of the unmerciful servant. The Apostle Peter goes to Jesus and asks, *Lord, how many times shall I forgive my brother or sister who sins against me? Up to seven times? Jesus answered, I tell you, not seven times, but seventy times seventy.* As the parable goes on, we see that a King wanted to settle debts owed to him by his servants. One man owed him ten thousand bags of gold and was brought to the King. As the story goes, the man could not pay his debt, and the King ordered that the man, his wife, his kids, and everything he had to be sold to repay the debt.

Hearing the consequence of his inability to pay his debt, the man fell on his knees, begging the king to be patient and promising that he would pay back everything. The king and Master of the man had compassion for him, canceled the debt, and let him go. However, the servant went out and found a friend who owed him a hundred silver coins, grabbed him, and Bart Simpson choked him while demanding that the friend pay him back everything, he owed him. His friend fell to his knees, begging him to be patient and promising that he would repay him, but the servant, whose debt was canceled by the king, refused, and had his friend thrown into prison. A crowd of witnesses who saw the interaction between the servant and his friend were outraged and went and told the King everything that had happened. The King called the servant back to his house and said, "You wicked servant, I canceled all your debt because you begged me to. Why didn't you have that same mercy on your friend?" Angry, the King handed the servant over to the jailers to be tortured until he paid back all he owed. At the end of the parable, we learn that our heavenly Father will treat each of us this way if we do not forgive our brother and sister from our heart.

First, we need to clarify that the heart in this parable, and in many instances throughout the Bible, is not a vital organ, a muscle that pumps blood throughout the body. Neither is it concerned with romantic, philosophical, or literary definitions. The Bible mentions the heart almost 1,000 times. Essentially, this is what it says: the heart is that spiritual part of us where our emotions and desires dwell. Before we look at the human heart, we'll mention that since God has emotions and desires, He, too, can be said to have a "heart". We have a heart because God does. David was a man *"after God's own heart"* (Ac 13:22). *And God blesses His people with leaders who know and follow His heart* (1 Sam 2:35; Jer 3:15). The human heart, in its natural condition, is evil, treacherous, and deceitful. Jeremiah 17:9 *says the heart is deceitful above all things and beyond cure; who can understand it?* In other words, the fall has affected us at the deepest level; our minds, emotions, and desires have been tainted by sin- and we are blind to just how pervasive the problem is. We may not understand our own hearts, but God does. He knows the secrets of the heart (Psa 44:21; 1 Cor 14:25).[155]

Jesus *"knew all men and had no need that anyone should testify of man, for He knew what was in man"* (Jn 2:24-25). Based on His knowledge of the heart, God can judge righteously: *"I, the LORD, search the heart, I test the mind, even to give every man according to his way, according to the fruit of his doings"* (Jer 17:10). Jesus pointed out the fallen condition of our hearts in Mark 7:21-23. *From within, out of men's hearts come evil thoughts, sexual immorality, theft, murder, adultery, greed, malice, deceit, lewdness, envy, slander, arrogance, and folly. All these evils come from inside and make a man unclean."* Our biggest problem is not external but internal; all of us have a heart problem. In order for a person to be saved, then, the heart must be changed. This only happens by the power of the Holy Spirit in response to faith. *"With the heart one believes unto righteousness"* (Rom 10:10). *In His grace, God can create a new heart within us* (Psa 51:10; Eze 36:26). *He promises to "revive the heart of the contrite ones"* (Isa 57:10).[156]

God's work of creating a new heart within us *involves testing our hearts* (Psa 17:3; Deut 8:2) *and fulfilling our hearts with new ideas, new wisdom, and new desires* (Neh 7:5; 1 Kgs 10:24; 2 Cor 8:16). The heart is the core of our being, and the Bible sets high importance on keeping our hearts pure: *Above all else, guard your heart, for it is the wellspring of life* (Prov 4:23[157]) In other words, the heart in the Bible was thought to be a sort of "control center" from which all our decisions were made. So, when we read about the heart in the Bible, it is about the place where you have your will, your attitude, and intentions, and which is the source of your thoughts, actions, and words. This heart is the core of who you are as a person, and with it, you choose between good and evil. Your conscience sends out a message of whether something is right or wrong, and your heart is what drives you to choose. The heart that is in connection with God is able to choose the good every time. The heart that opens itself to other, impure influences becomes blind and confused when it comes to discerning between good and evil. "How can a young man cleanse his way? *By taking heed according to Your word* (Psa 119:9)".[158]

My heart had been opened to other, impure influences, becoming blind and confused when it came to discerning between good and evil. Missing curfew was not inherently evil in my eyes when I was out with Joe and his family, nor was it when I was 19 years old, making the decision to skip the curfew to go to a party. The source of my thoughts, actions, and words was Satan and his kingdom, who claimed legal rights to my life well before I was born. However, Isaiah 55:11 declares *that it is the same as my word. I sent it out, and it always produces fruit. It will accomplish all I want it to, and it will prosper everywhere I send it* (NLT). Though the sins of my father and mother, along with those of my grandparents and those who came before them, were being punished through the generations to the third, fourth, and beyond generations, the LORDS word of training a child in the way he or she should go did not return to Him void. My heart had to go through a purification and transformation process to be purged of the contamination of my bloodline, events, circumstances, and people that shaped my worldview.

Operation *Healing God's Way: The Art of Spiritual Warfare, Healing, and Deliverance* was in full effect by God, though I had no awareness of what He was doing and how He was doing it in my life. The seeds of faith planted by my grandmothers and watered during my mom's personal salvation process starting when I was 15 years old was all that God needed to begin unraveling the sickness attitude [159] and intentions of my broken conscious mind. I do not believe it was by accident that when I was 15 years old, not too long after the Joe incident that, I went to Kids Across America, Jesus' camp, when I had my first encounter with the Holy Spirit drawing me to accept Jesus Christ of Nazareth as my personal Lord and Savior. It was also the time when I wrote in my camp journal to the Holy Spirit for the first time, asking Him to allow me to become an evangelist like my great-grandmother Eva Mae Buchanan. Little did I know that the Lord would answer that prayer fifteen years later after much heartache, which produced the healing ministry that has me writing this blueprint to *Surviving a Cheating Man's Heart.*

One area of my study in theology and ministry school at Oral Robert's University is the study, research, and teaching of the leadership emergence theory. Leadership emergence theory forces you to look at a lifetime with long-range perspectives. When you step back and view a person's life history telescopically, you see things that you may otherwise miss. First, I need some necessary background, so you'll understand my language. Leadership emergence theory begins with the concept of formulating a timeline. The timeline for everyone is unique. However, when you see enough timelines, you notice some overall general patterns..[160] The cycles and patterns notated about my life and my relationship with Derrick Jaxn in this book serves as a functional framework for providing insights that may help you see more clearly, God's presence working in my life and how He is using these five development phases to purify and transform my heart while maturing me in ministry. Sometimes, though rarely, there is a sixth phase called "After Glow" or Celebration."

Figure 1-1 Five-Phase Generalized Timeline + Rare After Glow

161

Utilizing Dr. Robert J. Clintons general timeline as a framework for this spiritual autopsy of my failed relationship where the Holy Spirit is exposing and examining why I stayed so long in a toxic situation for 14 years in a sequential pattern in each subchapter of the first part of this book. In phase I, God providentially works foundational items into the life of the leader-to-be, which is me in this book. Personality characteristics, both good and bad experiences, and the time context are used by God. The building blocks are there, though the structure being built may need to be more clearly focused. Character traits are embedded. These same traits in mature form will be adapted and used by God. Many times, the personality traits later will be seen to correlate with the spiritual gift-mix that God gives.[162] Looking back on or dealing with past events or situations during the natural and spiritual interactions makes it easier to clarify just how the foundations issues correlate with mature leadership. While everyone is not called to stand in a pulpit and preach, teach, and minister the word of God, everyone who calls on the name of Jesus Christ of Nazareth is called to minister or lead those in their sphere of influence.

Romans 12:4-8 (AMP)

[4]For just as in one [physical] body we have many parts, and these parts do not all have the same function or special use, [5]so we, who are many, are [nevertheless just] one body in Christ, and individually [we are] parts one of another [mutually dependent on each other]. [6]Since we have gifts that differ according to the grace given to us each of us is to use them accordingly: [7]if [someone has the gift] prophecy, [let him speak a new

177

message from God to His people] in proportion to the faith possessed; if service, in the act of serving; or he who teaches, in the act of teaching; [8]or he who encourages, in the act of encouragement; he who gives, with generosity; he who leads, with diligence; he who shows mercy [in caring for others], with cheerfulness.

In Phase II, an emerging leader usually receives some kind of training. Often it is informal in connection with their God-given purpose and destiny.[163] Likewise, my relationship story is not being poured out for the sake of being told, but more importantly so that those of you who resonate with any part of my story can receive training on how to survive a cheating man's heart after years of being enslaved to toxicity that produced offspring, your children. As the leader-to-be, I learned by doing in the context of the healing ministries of Oral Roberts, Katherin Kuhlman, A.A Allen and Amie Semple McPherson. The basic models by which I learned are imitation modeling[164], and informal apprenticeships [165]as well as mentoring[166]. Apostle Paul models this blueprint in 1 Corinthians 11:1, saying, *and you should imitate me just as I imitate Christ* (NLT). Sometimes, God prompts formal training (especially if He is calling a person into full-time leadership) like myself, to Bible school or seminary.[167]. Superficially it may appear that the ministry training is the focus of this development phase. But closer analysis shows that the major thrust of God's development is inward. The real training program is in the heart of the person, where God is doing some growth testing.[168] This testing is what I think is happening to me as I offer up my personal, romantic life as a training ground for equipping, rebuking, correcting, and teaching this generation of broken conscious women the process of *Healing God's Way: The Art of Spiritual Warfare, Healing, and Deliverance* by the power of the Holy Spirit.

Remember Proverbs 17:3, where the LORD tests the heart, which we've learned is the control center for which all our decisions are made. Many of us fail this test because we do not know or believe that God will test your heart in every circumstance, which includes your desire to be healed in mind, body, soul, and spirit from the wounds caused by your enslavement to a cheating man's heart. The first thing that you must do when pursuing your healing from this toxic web of man's unfaithfulness is to take your eyes off the man, as Leah did in Genesis 29:35, and focus on what the LORD is trying to teach you and how He wants to develop you through the healing process. Requiring you to know the truth of:

Jeremiah 17:10 (NIV)

[10] I the LORD search the heart and examine the mind, to reward each person according to their conduct, according to what their deeds deserve.

Time and time again, we see Jesus demonstrate this testing as he performed miracles, signs, and wonders in the areas of healing and deliverance. Followed by the imitation of these tests which Jesus taught to the disciples, sparking faith by means of hearing in the hearts of others who did not personally walk with Jesus in His earthly ministry like the Apostle Paul, whose faith was affirmed through an encounter with Jesus on the road to Damascus. Saul's metamorphosis into Paul manifests the rebirth of a new man in Christ. Saul's old identity is she for the Lord's glory (2 Cor 5:17). A mystery is solved as the Jewish Pharisees turn from persecuting the Gospel of Christ and the Church of God to the spokesperson of the Gospel of Christ and the Church of God. An assessment of the "methodological character"[169] needs to be unpacked to magnify the significance of Apostle Paul's conversion and the power behind the influence of this life-giving event that is winning souls for the kingdom of God today.[170]

The assessment will answer the following questions:

Why, and for what reasons, did he persecute the Church of Christ? What did this religious Jewish man experience on the Road to Damascus? Moreover, how did the Damascus Road experience work in reshaping this man's person, thoughts and even his vocation?[171]

Revelation concerning the conversion, methodology, teaching, community, leadership and theology of Paul's life and legacy lies in the answers to these questions. The same conversion, methodology, teaching, community, leadership, and theology principles are what I have applied to my life to survive a cheating man's heart and what I am using in the structure of this book as I tell my story with its failures that led to a very public and nasty death. Do you remember what I said in the *Two Sides to Every Coin section?* Simply, being alive after such trauma that has played out publicly does not make me a survivor. I was made a survivor going through the transformation process of identifying and acknowledging my toxicity, Derrick's toxicity, and the toxicity from which we came in our bloodlines. I then had a road to Damascus encounter with the one true living God (Ac9:1-9), and you do too if you want to survive a cheating man's heart with all your mental faculties intact.

Accomplishing that desired transformation with all your mental faculties intact requires you to allow the Holy Spirit to reveal the truth about the motives of your heart, followed by the heart of your spouse, which will automatically and naturally produce healing and deliverance from bitterness and deep hurt embedded in your soul. The best way to learn how to apply this to your life is to study the Apostle Paul's conversion from Saul to Paul on the Road to Damascus. The motives prompting the persecution of Christ Jesus and the Church are found in man's mindset. A direct reflection of Proverbs 23:7, *for as a man thinks, so is he.* An in-depth understanding of the mindset of Saul, religiously, spiritually, and theologically, highlights the integrity or trustworthiness of his devotion to the law as an "elite committed Pharisaic Jew During Jesus' three-year ministry, friction between the Pharisees and Christ is mentioned throughout the Gospels. The most notable is the dispute over whose children Jesus' opponents are in the book of John, chapter eight versus 31-47. Abraham as the father of the Pharisees, is the religious source supplying strength to the house of the strongman (Matt 12:29), enslaving (Jn 8:34) the Pharisaic Jew's mindset to the scrupulous observation of the rabbinic and Mosaic Laws. [172]

"Paul speaks about it in Galatians and calls it "the traditions of my father's"[173] hen referencing his former life in Judaism and his persecution of the Church of God. Therefore, Saul, with ignorance and indifference to the Old Testament Law. Saul was a "fanatic Pharisaic Jew" [174] with single-minded zeal for the traditions of men under the law. Passion (Col 3:5) fueled the anger provoked in Saul that had been rooted in wholehearted work for men (Col 3:23) under the disguise of the Lord. Saul led the charge in persecuting Christ and the Church, misguided by the belief that he was practicing righteousness under the law of God. Jesus of Nazareth confessed as the Son of God in the early church collided with the fanatic Pharisaism of Saul's zeal for the traditions of his fathers (Gal 1:15-16).[175]

"The reasoning for this collision is clear that the law placed anyone who is hung on a tree under a divine curse; therefore, Jesus who was hung on a tree could not be the Son of God. Damascus Road then becomes the stage for the abrupt crucifixion of Saul and the birthplace of Paul as experienced but all godly leaders who have "an intimate encounter with the living God". [176] Ironically, after the conversion, Paul speaks with great fanatic soteriological language as the dominant voice through the book of Acts and his own Epistles, displaying his methodology, teaching, community, leadership and theological principles and practices by which he lived. The principalities, powers, rulers of the darkness and spiritual wickedness in heavenly places (Eph 6:12) intended harm against the body of Christ using Saul. However, God turned his single-minded zeal for traditions of men into the single-minded zeal for the Gospel of Christ. As Paul was resurrected and called on the road to Damascus according to His purpose (Rom 8:28).[177]

Paul's transformation by renewing his mind took place over the three days he was blind (Ac 9:9) and deprived himself of food and drink. As Christ took three days to rise from the dead, so Saul took three days to rise as Paul when Ananias placed hands on him, immediately melting the scales from his eyes so he could see (Ac9:17-18). Lifestyle and leadership principles emerge "in the genre of Acts as a work of ancient historiography," [178] echoing a genre of farewell speech in ancient literature.[179] Paul's Miletus speech in Acts 20 shows elements typical of farewell speeches. An outline includes "announcement of approaching death, parenetic sayings or exhortations, prophecies or predictions, a retrospective of the individual's life, successors, prayer, instructions concerning burial, promises and vows requested of those assembled that they would fulfill these requests and final instructions."[180] Paul's retrospective account, as told through Luke, indicates that Paul fulfilled all that was commanded to him and demanded by him.[181] Paul's preaching and gospel teachings reveal his convictions about the Church as the body of Christ and the practices of its members in preparation for secession that imitates his leading well after the Apostolic Age..[182]

Oral Roberts expounds on this in his teaching on The Sickness Attitude [183] as it relates to Acts chapter nine detailing of Saul's metamorphosis into Paul on the road of Damascus. Paul's transformation by the renewing of his mind, as discussed so far, reveals God's divine plan to heal the issue of the sickness attitude in the mind as well as the healing of the sickness in the body. Roberts goes on to say in the healing ministry of our Lord Jesus Christ, as He walked the roads of this earth, He encountered the lost and suffering humanity. Scripture reveals to us the great problem that He faced on every side. The problem of the mental attitude of the people, for it seemed that some of the sicknesses of the people began in their minds, and in any event, their mind was always a part of the healing problem or in the problem that Christ had in healing their minds and bodies. As you see, what we are inside, how we think, how we believe, and the habits that we have built up over a lifetime have a great deal to do with the power of Christ and with the attitude of God between you and me.

Jesus had to deal with people's minds, even as He through us must deal with your minds through this book as you read why and how I stayed in a treacherous relationship turned marriage for 14 years. In the words of Oral Roberts, your mind is a part of the problem; your mind is a part of the healing process. You are a part of it, and God depends on the cooperation of your mind for you to cease being negative and start being positive while recognizing a part of this is inside yourself as the wounds of your own broken relationships are triggered through the horrors of my story that resonates with millions after speaking for the first time on the Dear Future Wifey Podcast. Regardless of how much power God has, that power will never fully be effective in your life unless you cooperate with the power, unless you lose your own faith unless you are willing to change some of your patterns of life or your life habits and let Christ show you exactly how to think and believe in these terrible days. Time and time again, we see Jesus' battle with the sick mindsets of the people, which again is demonstrated through the Apostle Paul, who was a murderer of Christians before he encountered the power of God which prompted him to co-operate with the power, loose his faith and willingly desire to change his zealous "elite committed Pharisaic Jew" mindset.

My mindset changed from being an "elite committed Pharisaic Jew" when I took my eye gates off Derrick and his poor behavior and began focusing my attention on discovering my God-given destiny and purpose. In doing so my eyes and my ears had to be rewired to see and hear the truth of God's word, so I could see and hear the truth about what God was saying about my marriage. In doing so I had to confront my adultery that I had and was committing against the LORD who is my bridegroom (Rev 19:7). What I discovered is that I was not ready to meet Him, nor did I know who He was, which meant I was on the path to hear the dreadful words "I never knew you; depart from Me, you who practice lawlessness" (Matt 7:32-23)! I was shocked, then immediately offended by this revelation, but I was willing to explore how I had played the whore by committing adultery against the LORD. It was this willingness and curiosity that made me a candidate to receive healing and deliverance from the sickness attitude that plagued my life.

On Instagram, I posted a video of Derrick at one of the earlier shows of the Self Love Summit, being introduced by Ace Metaphor. Derrick walks the catwalk of the stage, suited up and looking fine, the women are in the crowd are screaming for him and I'm recording it real time as Meeting in My Bedroom by Silk is playing as his theme song. At this point, I did not know that he had already had physical affairs with Ashton in December of 2018, which he claims was only an oral sex experience, along with countless other sexual and inappropriate conversations with hundreds of other women. I was willingly and comfortably aloof to this reality and the signs of it, which unfolded right before my eyes during the Self Love Tour. Looking back now, from a healed place, on that time in my life, the red flags scream, HE IS SLINGING THE DING to everyone who comes into his presence Da'Naia, WAKE UP! Unfortunately, my mind was so sick that I was consumed with the mirage that I had created from a dissociated place in my thoughts, emotions, and behaviors. Remember, dissociating is the experience of detaching from reality. Dissociation encompasses the feeling of daydreaming or being intensely focused, as well as the distressing experience of being disconnected from reality. In this state, consciousness, identity, memory, and perception are no longer naturally integrated. Furthermore, dissociation often occurs because of stress or trauma, and it may be indicative of a dissociative disorder or other mental health condition.[184] Again, while I was never clinically diagnosed with any mental illness or disorders except for severe postpartum depression, I was clearly living in a dissociated state in the first two years of my marriage with Derrick. Psychology without God is dead, so the dissociation of my reality with its glaring, and obvious signs of infidelity has a direct correlation to the sickness attitude described by Oral Roberts from the passages in Acts chapter nine. The eight months that I spent being nursed back to health, mentally, emotionally, physically, and spiritually, while sleeping on my mother's couch tore the self-made bandage off of this sick attitude wound. Forcing me to wrestle with the complexities of my wounds as I sought to understand the wounds of Christ.

In the words of the Apostle Paul in Romans 6:19, I am speaking in human terms because of the weakness of my flesh at that stage in my life. For just as I presented the parts of my body as slave to impurity and to lawlessness, resulting in further lawlessness binding me to a loveless marriage, so I began presenting my body parts as slave to righteousness during my separation and recovery time from Derrick in 2020, resulting in my sanctification as a leader and deliverer of this generation. The more, I desired to know and seek Christ for myself during this time the more my sickness attitude waged war against my spirit, soul, and body, creating the road to Damascus needed for me to encounter the One true and living Christ. Live footage of me playing the whore against God was pushed into the gates of my eyes when I was going through the archives of videos and images of Derrick that I needed to give to the divorce attorney, that I hired in 2020.

Rummaging through these files was utilized by Jesus Christ of Nazareth by the power of the Holy Spirit to shake the prison gates of my eyesight as I watched the video of Derrick Walk the stage on the Self Love Tour to *Meeting in My Bedroom*. The shackles and chains fell off my eyes and ears, and revelation hit me so hard that I fell to the ground and had a blinding experience induced by the brightness of the presence of the LORD, just as the Apostle Paul did in his experience. The reason we as believers in Christ Jesus need to stop listening to secular music is because *the power of life and death is in the tongue* (Prov 18:21). As I watched Derrick and listened to what was happening in the video, I was immediately shown, in what seemed to be in a dual monitor vision, me singing at the top of my lungs the song Superstar by Usher. Imagine watching your phone screen and seeing one video playing and then seeing another comparable screen simultaneously playing a completely different video in which you are the Superstar.

The LORD was showing me singing the lyrics that go with it, "This goes out to you, you, my #1. Spotlights, big stage, fifty thousand fans screaming in a rage, bodyguards, limousines, this is the way I see you in my dreams. Paparazzi flash, a hundred pictures, all of you hanging on my bedroom wall, I'm a kid again, I feel like thirteen, but I knew when we fell in love boy (my improv from the original "girl" line). I'd be your groupie baby because you are my superstar." I was horrified at what I was seeing, and I am not talking about Derrick posing for hundreds of women at that stop of the Self Love Tour. It was very clear from the vision the LORD showed me that I was an idolator, which meant I was acting like a prostitute and committing adultery against my personal LORD and Savior, Jesus Christ of Nazareth. I was fourteen years old when that song by Usher was released, and I had the album. Five years later, I would meet my superstar, Derrick Jaxn. The problem with this is spiritual and witchcraft because the song itself is an incantation that, when sung, worships someone and something other than the LORD our God.

Exodus 20:3 (NIV)

³You shall have no other God's before Me

When I was declaring out of my mouth the lyrics from the song Superstar and other songs like it, I placed an image of a person above God in my heart, which eventually manifested in the reality of my life with my demonic relationship and marriage with Derrick Jaxn. Being a groupie for my husband made him my #1 and God my #2 which was a direct violation against His above command. Immediately following this vision and revelation, I had my encounter with the LORD. He said,

> *"You (Da'Naia) erected a shrine and built a high place for your husband and his talents, listen to you yelling out his books, which Ace did not mention. Yet you were not like a whore because you got paid. You are like a harlot against ME YOUR BRIDEGROOM WHO SHED MY BLOOD DO YOU COULD LIVE. Men make payments for harlots (hoes). But you, Da'Naia made your payments to your lover by following him around being his #1 fan and groupie with your time, talents, and body that I, the LORD your God, gave to you. You made an Idol of a man and did not acknowledge ME in any of your wicked ways. You, Da'Naia are not like other women in your harlotry because no one solicited you to be a whore. In that you have made payment in the form of your time, talents and body to a man that didn't give any payment to you in safety psychologically, emotionally, physically and spiritually (Eze 16:31-34 NIV),"*

Like lightning, I fell to the ground in my mother's living room, crying. LORD FORGIVE ME. The realization that I had erected an altar of the lust of my eyes and the agreement of my words as I sang that incantation shifted the lens from which I looked at myself, Derrick, and the future of our marriage. In his videos, What Are Alters and How to Raise Them and The Hidden Truth about Altars that Satan Doesn't Want You to Know, Miz Mzwakhe Tancredi teaches about the dangers of altars and how they can be used to destroy, divert, or delay your life. Apostle Tancredi says altars are a system of authorization that gives permission to something. A place of spiritual activities, a place where divinity meets humanity. However, the law of balance must be applied so that you understand that an altar can authorize good or evil, and where there is more than one altar in a person's life, you end up having a battle of the altars. Serving as a spiritual airport, the reason why altars are something every believer needs to be aware of is because of the law of territory.

The law of territory says that no entity can enter that territory without a body, which is required to thrive in that territory. So, if a spirit does not have the right permission for that body, they are not allowed access to specific territories. Spirits are not allowed in the realm of men, so they need a body, which is why we are spirits, with a soul that lives in a body. Therefore, when an altar is erected, it gives a spirit permission; that spirit is either the Spirit of God or demonic spirits called demons. The patterns and cycles that I have highlighted in my generational bloodline when it comes to abuse, rape, pre-marital sex, abortion, rejection, trauma, sexuationships, divorce, addiction, birthing children outside of marriage, and the like were able to go from generation to generation because of evil altars. Evil altars are the illegal way that spirits enter into the realm in which we live, creating patterns and cycles of generational destruction in every area of our lives, especially that of love and relationships. If these evil altars are not dismantled from the foundation, then they are fighting against your life, as they did mine and those who came before me in my family.

What I've learned after receiving much deliverance through Ed Citronnelli Ministries and getting hands-on practical training for how to be free from demonic oppression in mind, body, soul, and spirit is that the power behind a cheating man's heart is supplied by an evil alter. Furthermore, all altars are powered by the sacrifice of prayer.

Unfortunately, we lack knowledge and fail to differentiate between types of prayer. Nor are we taught in church that agents of Satan pray and write incantation prayers in the lyrics of songs that we sing in the secular world. We know this is true because the law of balance tells us that if there are different kinds of prayer that we should offer to the one true and living God, then there are many types of prayers that are offered up to the father of lies, Satan. The Bible teaches several kinds of prayer-and the different rules that govern them. However, we simply put all prayers together in the same sack and shake it all out together. Due to this, many prayers, like those asking God to heal our broken hearts from the men who broke them, are not working because we are using the wrong rules and laws. Evil spirits have figured out a way to enter the realm, which we call the natural world, without a body through the illegal means of an altar. This is why we need to learn which rules and laws apply when we are seeking healing and deliverance from the evil altar that comes with a cheating man's heart. Again, altars are systems of authorization that give spirits and entities access to the natural world we live in without being in a body. The foundation of a soul-tie and trauma bond is built on an evil altar, which makes it difficult for someone to leave a toxic or abusive relationship though their life may be in jeopardy. Since an altar is a spiritual portal that summons spirits, and a soul tie is when two souls are joined together, creating a spiritual link or portal between two people in which they exchange spirits and demons, we have to acknowledge and deal with the spiritual component of staying or going back to toxic relationships.

Exodus 20:24 (NIV)

[24] Make an altar of earth for me and sacrifice on it your burnt offerings and fellowship offerings, your sheep and goats and your cattle. Wherever I cause my name to be honored, I will come to you and bless you.

God is so big that He does not need an altar, but because He is a Spirit, he must comply with the law of territory, which is why our bodies are the temple of the Holy Spirit (1 Cor 6:19). But an altar authorizes a spirit to be in the realm of men without a body, which is why we need to rebuild, and altar dedicated to God the Father, Son, and Holy Spirit in our hearts. So, when God gives the word, His word becomes the law, and He gives dominion to his children, male and female, over the earth. No matter what, He cannot break His word. This is why God can not intervene with matters on the earth, such as dysfunctional and toxic relationships, because He cannot violate His own word, which is why He works through men and women of God who have given Him permission to use them to intervene. The lesson here is that as believers in Christ Jesus, we have to learn how to give God permission to intervene with matters of our broken hearts. Altars, however, become a way for Him to intervene and bring deliverance to a person or a family who has dedicated one to Him in their bloodline.

We see God's intervention through an altar in the bloodline of the father of our faith, Abraham (Rom 4:16). Scripture in Genesis 12 records the call of Abram, whose name was changed to Abraham by God in Genesis 17. God's instructions to Abraham were to leave his place of birth, his family, and his friends to go to a place that God had prepared for him to enter into a covenant with the one true and living God. The consequence of his obedience would result in Abraham being made a great nation, blessed, protected, and provided for by God forever throughout his bloodline. The covenant is that God would intervene in the affairs of Abram's lineage because of his faith and obedience when he left his home of Ur. Genesis 12:4-6 tells us that *Abram went, as the LORD had told him, with his wife Sarai and nephew Lot. He traveled to the land as far as the site of the great tree of Moreh as Shechem. The LORD appeared to Abram there and said, to your offspring (bloodline), I will give this land. So, Abram built an altar there to the LORD, who had appeared to him.* It's important to note here that physical altars are no longer required for believers today in the same way that they were necessary for those who lived in Old Testament times. While we can, and most of us have physical altars called prayer closets to the Most High God, the requirements for the altar that we are to build have shifted to being in the place of our heart chambers that was made possible by the completed work of Jesus on the cross.

In other words, the first thing we must start with is building an altar for our LORD and SAVIOR Jesus Christ in our hearts, which comes from godly sorrow and repentance. Meaning our hearts must be repaired, fixed, or mended from suffering, damage, and fault. In the matter of *Surviving a Cheating Man's Heart*, the first step to being healed in our mind, body, soul, and spirit is to surrender our hearts to the Holy Spirit so he can examine the condition of our hearts, suffering, damage, and personal sin. I went through this process for eight months as I slept on my mother's couch in Denver. It was in this place that I was able to be completely broken, unorganized, an emotional wreck, and physically weak, leading me to a place of desperation and complete dependence on others to help me carry my cross in preparation for my death mentally, emotionally, and psychologically. Luke 9:23 describes the death that I am talking about when it says, *whoever wants to be a disciple of Jesus Christ of Nazareth must deny themselves and take up their cross daily and follow Him.*

The concept of dying to self is found throughout the New Testament. It expresses the true essence of the Christian life, in which we take up our cross and follow Christ. Dying to self is part of being born again; *the old self dies, and the new self comes to life* (Jn 3:3-7). Not only are Christians born again when we come to salvation, but we also continue dying to self as part of the process of sanctification. As such, dying to self is both a one-time event and a lifelong process.[185] However, the one-time event portion of this process is excruciatingly long and painful because we do not understand nor are we taught that dying to our selfish desires, pre and extramarital sexual appetites, lying tongues, greed, love of money and material things, our ideas of love, relationships, and marriage must be put to death in order for us to see clearly what God has authorized to be in our lives. I went through this excruciatingly painful process in those eight months away from Derrick, where I was going through withdrawal and relapses from my psychological addiction to the chase-and-trap dynamic of our 11-year relationship at that point and time.

I went through all the normal withdrawal symptoms or thinking, what if he changes? What do I need to change? Maybe if I had done this or that differently, he wouldn't have? I don't know how to forgive him or myself. I love him, but I hate him; what am I to do to move past that? Why has he never chosen me? Why would God allow this to happen to me and all people? My mind was flooded with all these questions, while my heart simultaneously was crushed, feeling like millions of microscopic pieces floating around my body with no hope of being put back together in the proper places. Not to mention the sleepless nights, uncontrollable crying, loss of appetite, chronic headaches, fatigue, lack of focus, inability to engage with people, extreme overwhelm, fits of rage and anger, depression, and anxiety that come along with the heartbreak of infidelity. All of these are signs of dying to self-process that are required for complete healing in mind, body, soul, and spirit.

Each year, Cahleen Shrier, Ph.D., associate professor in the Department of Biology and Chemistry, presents a special lecture on the science of Christ's crucifixion. The same crucifixion we must imitate when dying to ourselves as required in John 3:3-7. While our death is not a physical death, the process of dying mentally, emotionally, and psychologically produces the sense of physical death, which registers in our brain's processing center. However, we are saved by grace through faith, which is what sustains us through this process of feeling like we literally cannot cope with or get through the trauma of betrayal. The following details from Dr. Shrier's lecture help us to see our emotional and psychological brokenness through the suffering of Christ. It also brings clarity to the physical body responses we have when we experience such emotional and psychological distress and suffer from depression, anxiety, anger fits of rage, low appetite, chronic headaches, fatigue, lack of focus, and other physical medical conditions because of our soul pain.

It is important to understand that from the beginning that Jesus would have been in excellent physical condition. As a carpenter by trade, he participated in physical labor. In addition, he spent much of His ministry traveling on foot across the countryside. His stamina and strength were, most likely, very well-developed. With that in mind, it is clear just how much He suffered: if this torture could break a man in such good shape, it must have been a horrific experience, says Dr. Shrier, as in the introduction of her lecture. After the Passover celebration, Jesus takes His disciples to Gethsemane to pray. During His anxious prayer about the events to come, Jesus sweats drops of blood. There is a rare medical condition called hematidrosis, during which the capillary blood vessels that feed the sweat glands break down. Blood released from the vessels mixes with the sweat; therefore, the body sweats drops of blood. This condition results from mental anguish or high anxiety, a state Jesus expresses by praying, *"my soul is deeply grieved to the point of death"* (Matt 26:38). Hematidrosis makes the skin tender, so Jesus' physical condition worsens slightly.[186]

Let me pause here to note the similarities between Jesus dying to himself as He was in the process of being crucified so we can live and our feeling like we are dying inside and out when the man that we love and have kids with cheats on us. I felt like I was doing well mentally, emotionally, and physically in 2019 when I decided I needed to change my life and begin a weight loss journey, which I have documented publicly. I didn't stop there; I had narrowed the three therapists I had been seeing since 2017 down to one who specifically dealt with self-love. Evanye helped me to develop strategies to cope with betrayal from college and the period after college before marriage, which I internalized as being things that were hindering my marriage with Derrick because he had changed, but I was still stuck in the past, unable to move forward. Yes, I believed that he had changed and not actually cheating because he said he had changed, and I was the only one who had not changed when I called him out and confronted him about Dunnie being involved again in the MSM card game, scheduling appearances for him and labeled in his phone as Teresa Langly. Not to mention, he was giving her extra money so she could provide for "her" child since she was coincidentally going through a very public nasty divorce. Knowing what I know now makes me question if her divorce was related to her rekindled "business relationship" with Derrick and his brand. Nevertheless, the result of this situation resulted in me thinking and feeling like I was the only one who had not changed; according to Derrick, Dunnie and he had changed and moved on, I was the only one who had not, so that was my problem and I needed to change that or I would lose him because he could not live life with that negative outlook that I had.

Traumatized with severe diagnosed postpartum depression, anxiety, and emotional instability is what I began confronting in order to be what Derrick needed me to be personally and for the sake of his brand that required him to work with women, even women that he has had a sexual history with so that we could live. My healing journey at this point looked like working out and therapy, and the results were that I was losing weight, looking fine, and finally feeling like I was coming out of the depression and anxiety from betrayals from the "past", though I was actively still battling knowing her body better than I knew my own. The world is ignorant of real trauma and the impact it has on a person. In the pages of this book, I have been sharing the deep things that shaped my natural combative nature when it comes to protecting my well-being. I know how to heal because I've had things to heal from. I've fought some real demons personally and maritally. So, thank God Almighty for the ability to do the deep inner healing work years before the public at large knew I existed. I know what it's like to be at the lowest of lows, depressed, comparing yourself to other women, and trying to win the affection of a man who never cared for or about you.

My decision to take my eyes off my spouse and put my attention and focus on myself makes it clear just how much I suffered after building up physical and mental stamina through the modern psychological model combined with physical exercise. Remember that Jesus most likely had physical stamina and strength based on his occupation as a carpenter, painting a clear picture in our minds of how much he suffered on his way to the cross. Again, if the torture of Jesus could break Him, who was in good shape, it must have been a horrific experience. In a similar manner, my experience after losing over 80lbs in 2019 and being in the best physical and mental shape I had been in since before I met, Derrick, translated to a horrific experience when I discovered his infidelity in November of 2019. As a result, my physical and mental health began to deteriorate again. However, instead of becoming overweight again, I lost more weight and essentially stopped eating, which led to severe malnutrition, putting me on the cusp of the eating disorder anorexia nervosa. Between December 2019 and February 4th, 2020, I lost an additional 40 lbs. through starvation, though it was aided by my still working out at that time.

In this condition, my mental anguish and high anxiety went through the roof, exceeding my capacity to cope, meaning I was actively experiencing compound trauma. In the words of Jesus expressed in the garden of Gethsemane hours before He was to die on the cross, *"my soul was deeply grieved to the point of death"* (Matt 26:38). In other words, it was almost as if I was dying from deep distress caused by the loss and disappointment of what I thought was a monogamous marriage where I was the sole source of dysfunction. Leading to my physical condition worsening. Now, let's go to the next phase of Jesus' suffering as He prepared to go to the cross. Traveling from Pilate to Herod and back again, Jesus walks approximately two and a half miles. He has not slept, and He has been mocked and beaten (Lk22:63-65). In addition, His skin remains tender from the hematidrosis. His physical condition worsened further. Pilate ordered Jesus to be flogged as required by Roman law before the crucifixion. Traditionally, the accused stood naked, and the flogging covered the area from the shoulders down to the upper legs. The whip consisted of several strips of leather. In the middle of the strips were metal balls that hit the skin, causing deep bruising. In addition, sheep bone was attached to the tips of each strip. When the bone makes contact with Jesus' skin, it digs into His muscles, tearing out chunks of flesh and exposing the bone beneath.[187]

The flogging leaves the skin on Jesus' back in long ribbons. By this point, He has lost a great volume of blood, which causes His blood pressure to fall and puts Him into shock. The human body attempts to remedy imbalances such as decreased blood volume, so Jesus' thirst is His body's natural response to His suffering (Jn 19:28). If He had drank water, His blood volume would have increased. Let's take another moment to pause as I note the next level of Jesus' suffering before He completed His work on the cross and my suffering in the last two years of my toxic marriage. Traveling from Georgia to Denver by car took 28 hours, including a few hours of rest in Kansas. Weeks leading up to my abrupt departure with our two kids to Denver with my mom as my backup driver. I went on a no-food and minimum-water fast. Keep in mind at this point in January, I was already down 40lbs of unhealthy weight loss from starvation, mental anguish, and high anxiety. In the first 21 days of January 2020, all hell physically broke out between Derrick and I. Reading my Bible and binge-watching Ed Citronnelli teachings and deliverance services had become my new addiction to cope with Derrick's infidelity that, I discovered just before we hosted his entire family for Thanksgiving in our 9000 sq ft house in Alpharetta, Ga.

The things that I learned about demons, witchcraft attacks, and other wiles of the devil through the ministry were everything that I needed to keep functioning in somewhat of a normal way for my children, who were one and three at that time.

Deliverance from demonic spirits was not the only thing that I received from watching Ed Citronnelli Ministries; I also received deliverance in the form of healing. In December 2019, just before my 30th birthday, I started having abnormal bleeding from my uterus, and baseball-sized boils under my arm. I went to the hospital and took x-rays and ultrasounds, and there was nothing that the doctors could see that would be contributing to this abnormal bleeding. The bleeding did not stop for twenty-one consecutive days until I watched a video teaching from Ed Citronnelli on spiritual spouses, where he prayed at the end of the video for everyone who was watching. Ed proceeded to have a prophetic revelation about a woman who was watching and suffering from an issue of blood. No, it is not ironic that there is a scriptural reference to the woman with the issue of blood in Mark chapter 5. As Ed prayed for that blood issue to dry up and be healed now in the name of Jesus, he called for the woman to touch the screen of her device and receive her healing. I was lying in bed in our mansion by myself, as I was accustomed to doing most nights of the week, when I began crying and touched the screen by faith. Once I touched the screen of my phone, something happened; it was almost as if I could feel sickness leave my body, leaving me with the sensation of complete relaxation from the crown of my head to the soul of my feet.

All I know is that after touching the screen of my phone when Ed prayed and gave a call to action, I was healed from my twenty-one-day issue of blood, which doctors could not identify or help me with when I came seeking answers. I was in a desperate place; I had tried everything and went to every kind of doctor except one, the Great Physician (Mk 2:17). *Broken hearted and in contrite spirit* (Psa 34:18), I reached out to

Jesus by faith to receive living water for my body's natural unquenchable thirst triggered by my suffering. One contributing factor to my overall suffering at that time was my silence and willful refusal to disclose to Derrick that I was aware of what he was doing at the condo we had in midtown, which was not what he said he was going to do or what he needed for us to live a comfortable life. Again, my silence here highlights my toxic trait of withholding information and not confronting it, revealing once again the unhealed wound of my rape trauma that still was not even on my radar as something contributing to my fear of confrontation and standing up for myself. Further, it played on the wound that I was someone to use, consume, and feed off, meaning that I was worthless and anything I had to say or could say was valueless, and I had no power to spark change for anything.

Just when you thought it couldn't get any worse, it did! By the time my 30th birthday had arrived, I knew very well that Derrick was engaged with several women, though I did my best to doubt the truth about it. At that point, we had not spent a whole lot of time considering his full-time residence was at the condo, but he was making it a point to be in our large home for a few days leading up to my birthday. Unfortunately, while he was technically staying the night in our house, his mind and heart were elsewhere. He would come home at nearly midnight after dealing with Ashley, with whom he developed a full-blown relationship, down to meeting her mother, with alcohol on his breath. I would kiss him and ask if he had been drinking, and immediately, he would be irritated, rolling his eyes, and saying Man, don't start that shit. On my 30th birthday, he spent the first half of that day with his girlfriend, then came home to take me on a luxurious, exclusive helicopter tour of Atlanta. After that, he took me to a place called Trapeze in Atlanta, which is basically a club where you're free to have open sex with whoever, however you want in front of everyone in the club.

I honestly felt like I was in Sodom and Gomorrah, considering what goes on in that establishment. We sat down at one of the tables closer to the bar area, where we could grab some food and drinks. We ordered, had some drinks, and walked around. Let me back up to what was happening when we first arrived to get into this sex club. Upon arrival, there were lots of people, ready and eager to get the night started; I did not really know what to expect because, one, I had only been to a handful of clubs, and two, I had never been to a sex club. Derrick proceeded to the counter to pay, I asked him if he had been there before, and he said no, he had just heard about it; as he continued to check out, the host asked him if he wanted to get a membership, he says yes, pays for a membership and then we proceed to enter into a modern-day Sodom and Gomorrah.

As we walked through the building, people were literally stopping and staring at us, and one person gained enough courage to ask if he was Derrick Jaxn. In short, as we walked the building, there were different sex rooms and open orgy rooms that with different themes for people to get off on. After a certain point, there is a no clothes policy, so you must strip down naked, though they do provide towels for you to wrap around. We went into those areas, and I will leave that right there; however, I will note that Derrick did ask me in that exposed area if I would be open to inviting a girl into the mix. I declined the offer, and he proceeded to go on about his business while I was just trying to take it all in. Traumatized is not a big enough word to describe what was happening in this sex club on my 30thbirthday, with my foreknowledge of his infidelity, that I had not told him that I knew about, nor was it something that he acknowledged or admitted to at that point. Making matters worse than they already are, this day was the day I became the most ungrateful bitch that has walked the face of the earth that he knows personally, and that's almost verbatim. It was this event that ushered in my journey down the road to anorexia nervosa in January 2020.

Meaning my condition worsened, just like that of Jesus condition when he traveled from Pilate to Herod and back to Pilate again.

Moving forward to the next phase of Jesus' suffering before his final moments on the cross, Dr. Shrier details how Roman soldiers placed a crown of thorns on Jesus' head and a robe on His back (Matt 27:28-29). The robe helps the blood clot (similar to putting a piece of tissue on a cut from shaving) to prevent Jesus from sustaining more blood loss. As they hit Jesus in the head (Matt 27:30)., the thorns from the crown push into the skin, and He begins bleeding profusely. The thorns also cause damage to the nerve that supplies the face, causing intense pain down His face and neck. As they mock Him, the soldiers also belittle Jesus by spitting on Him (Matt 27:30). They rip the robe off Jesus' back, and the bleeding starts afresh. Jesus' physical condition becomes more critical. Due to severe blood loss without replacement, Jesus is undoubtedly in shock. As such, He is unable to carry the cross, and Simon of Cyrene executes this task (Matt 27:32). The key word in the third stage of Jesus suffering before His death on the cross is shock. Therefore, we must define and understand this term in order for you to understand exactly what I was experiencing before I fled to Denver with my two kids.

Shock is a serious, life-threatening condition that happens when your body doesn't get enough blood flow. Lack of blood flow to your organs means they won't get enough oxygen, which can cause them to fail. Shock may also lead to a lack of oxygen in your body's tissues (hypoxia) and can cause your heart to stop (cardiac arrest). Several medical conditions may cause shock, including low blood volume, inadequate pumping action in your heart, excessive widening (dilation) of your blood vessels, certain medications that reduce heart function and damage to your nervous system. There are several different types of shock, these include hypovolemic shock, cardiogenic shock, obstructive shock and disruptive shock. Hypovolemic shock occurs due to low blood volume. Low blood volume means the amount of blood entering your heart with every heartbeat is lower than normal. So, the amount of blood pumped out to your body is lower than normal.[188]

Hypovolemic shock may be caused by excessive external bleeding due to cuts or other injuries, severe internal bleeding due to an ulcer, a ruptured blood vessel or a ruptured pregnancy outside of your uterus (ectopic pregnancy), loss of other bodily fluids due to major burns, inflammation of your pancreas, a hole in your intestinal wall, severe vomiting or diarrhea, certain kidney disorders, excessive use of diuretics and severe dehydration. Cariogenic shock occurs when damage to your heart leaves it unable to pump as much blood as your body needs. The most common causes of cardiogenic shock include heart attack, malfunction of heart valves, abnormal heart rhythm, heart muscle rupture or infection, and heart valve tear or infection. Obstructive shock occurs due to a blockage in your heart, arteries, or veins, which prevents blood from flowing properly. It can also occur due to a buildup of fluid in your chest cavity. Causes of obstructive shock include blood clots in your lungs, air trapped between your lung and chest wall (tension pneumothorax), and blood or fluid buildup in the space between your heart muscle and outer heart sac (cardiac tamponade).[189]

Disruptive shock occurs due to excessive widening (dilation) of your blood vessels. When this happens, your blood pressure lowers, and your organs don't receive enough blood flow and oxygen. There are several types of disruptive shock, which include anaphylactic shock (severe allergic reaction), septic shock (severe bacterial infection in your bloodstream), and neurogenetic shock (damage to your nervous system caused by spinal cord injury). The symptoms of shock depend on the cause and type of shock. Extremely low blood pressure is one of the most common signs. Other signs and symptoms of shock may include dizziness, lightheadedness or faintness, anxiety, blue or gray lips and fingernails, confusion, excessive sweating, low or no urine, fatigue, rapid but weak heartbeat, and shallow breathing.[190] It's important to note that

Jesus experienced all these forms of shock on His way to the cross to die for you and me to live. While my crucifixion was not a physical one like that of our Savior Jesus Christ of Nazareth, the shock in my trauma was eerily like that of the experience of Jesus' physical phases of death before He died on the cross.

Shock in trauma is any sudden, terrible experience that disrupts your well-being and overwhelms you. A traumatic experience can shock your system, causing you to go into a state of dissociation where your body and mind feel disconnected, and nothing feels real.[191] Your brain resorts to this adaptive defense mechanism when trying to cope with stressful or overwhelming events that it cannot prevent or escape. [192] Shock helps reduce your awareness of your physical or emotional pain by dulling your senses, making you numb, and reducing your conscious cognizance of the event. Symptoms of traumatic shock can cause a wide range of physical and emotional symptoms. However, every individual reacts to it differently.[193] These are some of the physical symptoms that may accompany traumatic shock, chills, dizziness, shakiness, lightheadedness, unconsciousness, nausea, committing, stomach pain, rapid heartbeat, headache, muscle tension, elevated blood pressure, rapid, shallow breathing. Emotional symptoms that may accompany traumatic shock are fear, panic, denial, anxiety, anger, irritability, helplessness., brain fog, confusion, disorientation, numbness, withdrawal, emotional outbursts, inability to concentrate, difficulty making decisions, decreased awareness of surroundings, a feeling of being unsafe.[194]

The dissociative state typically lasts for a short time, such as a few minutes or hours; however, in some cases of repeated and prolonged trauma, like mine, it can persist for much longer periods of time. [195] Afterward, it is not uncommon for the person to be preoccupied with the event, forget it entirely, or have flashbacks or nightmares of it.[196] What causes traumatic shock? While anything that significantly disrupts your emotional equilibrium can be considered a traumatic event, these are some examples of events that can cause traumatic shock, abandonment, abuse, accident, argument, bankruptcy, breakup, bullying, crime, death, divorce, domestic abuse, financial crisis, illness, imprisonment, infidelity, injury, job loss, life-threatening event, natural disaster, racism, sexual abuse or assault, terrorism, violence, war and witnessing a traumatic incident that happens to someone else [197] Due to this traumatic shock can be categorized into different, types, depending on how it affects the brain and body.

Traumatic events can sometimes cause a person to go into shock and disconnect from either themselves or the people around them. People who experience dissociative shock may feel disconnected from reality, suffer memory loss, or develop dissociative disorders.[198] While these types of shock are psychological and emotional, they can also affect a person medically because the body and mind are interlinked. For instance, someone who has been shot at or been in a car accident may have severe blood loss and go into hypovolemic shock; however, they may also sustain severe emotional trauma. Similarly, someone who receives devastating news or experiences a trauma may have a heart attack and go into cardiac shock.[199] The emotional effects of trauma are thought to be best treated by healthcare providers who specialize in trauma-informed care, which takes a different approach from other types of mental healthcare. However, I am demonstrating through my life story that professional medical and psychological treatment plans without God is dead! The Holy Spirit must be at the center of our healing in mind, body, soul, and spirit as He ministers to us through the wounds of Christ while utilizing medical and psychological practices. In my book, *Traumatized is God a Monster or Healer? A Trauma Informed-Guide for Ministers to Understand the Mind of the Wounded*, I emphasize that trauma-informed care recognizes the need for spiritual and psychological elements of the whole person to providers who believe in Jesus Christ of Nazareth. It is the missing link that we need to understand the person's life experience to deliver effective care.[200]

Pause and track with me through January of 2020 when I was already silently sliding down the hill towards anorexia nervosa in my suffering. My mom's Bible study group was doing their yearly Daniel fast, and I decided to join in on that since I had nothing else to lose, and God was something I was willing to try. Since I was already not eating much of anything, the fast was fairly simple; from a physical standpoint, I actually felt great the whole time, though my body was actually deteriorating from the inside out. Seven days into the fast, I discovered that Derrick had been spiritually manipulated when he went to see a person who does hypnosis to get over his fear of speaking. I learned this after watching Ed Citronnelli's How to Know if You are Under Witchcraft attack on YouTube. In short, Ed revealed from a scriptural standpoint that anyone who was doing psychic readings, tarot cards, and hypnosis was practicing witchcraft, and if you have seen someone like this, you need deliverance. Believe it or not, I didn't actually connect Derrick, having demons inside of him until the last day of the fast, I attribute this lack of connection to the active dissociation I was experiencing.

By day ten in the fast, I had already been texting Derrick about him needing deliverance and how the woman he had seen for hypnosis had opened him up to demons. I also asked him to send me the audio recording of his session with her, and what I heard confirmed everything that Ed Citronnelli had taught in his video. The woman, who had the title of Reverend something, began the session by asking him to lie down and get comfortable and letting him know that if he fell asleep, that would be okay. She did a quick prayer that did not acknowledge God the Father, Son, and Holy Spirit before she got started; after that, she played some nature sounds with water running in the background. I know Derrick drifted off to sleep because she made a note of him going deeper into sleep, and then she began to say that she had seen an aunt-like figure standing beside him; she was protecting him. Then she said, I also see a spirit guide that chief Indian spirit, and she spoke over Derrick, I open your soul and spirit to allow the Indian Chief to help guide you further; you'll know he's leading you because you'll be drawn to the water and find your peace close to bodies of water. More things were said, but I leave this portion of the story here because what I shared so far is enough to let you know that we were dealing with real witchcraft, sorcery, and divination. Derrick was not receptive to me talking about demons and deliverance, nor was he jumping for joy when I told him he needed deliverance because that woman opened him up to the demonic world.

I honestly could not understand why this was not good news and why he was not jumping for joy that all our problems could be tracked to a source outside of him and me but to Satan and his kingdom. In my mind at that time, he just needed to get delivered by Ed Citronnelli or Marcella, a prophet and deliverance minister that I personally knew from Denver, and we could be on our way to living a happy and less painful life. As I've stated several times in this book, boy, oh, boy, was I wrong!. Not only was he not feeling anything I was saying about Jesus, deliverance, and demons, but he literally began to speak out and tell his family and friends I was mentally ill. Friction grew so much between us that by the time our second wedding anniversary came along, thirteen days now into my fast, Derrick was locked in at the condo, refusing to come anywhere near the house. In fact, on our second-year wedding anniversary, we barely spoke on the phone or text. I found out in March of 2020 that, the day before and after our second wedding anniversary, Derrick had been balls deep in Ashley and Autum raw. I want to pause here and make a statement. Men wonder why women hate men; what I am disclosing to you in this book is how that happens, and no, they can't just get over it; they need to be healed in mind, body, soul, and spirit by the power of the Holy Spirit and the blood of Jesus.

Moving forward, Derrick's response to what I was saying about deliverance and demons added to my confusion about our whole relationship dynamic. Once day sixteen of my fast came along, I spent hours on my face crying to the LORD, asking Him to help me because I did not have the strength to go on and fix my marriage. At that time, an idea came to me: to take the repentance and renunciation prayers in Ed Citronnelli's book, *Prayers of Warfare*, and ask Derrick if he would be open to seeing how I worship God and pray. I sent a text message, not thinking he would respond, after about an hour:

He replied, "yes, when?"

I said, "tonight, will you come home?"

He replied, "aite bet."

When he arrived home, I greeted him and waited for him to get situated before sharing with him how I worship and pray to God. I was nervous because we had not really prayed and worshipped together in any fashion since 2009, when we dabbled in a church here and there in Tuskegee.

Once Derrick settled in and began to settle down, I slipped into the bed next to him, though we were not in touching distance of one another. An awkward silence filled the room as we sat there, avoiding eye contact with one another. He grabbed his phone and began engaging with those who had been occupying his attention for some time. I said a quick prayer to the LORD to strengthen me and give me the courage to share my faith in my heart. Then I said in a soft and timid voice, can I show you how I worship? He rolled his eyes which I perceived as irritation and said yeah. I got out of bed and turned on *The Call* by Isabella Davis, which started playing through the sound bar in our bedroom. I got on my knees beside the bed and began singing along with the track. My heart was racing and felt like it was continuing to increase in speed. The palms of my hands became filled with sweat, and my forehead began to drip large drops of sweat that were running down my face. At first, I was holding back on passion and conviction as I sang the first verses of the song. However, by the time the chorus came along, I had my eyes closed, and for the remainder of the time I was singing, it was almost as if it was just me and the LORD, as it had been since November 2019 when I really started trying to figure out who He was and if He could heal this aching pain I had inside. Near the end of the song, I was in full-fledged tears and felt like the thermostat heat setting was 100 degrees Fahrenheit.

Once the song stopped, I wiped my eyes, stood up, and got into bed. Derrick was slumped down in the bed in a lying position, with the covers pulled all the way up to his nose with just his eyes peering out. I sat in the bed next to him and then asked him if he would be willing to pray with me. He responded, "yes", then sat up with his back against the headboard. I grabbed two sheets of paper that I had printed off with the Prayers from Ed's book and told him we would read these together. He looked at the sheets of paper, then asked, "what kind of prayers are these?" I told him "they are some basic prayers from the Bible that I got from the book, which are all rooted in scripture." He rolled his eyes and fixed his gaze straight ahead in the direction of the fireplace in our room. I grabbed his hand and said, "it is better that we hold hands and say these prayers together". Before I go on with what happened next, the back story to this, in brief, is that hours before, I had told my mom that I felt like God was telling me to pray with Derrick. She agreed that would be a good idea, but she also warned me that doing the prayers from Ed's book would make demons manifest. So, I should expect and know that doing those prayers with him would cause demons to manifest, and I needed to be prepared to call on the name of the LORD.

As Derrick and I intertwined our hands together, I held the repentance prayers up for us to recite. He looked at the paper and said, "Do we have to do this"? I said, "yes, we do," with no hesitation and with authority. I did not know this at the moment, but when that question was asked; it was not Derrick, my husband, talking to me; it was one of the many demons in him, asking permission to stay by not repeating the repentance prayer. Remember, what we learned in Chapter 1 about demons, they speak.

ACTS 19:13-15 (AMP)

[13]Then some of the traveling Jewish exorcists also attempted to call the name of the Lord Jesus over those who had evil spirits, saying, I implore you and solemnly command you by the Jesus whom Paul preaches! [14]Seven sons of one [named] Sceva, a Jewish chief priest, were doing this. [15]But the evil spirit, retorted, I know and recognize and acknowledge Jesus, and I know about Paul, but as for you, who are you?

Demons will speak to you when you are casting them out. Remember, they are masters of deception. Do not attempt to hold conversations with them or ask them a lot of questions. They are liars! [201] Though they will tell the truth when it suits them and paralyzes a person enough to get them to stop their pursuit of casting them out in the name of Jesus. Anytime demons spoke in the presence of Jesus, He commanded them to be quiet, or He asked them what their name was. When a demon is about to be cast out, it will speak to declare its rights to the person's soul. They will threaten you, and they will even mock or attempt to taunt you. Never lose your focus. Command them to come out![202]

Again, I did not have that revelation or know that the demons in Derrick had already manifested when I was down on my knees, singing my lungs out to the LORD. I was so ignorant of spiritual warfare and the things of God that I did not even know the Bible *declares let them shout aloud as they praise God, with their sharp swords in their hands* (Psa 149:6 GNB). Nor did I really expect demons to manifest and talk to me through Derrick. As we said the prayers, I could feel my heartbeat steadily increasing, and the palms of my hand began to sweat, making Derrick's hand sweaty too, but we kept on doing the prayers on the first sheet until we completed them. Immediately, Derrick threw his head back towards the headboard looking up at the ceiling. I could tell it had taken a lot out of him to say the prayer, but again, I did not know that Derrick was no longer available and that demons had come to the surface. After a few seconds, I asked him if he was ready to do the repentance prayers. I was hit with the question; "can we do this later?" I responded, "no, we must do this now; it's not that much." Eyes rolled again, and Derrick's head came forward with fixed eyes on the next page. Hand in hand, we repeated the prayers of repentance; at the end, I made a declaration that was not on the page, that as we said the prayers together, we were delivered together because the two of us are one flesh, in Jesus' name.

Our hands unclasped and Derrick immediately laid flat down, scooting on the far end of the bed, pulling the cover all the way up, where only the top of his head and eyes were out. I thought it was odd but did not think demons had shown up, which meant I was not dealing with Derrick. The room was silent, yet everything in me felt like I was shaking, and my skin felt like it was about to jump off of my body; the hairs on my arms were raised, sticking straight up. I looked at Derrick, and he was looking at me with bloodshot red eyes, fixed, not moving or blinking. I figured he didn't have anything to say, so I said" OKAY, good night", and then reached over to kiss him before shutting off the lights. As I reached in for the kiss, he ducked his head and scooted away from me, not batting his eyelids. My thoughts were about what was going on. This was so weird, so I turned off the lights. The second I turned off the lights, I heard Derrick's voice say, "so, how was your day?" My thoughts were wtf. You want to talk now that I have turned off the lights and we are sitting in complete darkness, which was not an exaggeration because blackout curtains covered the windows in our room.

I turned on the light and noticed Derrick had pulled the covers down to his waist; then I responded to his question;" I thought it was good overall". I then asked, "what did you think about how I pray and worship?" Derrick then grabbed one of the four pillows on our bed, placed it between us horizontally, slipped his left arm up to the elbow into the pillowcase, and began making S-like motions inside. His arm movements resembled that of a snake slithering on the ground. As I was watching this, I was thinking wtf? Why is he doing that? Suddenly I had thought that this was a snake demon that had manifested because I could see Ed Cirtronnelli's deliverance of a person with a snake spirit. I'm not going to lie; fear consumed me because I realized then that I'm not dealing with Derrick, I'm dealing with a demon, and I don't know what to do next. The demon kept on trying to make small talk with me about my day while still moving his hand in an S pattern inside the pillowcase. I stopped talking to it and started saying, I plead the blood of Jesus over me and my children. Then I took my finger and acted out, drawing a line of protection while saying, "I draw a line of protection around me and my children."

I can't even tell you how many times I repeated the phrase I plead the blood of Jesus and I draw a line of protection around me and my children, which are things I heard watching Ed Citronnelli videos. But I can say I managed to say, Holy Spirit, I ask you to come into this bed and save me and my children. As I called in the Holy Spirit, the demon in Derrick said, "I am going to put on my boxing gloves and keep fighting you." Then, all of a sudden, fire, which looked like literal fire to me, came from the ceiling of our room into the bed, separating me and the demon in Derrick. The time the fire was in the bed felt like hours, but it was probably mere seconds. All I know is that when the fire cleared up, Derrick's body was facing away from me towards our bedroom windows, and he was sound asleep. All I could think was thank you, Jesus, and wtf was that? I did not sleep well that night, I kept waking up every couple of minutes, looking across the bed to see if Derrick's body had moved, but he had not moved an inch since the fire from the ceiling touched down in our bed.

Since I was waking up every couple of minutes, I would pray and ask God to protect me and my children and to keep that demon from waking up while I was drifting into sleep. I would also take my finger and touch Derrick's arm and ask God to deliver him; as I did that, I was saying, "I release the Holy Ghost shot gun anointing and Holy Ghost ricochet anointing into Derrick". Each time I said this phrase through the night, Derrick's body would shake, but he would never wake up or move an inch from the spot he had been in since the fire came. Once in the night, after three of four rounds of releasing Holy Ghost shotgun anointing, I heard a voice say, "hey hey, hey, hey", but Derrick's body was snoring. I was terrified and asked God to help me, and the voice did not speak again for the rest of the night. During one of my phases of minutes of sleep, the sun came up, and Derrick got out of bed without my noticing. I was sleeping on my back and felt the urge to wake up; as I opened my eyes, I noticed Derrick was sitting on the black couch in our bedroom, head down as if he was in deep thought, and his facial expression was filled with the expression of anger and defeat.

When he raised his head from looking down, I closed my eyes quickly to pretend I was still sleeping, and inside of my thoughts, I was asking God to please keep him away from me. God delivered, and Derrick walked straight into the bathroom, got himself together, got dressed, and left the house. About an hour after he left, I got a call from him, saying, "I don't know what kind of stuff you're on, but it doesn't align with what I had planned for my life; I don't know if we need to separate or divorce." I was silent for a few seconds, and I heard the word separate, so I replied to him, "I think we need to separate and then decide after that what we are going to do." He said" OKAY," then hung up the phone. I remember like it was yesterday, I was sitting on the edge of our jacuzzi tub when the phone hung up, and reality settled that we had just agreed to separate. Ugly, deep, and nasty tears welled up from the depths of my belly, rising up within me until I was ugly, crying in the bathroom. No words in any language or dialect can describe the type of pain I was feeling. After about 10 minutes of bawling my eyes out, I picked up the phone, called my mom, and said in a defeated voice, "I need you to come get me and the kids." Her response was, "I will be on the next flight out". I had her redeye flight itinerary within the hour, and I was charged with packing bags so that my children and I could go to Denver during this time of separation.

Remember, shock in trauma is any sudden, terrible experience that disrupts your well-being and overwhelms you. A traumatic experience can shock your system, causing you to go into a state of dissociation where your body and mind feel disconnected, and nothing feels real. The whole situation I described qualified me for trauma shock. If it had not been for the LORD holding me together in mind, body, soul, and spirit, I never would have made it to write this book. It also provides a timeline of how quickly I was taught, developed and matured in the LORD. What I teach, preach, and do now, I did not know, just four short years ago, which should be proof that there is one true and living God! My journey to take up my cross and die to the old me accelerated when the demons in Derrick manifested in our bed. Leading me to the next phase of Jesus' crucifixion, that my suffering reflected. Going deeper into what it means to be crucified requires a brief history of how it started. In Dr. Shrier's lecture, she explains how crucifixion was invented by the Persians between 300-400 B.C. It is quite possibly the most painful death ever invented by humankind. The English language derives the word "excruciating" from crucifixion, acknowledging it as a form of slow, painful suffering.

Its punishment was reserved for slaves, foreigners, revolutionaries, and the vilest of criminals. Victims were nailed to a cross; however, Jesus' cross was probably not the Latin cross but rather a Tau cross (T). The vertical piece (stipes) remains in the ground permanently. The accused carries only the horizontal piece (the patibulum) up the hill. Atop the patibulum lies a sign (the titulus), indicating that a formal trial occurred for a violation of the law. In Jesus' case, this reads *"Jesus the King of the Jews"* (Lk 23:38). I am being intentional here to connect each part of my suffering that played out in the public eye to that of the suffering of Christ because it's the only way that I had hope for a future. Jesus Himself also showed me the way out as I focused my eyes on Him while exploring who exactly He was and is and is to come (Rev 1:8). In an Instagram post, I shared a side-by-side picture of me from 2019 to 2021, when I made my public debut. The caption reads, "The two phases of me are not the same." However, this portion of the lesson from my life that contributed to my death and rebirth in Christ is called, you cannot escape the consequences of playing the harlot against the Lord!

When you love a man (not limited to the gender) more than you love God, you have made an idol of the person. Remember my Superstar confessional led by Usher Raymond when I was fourteen years old? I created an image of the ideal person in my heart, and five years later, I met that person who became the superstar the world knows as Derrick Jaxn.

This is a direct violation of **Deuteronomy 6:5-7 (NIV)**:

⁵Love the LORD your God with all your heart and with all your soul and with all your strength. ⁶These commandments that I give you today are to be on your hearts. ⁷Impress them on your children. Talk about them when you sit at home and when you walk along the road, when you lie down and when you get up.

and the consequences is **Ezekiel 16:35-43 (NIV)**:

³⁵Therefore, you prostitute, hear the word of the LORD! ³⁶This is what the Sovereign LORD says, Because you poured out your lust and exposed your naked body in your promiscuity with your lovers, and because of all your detestable idols, and because you gave them your children's blood, ³⁷therefore I am going to gather all your lovers, with whom you found pleasure, those you loved as well as those you hated. I will gather them against you from all around and will strip you in front of them, and they will see you stark naked. ³⁸I will sentence you to the punishment of women who commit adultery and who shed blood; I will bring on you the blood vengeance of my wrath and jealous anger. ³⁹Then I will deliver you into the hands of your lovers and destroy your lofty shrines. They will strip you of your clothes and take your fine jewelry and leave you stark naked. ⁴⁰They will bring a mob against you, who will stone you and hack you to pieces with their swords. ⁴¹They will burn down your houses and inflict punishment on you in the sight of many women. I will put a stop to your prostitution, and you will no longer pay your lovers. ⁴²Then my wrath against you will subside and my jealous anger will turn away from you; I will be calm and no longer angry. ⁴³Because you did not remember the days of your youth but enraged me with all these things, I will surely bring down on your head what you have done, declares the Sovereign LORD Did you not add lewdness to all your other detestable practices?

May God grant you repentance and acceptance to come to this level of self-examination, knowledge, and truth (2 Tim 2:25). If conviction hits you as it did me in 2019, you will begin to do the natural and spiritual work to give the Holy Spirit permission to change your life. How did I go from physically being 225lbs in early 2019 to 170lbs in

2021 when the world was introduced to me for the first time? Answer, deep inner-healing work, which reflects in the drastic difference between 2019 me and 2021 me. A part of that deep-seated inner healing work required my repentance for being a HOE against God with my husband. The consequence of my harlotry, however, was inescapable. Emphasis on Ezekiel 16:41 says, *they will burn down your houses and inflict punishment on you in the sight of many women. I will put a stop to your prostitution, and you will no longer pay your lovers.* I faced my judgment live across the world for my prostitution against the LORD, enduring your gossip, slander, lies, and mockery. It taught me to REMEMBER what the LORD brought me through, even with His rod of correction on my head. His helmet of Salvation (Eph 6:17) kept me sane during my chastisement by the LORD (Rev 3:19). If I endured this test of proving my love for God more than any person or thing, I would *be recompensed for my own deeds, says the LORD.* I've kept my eyes on the LORD through great heartache, persecution, and false witnessing.

Some of you want to become a stronger woman, but you do not want to go through the fire and take responsibility for your part in your suffering, which is directly related to your prostitution against the LORD. The key to achieving this requires you to take your eyes off of the cheating man in your life and focus on what God is saying to you about your suffering. Additionally, the takeaway you can leave with from my story is that when you watched me on live stream for the first time, showing up exactly how I did, beret and all, the LORD was testing me to see who I would choose. Would I choose the idol that I had been choosing in Derrick, like I have done in times past, paying my lover in terms of my time and talent, that Derrick had only devalued, dismissed, and discredited, or would I use the opportunity to show who I love more by proclaiming the word of the LORD amid my suffering, with the helmet of salvation statement.

My eyes got me into this situation, staring into Derrick's eyes at the party in Auburn twelve years before I earned the title "Miss Helmet of Salvation", written atop the patibulum with the sign (the titulus) indicating that a formal trial had occurred for my violation of the law. Do you see the correlation between Jesus' sign atop his patibulum that read, *"This is the King of the Jews,"* and mine, "Miss Helmet of Salvation"? In both cases, these inscriptions gave the charge against Christ. Jesus was killed for who He is, and I was killed for being who I am in Christ and for whose image I am made. All this occurred well before the 2022 controversial "curse" video that had people in an uproar. It's also a reflection of the twelve years I spent with the issue of blood of being the unloved wife in the heart of a man who cheats. My eyes, which were full of darkness, had begun the process of being transformed by the renewing of my mind as I pushed through teaching, preaching, and ministering the pure, unfiltered word of God on my social media handles. Evidence of this transformation is what was and is currently coming out of my mouth that scripture declares when it says, *for out of the abundance of the heart, so the mouth speaks (Lk 6:34).*

The Holy Spirit has determined in this section of the spiritual autopsy that I had a heart issue that was in rebellion against God and His kingdom. Due to this heart issue, I was led by the lust of my eyes when Derrick and I had our first date. Since my eyes were not only full of lust but unhealthy, I never developed boundaries, barriers, or standards that would sound off to alert me of red flags and issues of the heart within Derrick from day one. *Surviving A cheating Man's Heart* then requires you to come to the realization granted by the Holy Spirit that you have a heart issue that is in direct violation of the laws of God. The question is, can you accept that truth, and are you ready to be made well?

The Two have Become One Flesh

By day twelve, Derrick and I knew each other, so I was bent over doggy style in his Russel Hall dorm room while his roommate "slept" on

216

the other side of the room. The Bible declares, *that is why a man leaves his father and mother and is united with his wife, and they become one flesh"* (Gen 2:24). It is this verse that gives us a picture of the marriage bond before sin entered the world. The question is, was Derrick and I smashing session, day twelve, in his dorm room in alignment with God's perfect design for marriage? The answer to that is no, which means both of us were operating based on the lust of our flesh and eyes, qualifying for the perversion of God's perfect design that the Apostle Paul talks about to the sexually immoral Corinthian church. "One flesh echoes the language of the preceding verse when Adam first meets Eve and exclaims, *this is bone of my bone, and flesh from my flesh* (Gen 2:23 NLT). The two becoming one in marriage involves uniting two whole and separate people into a new, God-designed, God-purposed life.[203] Marriage was intended to be an unbreakable, lifelong union. Termination of marriage in divorce was not considered before sin came into the world when Satan deceived the woman in the garden, according to Genesis 3.

Husbands and wives become one flesh in sexual intimacy, as reflected literally in their children's lives. A child is one, new, whole, individual, and separate life created through the physical union of two people, a man, and a woman.[204] Since Derrick and I had sexual intimacy, outside of God's perfect design for marriage, we became like those in the sexually immoral Corinthian Church that the Apostle Paul wrote to saying, *do you not know that he who unites himself with a prostitute is one with her in body? For it is said, "The two will become one flesh"* (1 Cor 6:16). Derrick was already married based on the spiritual law concerning marriage being the sexual intimacy with another, to those who proceeded me like Rochelle, Brittany, Januar, his neighbor that took his virginity, Ciera, Meghan, Jazmin and many more. In like manner, I had become one flesh with my rapist, Brian, and James, a Kappa at Tuskegee that used me like a cum dump and threw me away like the used condom, full of nuts thrown on the ground beside the trash can in the same way that Derrick has carried out. The difference is that Derrick married me for his own purposes, which did not include any plans of being monogamous, liking, or loving me. I was only a muse for inspiration to build his brand based on how I responded to his mental, emotional, and psychological abuse tactics to educate women of what to do when a man who is not good to them does the exact things he was doing to me.

While many want me to relish in murdering Derrick as a male whore, it is clear that I would not be able to do that according to the spiritual law of one flesh. If the two are one flesh upon sexual intimacy, then I became just as much of a whore because we married sexually and legally. This led me to the next phase in the crucifixion process, as described by Dr. Shrier in the Science Behind Jesus' Crucifixion lecture. The accused needed to be nailed to the patibulum while lying down, so Jesus was thrown to the ground, reopening His wounds, grinding in dirt, and causing bleeding. They nail His "hands" to the patibulum, notates Dr. Shrier. The Greek meaning of hands includes the wrists. If the nails were driven into the hand, the weight of the arms would cause the nail to rip through the soft flesh.

Therefore, the upper body would not be held to the cross. If placed in the wrists, the bones in the lower portion of the hand support the weight of the arms, and the body remains nailed to the cross. The huge nail (seven to nine inches long) damages or severs the major nerve to the continuous agonizing pain up both of Jesus' arms. Once the victim is secured, the guards lift the patibulum and place it on the stipes already in the ground. As it is lifted, Jesus' full weight is down on His nailed wrists, and His shoulders and elbows dislocate (Psa 22:14). In this position, Jesus' arms stretch to a minimum of six inches longer than their original length[205].

It is highly likely that Jesus' feet were nailed through the tops as often pictured. In this position (with the knees flexed at approximately 90 degrees), the weight of the body pushes down on the nails, and the

SURVIVING A CHEATING MAN'S HEART

ankles support the weight. The nails would not rip through the soft tissue as would have occurred with the hands. Again, the nail would cause severe nerve damage (it severs the dorsal pedal artery of the foot) and acute pain. Jesus was broken, but none of His bones broke (Psa 34:20-22).[206] Take a moment and let that sink in! Some things need to be broken so the Holy Spirit can be made strong in you. And that is exactly what happened to me when I decided to give it another shot with Derrick.

The decision came after watching him fly state to state every weekend to the crusades that Ed Citronnelli was scheduled to heal the sick and cast out demons. Derrick's attendance in the states across America didn't just catch my eye but warranted acknowledgment from Ed Citronnelli himself when he was in Pasco, Washington, delivering a message to Hungry Generation. In fact, it was at that service that Derrick was serving as a catcher as Ed started the deliverance process, and demons began to manifest in people. I watched live on YouTube from my mother's couch. I began having thoughts that there could be a chance for reconciliation to happen. Not only was it possible, but the only hope for us to come together united in Christ Jesus.

Besides, I had never given him a chance to do it God's way with spiritual and clinical counsel to fight the witchcraft that had been plaguing our lives since he went to see a hypnotist in 2018. On top of that at Essence Festival, there was a covenant of witches specifically targeting and attacking Derrick's booth. One of them made him a necklace that was comprised of three ropes and a bell-like shape at the bottom. My mom was there, and she was the one who spotted the witches and began praying against their plot. She then found me, pulled me to the side, and told me there were witches targeting my husband and that I needed to pray for him. Immediately, I sprang into action, pulled him to the side, and told him, "There are witches here attacking you; do not accept anything from them." He responded "okay". However, he did not listen; as I was working to manage the crowd that had gathered around, I turned to look at him, and one of the witches was putting this necklace on him and touching his chest. I was pissed but also alarmed because I knew that it was a matter of life and death, and I didn't know how to fully fight it.

Let me rewind to 2018 when he went to a hypnotist, who is a witch, though I had no clue this was a witch at the time, who put him to sleep and called in demonic spirits of an Indian Chief and other marine spirits. It was around that time that I began having dreams of snakes attacking my children, which manifested in the natural world as things in our house began to move on their own and my oldest child began having night terrors. It didn't stop there; Marlee would be picked up and tossed on the floor, which could be seen on our in-home surveillance system. So, I was encouraged in my faith by watching Derrick attend the services of Ed Citronnelli in many different states so that true healing, deliverance, and restoration could happen. After all, there is nothing impossible for God (Lk 1:37). What I did not account for was whether or not Derrick wanted to be saved, healed, and delivered.

My list of thirteen things that I needed for reconciliation showed his lack of interest in true healing, deliverance, and reconciliation, but I did not see it or understand it at the time these events took place. Yes, I had terms and conditions for reconciliation that I developed during a seven day fast with the LORD. I discovered I needed terms and conditions, boundaries, and barriers after having weekly 1 on 1 Bible study and counseling sessions with Marcella. In one of my sessions, Marcella said, "the LORD is saying that you need to develop some things that you need to happen for reconciliation." At that time, reconciliation was not at the forefront of my list considering, Derrick had just confessed to another six women after telling me there were only two women with whom he had become close, whom I've already identified as Autumn and Ashley. Now, if you are good at math, you will realize that he only confessed to me eight of the "eleven" women.

I had no idea what I needed for reconciliation, so I went on a seven-day fast for clarity on what I should do. I developed the discipline to write specifically to the Holy Spirit during this time, which is what I teach, preach, and encourage women who are struggling to navigate the hearts of their cheating men. I purchased several composition notebooks, so I cracked one open and began my first entry to the Holy Spirit to figure out what I needed for reconciliation because I was coming up short on anything that could fix it in my own thoughts.

March 27th, 2020

> *Lord Jesus, I am at a point where I'm saying fuck this shit, please release me from this marriage. I give this to you because I can not bare it. I don't know if it's partly my emotions or my free desire but I'm feeling done with this marriage. Only You can turn this marriage around if I'm not released. I'm asking for complete clarity in these seven days of fasting. I need a clear direction of which path to take. Divorce with your permission or stay with your mercy and grace? In Jesus name I pray. Amen.*

I continued writing to the LORD during the seven days. However, I had my answers on the 4th day as they pertained to my terms for reconciliation. So, I crafted my text message threads to send to Derrick. My terms were as follows:

March 30th, 2020, 4:22pm

> Thread 1: "You said you hope for the chance to show me this is not who you really are. This is required for that chance."

Thread 2: Symbol key reference:

* Equals: created and setup to give me proof you're all into this (Phone virtual or physical counseling are options).

♦ implemented withing two weeks of arrival home.

(includes implementation of schedule you put together).

♥ Birth of new marriage.

Thread 3:

* Commitment to God led marriage counseling. Mutually agreed on councilor for minimum 6 months. (Includes switching councilors if need be)

* Create a documented schedule we can have physically posted and programmed into phone calendar Mon-Sun.

1. That allows for 30 min of break with me virtual or physical uninterrupted

2. Allows for 2 times a week for bathtime which is 7:45pm (15-20 minutes)

3. 2 days a week of drop off or pickup to school. Unforeseen changes are expected and delt with as they arise. (Rough Draft to me by April 2nd, 2020)

* Change both numbers w/no non platonic female friend contacts

* Thursday night studies of the word together and prayer 9pm-10pm

* Full disclosure of all female friends and business partners

- 3 in home dates a week (includes weekends and two dates in one day)

- Passwords and codes to everything in google drive document. Mine included.

- Once a month you cook for us

- Vow renewal with new vows with our mothers and children only as witnesses. Small intimate with God being at the center. January 13th, 2021

- Post us publicly after new marriage renewal vows in the first 6 months of 2021."

I pressed send and waited for a response.

At 4:31 pm Derrick replied.

Thread 1: "Would you like to have a discussion about what we both would need in order for me to have that chance?

Thread 2: "Or is it just me that's earning the chance to move forward?"

I replied 4:41pm

Thread 3: "Yes, I would like to have that discussion. If you have your requirements for me already, can they be sent prior to the discussion."

Derrick Replied 4:43 pm

Thread 4: "Can we stop talking so formal."

I Replied 4:43 pm

Thread 5: "Yes"

Derrick Replied 4:45 pm

Thread 6: "Nd yeah that's cool. I'd also like the floor to open for us to offer our thoughts on each other's requirements as well before we finalize them as the determining factor of our marriage. Would you be okay with that?"

I Replied 4:45 pm

Thread 7: "Yes"

Derrick Replied 8:30pm

Thread 8: "Gonna get some rest early tonight. Talk tomorrow ♥

I Replied 9:20 pm

Thread 9: okay, gn ♥

Let's pause here before I share Derrick's requirements for him to come back to the relationship. After sending him my requirements for returning after his cheating with "eleven" plus women that I did not sign up to be in rotation with, his response was let's look at what "we would both need". Both people's needs in a marriage are normal and healthy; however, when there is a betrayal, a spouse who has compassion in their heart would be able to see their spouse and desire to create that psychological safety with them. However, in Derrick's actions to my need for psychological safety, his response was centered around how he could be served and what he would get out of doing the things that I needed.

Do you remember our working definition of a toxic man provided by Devon Franklin? The man whose toxic is looking to be served. Devon then says, "If I am a man that's only looking to be served, I'm not going to see you because I'm only going to see you through the lens of how you service me." Applying this to my life, Derrick was only able to see me through the lens of how he could be serviced after his cheating to consider my requirements for restoration. At the time, I did not know this was the case; I just knew something was wrong, but I did not know what to call it. The next morning, I woke up to text messages from Derrick.

March 31ˢᵗ, 2020

Thread 1: "Good morning" 3:49 am

Thread 2: "I wrote down a few things I would like from you yesterday but it's important that I contextualize before I send them. These aren't things I require in order for us to have a chance. I'm going to give us a chance regardless, even if you ball this list up and trash it (figuratively speaking). We are going to have a chance (as far as I go) because I love you and I'm willing to do anything to make this work even accept less than what I currently think I deserve as we work towards common ground. Unless I'm at a place where I honestly don't believe I can anymore, I don't really want to entertain the thought of not having a chance, so this list isn't made with that in mind. When I give you this list, it's no different than the things we discussed within our marriage that we needed to better serve each other. They are merely clear communications of my desires and I'm trusting that your love to treat them as requirements of yourself to deliver on the strength of that alone. Not on the strength of us even having a chance. I want to get away from this "do this or else" dynamic. IDK if it's the hurt, outside voices speaking into our relationship, demons, pride or what. But that's not fertile ground for loving, compassionate, forgiving yet genuinely best effort in marriage. My "requirements" are simply requests and as I grow old WITH you, they will change. I'm simply making them known because I trust your heart." 4:13 am

I Replied, 7:13 am

Thread 2: "Good morning. What did you come up with?"

Derrick Replied 7:31 am

Thread 3: "#1 Heal before you come home and don't come home until you do. At least to the point where you recover the capacity to appreciate the type of husband you say I should be. I.E., in situations like this morning where I put all pride aside and tangibly show you exactly what you say you need from me, that you do not gloss over it like it means nothing. I would like you to become the type of wife that deserves the husband I'm capable of being and have been to you. In year one of our marriage, you were not that."

Thread 4: #2 At least five times a week, the first thing you say, text, or communicate to be besides "Good morning" be a positive thought specifically about me. A thank you, acknowledgement or a positive trait or action recently, encouragement to face the world, etc. This is a tangible way to show me you're committed to #1.

Thread 5: "#3. You get your hair done by a professional stylist at least twice a month.

Thread 6: "#4 When I come home, you pause what you're doing or who you're talking to long enough to hug/acknowledge me in the first 15 minutes unless you're sleep or in the shower or putting kids to bed. Even if it's just to say hello.

Thread 7: If I tell you you're yelling at me, that you do not continue to use the same level of voice due to disagreeing that you are yelling. Or if I say you're being disrespectful, you apologize, first and then second explain why you were being unintentionally disrespectful."

Thread 8: "You return the calls and texts of my mother and sisters within 24 hours of them calling you."

Thread 9: "You brush your teeth and tongue at least 5 nights a week before you settle into bed."

Thread 10: "If you're not back home by April 14th, the children come stay with me for the remainder of the month until May 1 or longer if travel is restricted."

Thread 11: "Whether suspected or confirmed, if you plan to reach out or reply to any woman associated with me about dealing outside our marriage, you come to me first and we both agree that it be the right thing to do. If we don't agree, you don't respond or reply anything."

Thread 12: "You divulge/ tell me what your spiritual counselor, therapist and mother have been told by you about our marriage. I will do the same, but I'd like us to decide together what is appropriate to tell outsiders about what's going on in our marriage."

Thread 13: "To adjust to your requirements for me to now do more task of upkeep for the children that you would normally do...

Thread 14: #11 "You officially step down as an officer of any of my companies and strictly be my wife (not business partner or employee) by July 1st. We can make the adjustments and re-file with the accountant.

Thread 15: # 12 Hire yourself as an employee of SDJ, y by April 15th. Pay rate: 5000 a month. By July 2020, have another job or some way to meet financial contributions to the household whose schedule also provides both your requirements and my requests to be met. I.E., allows you to take the kids to school for 3 days and put them to bed 3 days, etc.

Thread 14: "Financial Contribution: Bills account. You contribute? 2,000 a month. I contribute the rest (? 20,000+). Vacation account: ?100 a month from you. ?1000 a month from me. Savings: ? 100 mo. from you.?5000+ from me max until at ?100k. All money pulled out of SunTrust account, split between us, and put into safes until joint account created for savings. Fun/Personal accounts, completely separate. No limitation or monitoring on personal accounts so long as contribution expectations are met."

Thread 15: #13 "Your mother is not allowed into our home or to keep our children unattended until she and I are able to have a conversation and she apologize for the verbally abusive way she has spoken to our children/ daughter. She didn't just wrong you when she did that, she also wronged me and my trust in her must be restored unless you don't require her to respect me as an equal parent the same way you respect me as an equal parent."

What differences do you notice between Derrick's "requests" and my requirements? Let's start with the word salad, used when they are confronted with something that they do not want to talk about or if they are being called out.[207] I called Derrick out by making my standards and requirements known for me to return to the relationship. How do I know it was the word salad? He began talking in circles and condescending me by saying, "I am not going to give you requirements but requests," to let me know that my requirements for his cheating were not acceptable, but he is more superior because he was able to give requests that he expects me to treat as requirements because he "trusts my heart". The flashing, neon sign that you are in a word salad conversation is that you feel as if the person is talking in circles and keeps bringing the same thing up over and over again. You may think that a point has been resolved, and they bring it back up a few minutes later, making the same points. They are trying to keep you engaged and keep it going so you get frustrated and accept blame and the conversation. They continually repeat themselves, and there will never be a resolution.[208]

Next, you see that he started the process of shifting blame and positioning himself as the one who needed things for his return to the relationship. Blame-shifting is a specific form of verbal abuse, although it may coincide with gaslighting and other forms. A blame shift is meant to absolve the abuser of responsibility, but it also effectively makes the target feel guilty or shamed. Blame-shifting is effective because the abuser knows the other person's insecurities and vulnerabilities. [209] Derrick knew all of my insecurities and vulnerabilities because I had been vocal about them since our Dr. Turpeau counseling sessions that we never completed. I continued to be vocal about what I saw or what I was feeling about situations until November 2019, when I stumbled upon information about his cheating.

So, the requests that he sent specifically targeted my insecurities, automatically triggered me. One thing you need to know is that this behavior is intentional, calculated, and designed to elicit a negative response from you. It's also known as reactive abuse. Reactive abuse occurs when the victim reacts to the abuse they are experiencing. The victim may scream, toss out insults, or even lash out physically at the abuser. The abuser then retaliates by telling the victim that they are, in fact, the abuser. [210] When looking at Derrick's response, he began shifting the blame when he said, "We are going to have a chance (as far as I go) because I love you and I'm willing to do anything to make this work even accept less than what I currently think I deserve as we work towards common ground." The key phrase is "even accept less than what I currently think I deserve" as if his cheating was a result of him getting less than what he deserved. Therefore, he is willing to continue getting less than he deserves, which triggered the cheating in the first place to make it work. What kind of sense does that make? None!

How manipulative and cruel to use such language to play on the existing wound of feeling inadequate, which he taught me through his words and actions. Over the entire course of the marriage and even before marriage, there would be comments of, "Are you going to wear your hair like that? Are you sure you're going to wear that? Or I would ask him what he thought about an outfit, and he would be like it's cool. Furthermore, he would say you're enough; I never wanted the others; they could never be half of you. Yet when I would go through messages on his phone or social media, he would tell people like Wifey N' Training owner, "She's a nice girl; she's just not for me," which came with some nudes through the inbox.

While all of this sounds very narcissistic, believe it or not, a therapist told me to my face Derrick is not a narcissist. Imagine my surprise, after talking to my mom, Marcella, and my mom's best friend Tabitha that I believe he is a narcissist behind his back. He found out about this because he had bugged my car, phone, and room without my knowledge. So, while I am not a licensed professional, I can only speak about my personal experience, which strongly resembles that of narcissistic abuse. The mental, emotional, and psychological impact created land mines of triggers that I experienced day after day, year after year, producing severe anguish. So, the blame shifting in his reply to my requirements set me off, and of course, it was intentional. He then moves into reframing his indiscretion so that he could be served in order to meet my required need for mental, emotional, and psychological safety after his profound violation of trust.

Again, while it is not inherently bad for both people in the marriage to be serviced, in the case of a profound violation of trust, more care and consideration should be taken when there is genuine care and desire to earn back trust and build psychological safety. Highlighting that my safety was not a concern or true desire for Derrick's claim to wanting to be with me. Furthermore, he revealed to me in his message exactly what he did with my requirements when he said, "I'm going to give us a chance regardless, even if you ball this list up and trash it (figuratively speaking)." Just as the text reads, he balled up my requirements and trashed it figuratively. It was not uncommon for this to happen when I brought my true grievances to him concerning suspicions that I had about him and other women, including his plutonic friends.

Are these characteristics of a relationship built on a sturdy foundation? It's clear that the cycle of chase and trap is in full effect through this communication between Derrick and I. Serving as living proof that you pick up the habits and traits of the person you have a sexually intimate relationship with. Power is in soul ties, and it is either a positive or a negative. Our soul ties had negative connections, and there was suffering through it. The hardest part about this, though, is that you have to get to a point where you realize that your behavior is a mirror reflection of your spouse and then choose to do something about it. Yes, all the messages with Derrick's requests, are controlling, manipulative and abusive. However, I had to start shifting my focus and attention to how I had done the same things he was doing.

I was mentally, emotionally, and psychologically abusive in the same way that he was, it just looked different. Forcing me to go deeper into my bitter roots and deal with my demon of revenge. Fabian and I worked together at Sonic in Auburn, Alabama, and became friends. I actually have to mention that Derrick was left hanging in the balance about the details and nature of Fabian and my relationship dynamics until September of 2021. What I am revealing is emotional and psychological abuse that I intentionally inflicted on Derrick as a "lick back." Meaning I intentionally mentally and emotionally abused and gaslighted Derrick on the subject for nine years, though I did not call it or recognize it as that at the time. On the flip side, Derricks manipulation tactic to avoid responsibility and accountability for his unfaithfulness in our marriage positioned this as me getting a "lick back" in the marriage.

Remember what we learned about oppression in Chapter 1? Oppression doesn't have to bring the person any pleasure at all. If there is something he or she wants to stop doing and can't, it should be dealt with through deliverance. I wanted to stop being an abuser, but I didn't know how to or where to start. As I began learning about abuse from a psychological standpoint and understanding that abuse is usually a learned behavior, it forced me to look at my own family and upbringing in more detail. At the same time, I began to investigate this from the spiritual standpoint and discovered a system of patterns and behaviors displayed in each bloody, painful memory or experience between Derrick and me. In a much larger picture, it revealed our sin cycle, which at the root is witchcraft.

Can you identify the pattern here? Addiction! We became addicted to mentally and emotionally abusing each other in different ways. At the time that these back-and-forth abusive tactics between Derrick and I occurred, I had no knowledge or awareness of addiction, nor did I know I, too, was abusive. I absolutely could not see how I was an abuser, nor did I understand the concept of the two becoming one flesh.

In order to be healed, you have to do the hard work of looking at the bloody, nasty, deep, and painful wounds of Christ so you can look at, heal, and move forward in your own healing. During my time in Denver, on my mother's couch, I would write to the Holy Spirit in detail about what was going on in my life and why I was so hurt. One of the deep and painful wounds that uncovered the nasty addiction of abusive behavior I was displaying is my dealing with Fabian. As I sat down to write to the Holy Spirit, my toxicity began to unravel even more as I went through the details of what took place between Fabian and I that had Derrick in torment for nine years. The lick back or murder plan was conceived in my heart when Fabian came to me at work one day and told me that he had seen Derrick at his house party.

Instantly, I was triggered, and the flood of unhealed and buried traumas of seeing Derrick's archive of women rushed back to my mind in full color. One of which is his longtime friend Zoe, who I found a photo of in his phone with red panties and a team Jaxn wife beater on with leg and booty propped up on the bathroom counter looking back at the mirror to take a picture. Sparking the fire for Operation Good Girl Gone Bad. Now, Fabian and I have the same type of car, a Subaru Impreza; the only differences are the year and shade of blue. Since I was tomboyish growing up, I actually had a bent towards racing and more sporty things, though I would not consider myself an athlete by any means. Fast and Furious was one of my favorite movie series, and as I mentioned before, movies shaped my reality.

Of course, that meant that I was racing Fabian on the back roads of Tuskegee at every opportunity that I got. At the time, I did not consider my behavior spending time or cheating. However, that is exactly what it was: emotional cheating because Derrick did not know about it, and I was intentionally working with this man to steal, kill, and destroy Derrick's psychological safety in the same way he did to me. Can you say demonic? My agenda was one hundred percent backed by the demons of cheating, lying, manipulation, witchcraft, gaslighting, stealing, and murdering. Yes, I had all the same demons as Derrick because, at the time of intimacy, we became one flesh, and we swapped spirits, souls, and demons.

This brings me back to the scriptural reference that says, *"Do you not know that whoever is joined to a harlot becomes one flesh?."* It is impossible to call Derrick a liar, cheater, manipulator, and gas lighter without calling myself the same thing because I became a mirror image of him. And this is why God tells us not to have sex before marriage or to be unequally yoked with an unbeliever. In my demonized mindset, I was going to make sure that Derrick felt every bit of doubt, anguish, bitterness, and resentment towards me for cheating on him in the same way I felt with him cheating on me. Unfortunately, I dealt with this all the way until our last year of active marriage, as Derrick expressed how I did the same thing he does by not being forthcoming with the whole Fabian situation.

I'm not going to lie; I tried to deny it at first, but the more I sat within the presence of the Lord, the more I had to acknowledge the power of being one flesh, which meant I was an abuser. What a tough pill to swallow, but it is a pill we all must accept if we want true freedom. It was in this space that a flood of memories began to bubble to the surface as the Holy Spirit began tearing down the wall of pride that kept me from seeing all the ways in which I contributed to the abusive relationship, which was keeping me bound in a loveless marriage that not only had similarities to that of the story of Jacob and Leah but more closely resembled the relationship of Abigail and Nabal.

At this point, it became critical that I search the scriptures as the Holy Spirit began to search and pull up all the wickedness of my heart that I had not been forthcoming with and buried deep inside. I did this by searching the Holy Scriptures for answers, and the Holy Spirit led me to pay attention to the details of the story of Abigail and Nabal. 1 Samuel 25 introduces us to the Abigail and Nabal relationship dynamics. Scripture describes Nabal as a man in Moan who had property there at Carmel and was very wealthy. Pause here as I embed my real life into the story relationship dynamic of this biblical couple. Derrick is a man who has property and is very wealthy, in the same way Nabal was, as described above. Now, let's hop back into the text starting in verse three, His name was Nabal, and his wife's name was Abigail. She was an intelligent and beautiful woman, but her husband was surly and mean in his dealings.

In the same way, Derrick walked in the path of Nabal, so I walked in the path of Abigail. The scripture does not give us a lot of background information on how Nabal and Abigail came to be because it is not the focal point of the message the LORD is communicating to the intended audience. God's focus is on Nabal's behavior, which qualifies him as a man who is "surly and mean." Further, the text provides evidence of his meanness by describing his interactions and treatment of King David and his servants, who had been watching over Nabal's property day and night, according to verse twenty-one. The key to my next phase of healing God's way came with me going through the evidence of the bloody, nasty, deep, and painful wounds the LORD began to bring to the surface when I realized that I, too, had been just as abusive to Derrick as he had been to me. The difference between us was our heart condition.

One of our therapists told us both in one joint session that we had both been mentally and emotionally abusive to each other in different ways. At first, I didn't understand how I was, however after being healed enough to teach and talk about the experiences laid out In this book, the details of the abuse begin to come together piece by piece to form a larger picture that is much bigger than Derrick and me. Salvation, healing, and deliverance are for the generation of children we birthed, but in a much larger scheme of teaching the generations in our sphere of public influence. The problems were highlighted when we did not agree to receive salvation, healing, and deliverance together. Revealing the differences in our heart condition. I wanted complete healing and deliverance, and Derrick wanted things to stay the same.

The first evidence of this heart condition can be found in the text of the first book of the trilogy *A Cheating Man's Heart*. Remember when Derrick's alias Shawn "decided to become spiritually in tune with himself?" A written decree was made, becoming the legal ground demons needed from Derrick to maintain their positions. The book's text became an evil altar fighting against him, me, and our marriage. In the same way, this book is a written decree made as the legal ground God the Father, Son, and Holy Spirit needed to maintain their position as the head of my life, but more importantly, the head of our children's lives. Altar verses altar, as mentioned earlier in this section of the book.

Careful examination of each bloody, deep, painful wound had to be examined to get to this place in the spiritual autopsy to diagnose the cause of death of my infamous marriage. Opening up several wounds that had been covered, festering, infected, and decaying that neither one of us dealt with contributed to the overall death of the marriage. It was here that led me on a whole new journey to discover and confirm the foundation upon which my marriage was built. Originally, I had identified with Leah, the wife of Jacob, who suffered from being unloved. However, the more I sat with my newly discovered wounds in the presence of the Holy Spirit, I began to realize that one of the reasons the marriage died was because our whole marriage was built on the foundation of a lie!

Since the foundation of my marriage was built on a lie, there is no wonder as to why there was never true friendship, mutual respect, trust, and care. Clearly, this did not stop us from having kids, though Derrick's view of me in his heart never changed from being someone who was just one of several players on his team. And just like that, an abrupt shift in our relationship pointed me in the direction of Abigail and Nabal. Which meant I had to start going through all the evidence, sorting it out, and confronting the excruciating pain from each experience that Derrick and I had transpire between us. This led me to revisit my sin of dressing to impress the man who didn't have any investment in me beyond what was between my legs when one of the others was not available to service him. That statement alone was a painful one to express because I began to realize I became exactly the person I dreaded becoming, an abused, abusive woman.

Acknowledging that was just the confession I needed to give in the presence of the Lord sent a flood of other memories that I needed to confront to the surface. Betrayal from "friends" like Barnes, Zoe, and Adrian, who all knew about infidelity and even kicked it with them while smiling in my face. The heartbreaking and soul-crushing realities of women like Watch Jazzy, Nicole Chaplin, a producer from the Breakfast Club, Candace, and just about every woman that Derrick had ever introduced me to or knew personally not only knew him but smashed him under my nose and in my face. At the same time, my own hidden secrets of dealing with men like Brandan, who was around at the time I was single yet in rotation with Derrick. Or my deepest and closest-kept secret, James, who was around in the same month before Derrick and I became an official couple on February 14th, 2009. I have never told anyone about James, not even my mother, who will be reading this for the first time with the same anticipation as all of you as I go into how it started and how it ended, while I was also in the getting to know Derrick stage, in book 2.

Discussion Questions & Topics:

How many soul-ties do you have? When you identify the number, write the names down, so you can begin breaking the soul-ties with each person for your freedom.

Identify all the ways that you have been an abuser or manipulator in your relationship. Grab a notebook and write, "Holy Spirit, I invite you into this writing time". Then write to him all the things you identified as abusive or manipulative that you have done and ask Him to take in out of your heart.

How many cycles or patterns of toxic behavior can you identify in your relationship? Write it down and begin to ask God to help you move towards healing and deliverance.

Are you addicted to your spouse? Or Ex? If so, list out all the ways addiction has shown up in your life. Then ask the Holy Spirit to help you break the addiction.

Chapter Summary/Key Takeaways

1. Dysfunctional families sweep things under the rug.

2. Model Homes impact your relationships.

3. Character is defined as the mental and moral qualities distinctive to an individual.

4. Stronghold is a place where a particular perspective or belief is strongly defended.

5. Fact based lies act like the glue to keep the trauma bond and soul tie.

6. The Two become one flesh at the time of sexual intimacy.

7. Eyes are one way demons enter your body.

Epilogue/ Conclusion

Al was a classmate in college who was in my supply chain management class. I introduced Al to Derrick which is how they became cool at one point. Fast-forward, out of college during my time of willing participation in rotation with the 99 plus in 2016. Note this was also the year our first daughter was born. I found out Al was in ATL, and I had just moved there as a single person. Clearly, I was still in rotation with Derrick, so I say single loosely. I bought a guitar and asked Al to give me lessons. He accepted and began teaching me how to play the guitar. Al literally rocks out, but he is also very intelligent.

In all transparency Al and I did have dinner twice and coffee and he took me on a ride in one of his fancy cars. Nothing sexual happened between us, but I think we had continued to hang out it could have, but I'll never know. My tail got pregnant which sucked me back into the emotional roller-coaster with Derrick that has be given me books of material to write.

Fast forward again, to September of 2022, about a week before the text message divorce discard from Derrick, I was accused of hooking up

SURVIVING A CHEATING MAN'S HEART

with Al. Honestly, in that moment I was thinking, I should have, but in reality, it would have been another tack in our addictive psychological games. Derrick said, "I spoke to Al, and he said, y'all hooked up."

I responded, "that's a lie, call him."

Derrick said, "No I don't need to call him, I already know the answer."

I responded, "You're lying because I know for a fact we did not hook up."

Derrick said, "So you're the one hooking up with my friends."

I responded, "Uh, No! Al was my friend that I introduced you too, so I'm going to call him and ask him if he said what you're claiming he said."

I grabbed my phone and began searching...

Derrick is furious and says, "So You're Just going to disrespect me and not honor my wish for you not to call him. God says to respect your husband, so you're not even following His command."

I responded, "I'm not going to be falsely accused when I know the truth, and I can call to fact check."

Derrick then switched to another issue that I got ensnared in trying to defend, so I never got to talk with Al.

Is it Narcissistic Abuse?

241

Acknowledgments

Oral Robert's University professors of the Master of Christian Ministry program were outstanding Bible teachers. The university shaped, guided, and developed me as an emerging leader of this generation.

In addition to the Oral Roberts University, the ministries of Ed Citronnelli, R.C Blakes, Frank and Ida Mae Hammond, Miz Mizwake Tancredi, and Bridge Ministries have been critical in many areas of my life and ministry concerning prayer, deliverance, and healing.

Each ministry God used for different functions, working together as one body to birth Da'Naia Jackson Ministries, the H.E.A.L.E.D school, and *Surviving a Cheating Man's Heart*.

About the Author

At the time of writing *Surviving a Cheating Man's Heart*, Da'Naia Jackson, M.A was a full-time student at Oral Robert's University School of Theology and Ministry. Prior, she has written two additional books, Healing God's Way: The Art of Spiritual Warfare Healing and Deliverance and Traumatized Is God a Monster or Healer? A Trauma Informed Guide for Ministers to Understand the Mind of the Wounded.

In addition to an M.A. in Christian Ministry from Oral Robert's University, Da'Naia received a B.A in Sales and Marketing, as well as a B.A in Hospitality Management from the prestigious Tuskegee University in Tuskegee, Alabama.

Her ministry experience at the time of writing *Surviving a Cheating Man's Heart* included pastoring her online community of 113k followers on Instagram and 1.7k on Facebook through emotionally healthy discipleship.

Da'Naia Jackson, M.A., became the founder and teacher of the H.E.A.L.E.D school for whole person healing and recovery birthed in 2022.

Surviving A Cheating Man's Heart was based on Da'Naia Jackson M. A's first seven years of life experience, study, and research of God's shaping, saving, and healing power in His rescue plan to save the traumatized believer.

Da'Naia Jackson, M.A. specializes in Trauma Informed Care through the American Association of Christian Counselors, Suicide prevention, and Youth Mental Health Coaching.

She is a mother to three beautiful children, Marlee, Derrick Jr., and Eliy'Sha.

Bibliography

[1] 2020.Blakes, RC.THE PSYCHOLOGICAL DEFECTS OF A WOMAN'S BROKEN CONSCIOUSNESS with R.C. BLAKES- https://www.youtube.com/watch?v=bHJ4ssECMvQ

[2] 1996.Hammond, Frank and Ida Mae. A Manual for Childres's Deliverance. Page 78

[3] How to Trust Yourself after Narcissistic Abuse-3 Tips. Patrick Teahan

[4] Solomon, D. Torace.2020. The Finger of God a Practical Manual for Deliverance Ministry. 2nd Edition. ISBN:9798479213557

[5] See Soloman, D. Torrence in reference 4

[6] James and Robert Morris. Jesus at the Center Sermon Series. Gateway Church 2024

[7] Jackson, Da'Naia. 2023. Traumatized: Is God a Monster or a Healer? A Trauma-Informed Guide for Ministers to Understand the Mind of the Wounded

[8] Strickland, Darby.2022. Foundations of Trauma Care for Biblical Counselors. JBC 36:2 (2022) p.29

[9] World Health Organization. April 10th, 2024

[10] See Traumatized Is God a Monster or Healer p.3

[11] American Association of Christian Counselors: YMHC 201: Childhood Trauma and Adverse Childhood Experiences

[12] Mental Health America: Dissociation and Dissociative Disorders

[13] Cymorth I Ferched Cymru Welsh Women's Aid. May 22,2023. Understanding Victim Blaming and Why it's harmful to Survivors

[14] See Welsh Women's Aid. May 22,2023.

[15] See AACC YMHC 201: Childhood Trauma and Adverse Childhood Experiences

[16] Hammond, Frank, Ida Mae.1996. A Manual for Children's Deliverance p. 19

[17] See Hammond, Frank, Ida Mae p. 19-20

[18] Solomon. D. Torace.2020. The Finger of God a Practical Manual for Deliverance Ministry

[19] Hammon, Frank, Ida Mae. The Breaking of Curses and the DVD Breaking Curses. Impact Christian Books at www.impactchristianbooks.com/frank

[20] See Solomon, Torace. The Finger of God p. 24

[21] See Stricklan, Darby. 2022 Foundations of Trauma Care for Biblical Counselors p. 26-7

[22] MSc. Guy-Evans, Olivia, Saul Mcleod, PhD.2024. How Anxious Ambivalent Attachment Develops in Children. Simplypsychology.org

[23] See AACC YMHC Childhood Trauma and Adverse Childhood Experiences

[24] See Strickland, Darby. Foundations of Trauma Care for Biblical Counselors p.27-8

[25] Strickland, Darby. Foundations of Trauma Informed Care for Biblicak Counselors p.27-8

[26] Stickland, Darby. Foundations of Trauma Informed Care for Biblical Counselors. P.27-8

[27] The Spiritual Impact of Sexual Abuse-Clinical Psychologist Diane Langberg YouTube

[28] Jackson, Da'Naia.2023. Traumatized: Is God a Monster or a Healer? A Trauma Informed Guide for Ministers to Understand the Mind of the Wounded. Also see Stickland, Darby. Is it Abuse? A Biblical Guide to Identifying Domestic Abuse and Helping Victims. Audible section 4. Understanding the Impacts of Abuse

[29] Evans-Guy, Olivia, Mcleod, Saul, PhD.2024. Fearful Avoidant Attachment Style: Signs & How to Cope simplypscyology.org

[30] Tanasugarn, Annie Ph.D., CCTSA. 2023. Fearful-Avoidant Attachment and Romantic Relationships. Psychologytoday.com

[31] See Frank & Ida Mae Children's Deliverance Manual p.21

[32] Jan, Misha, Mcleod, Saul, Ph.D., Evans-Guy, Olivia, MSc.2024. Secure Attachment Style Relationships & How to Form. Simplypsychology.org

[33] See Secure Attachment Style Relationships. simplypsychology.org

[34] See Children's Deliverance Manual Frank and Ida Mae p. 22

[35] See Children's Deliverance Manual Frank and Ida Mae p. 22

[36] Cleveland Clinic. Autopsy.my.clevelandclinic.org

[37] Jackson, Da'Naia.2021. Healing God's Way: The Art of Spiritual Warfare, Deliverance and Healing

[38] See Jackson, Healing God's Way: The Art of Spiritual Warfare, Deliverance and Healing p.1

[39] See Cleveland Clinic Autopsy

[40] Clinton, Robert. 2018. The Making of a Leader: Recognizing the Lessons and Stages of Leadership Development. (2nd ed.). Tyndale House.

[41] Jackson, Da'Naia.2022. The Birth of Da'Naia Jackosn Ministries Essay Oral Roberts University

[42] Jackson, Da'Naia.2022. The Birth of Da'Naia Jackosn Ministries Essay Oral Roberts University

[43] See Clinton p. 135

[44] Walling-Sprague. Major Role Reader Handout

[45] See Tanasugarn, Annie Ph.D., CCTSA. 2023. Fearful-Avoidant attachment and Romantic Relationships. Psychologytoday.com

[46] See The Birth of Da'Naia Jackson Ministries Essay

[47] See Torace D. Soloman p. 36

[48] Khan, Nyria.2020. Anxious- Avoidant Attachment relationship chase and trap

[49] Drescher, Anna, Mcleod, Saul PhD, Guy-Evans, Oliva.2024. Dismissive Avoidant Attachment Style: Signs and How to Heal

[50] Torace D. Soloman The Finger of God

[51] See Torace D. Soloman Finger of God p.25

[52] National Institute of Mental Health nimh.nih.gov

[53] Scazzero, Peter. Emotionally Healthy Discipleship p.5

[54] Scazzero, Peter, Emotionally Healthy Leader

[55] See Jackson, Da'Naia. Traumatized: Is God a Monster or Healer? p.18

[56] See Scazzero, Peter. Emotionally Healthy Discipleship p.6

[57] See Jackson, Da'Naia. Traumatized: Is God a Monster or Healer? p. 19

[58] See National Institute of Mental Health. Schizophrenia

[59] See Torace D. Solomon Finger of God p.27

[60] See Torace. D. Solomon. Finger of God p.27

[61] Freeze- Complex Trauma Resources complextrauma.org

[62] See Jackson, Da'Naia. Traumatized: Is God a Monster or Healer p.35

[63] AACC YMHC 201: Childhood trauma and adverse Childhood Experiences

[64] Srickland, Darby. Is It Abuse? Audiobook. Audible

[65]Yahmas Budiatro, Avin, Fadilla Helmi. 2021. Shame and Self-Esteem: A Meeta Analysis. National Library of Medicine

[66] Dyer, K.F., W. Dorahy, M.J, Corry, M., Black, R., Matheson, L., Coles, H., Middleton, W,.2017. Comparing shame in clinical and non-clinical populations: Preliminary findings, Psychological Trauma: Theory, Research, Practice, and Policy,9 (2), 173-180. 10.1037/tra0000158 [PubMed][CrossRef]

[67] See Jackson, Da'Naia. 2023. Traumatized: Is God a Monster or a Healer? P. 11

[68] Henri Nouwen's "The Vulnerable Journey" Chapter 2 The Way of Jesus YouTube

[69] Evans-Guy, Olivia. Mcleod, Saul PhD.2024. What is Masking? Simplypsychology.org

[70] See What Is Masking? Evans-Guy, Oliva. simplypschology.org

[71] Jackson, Da'Naia.2022. The Birth of Da'Naia Jackon Ministries. Essay. Oral Robert's University

[72] See Jackson, Da'Naia. Traumatized: Is God a Monster or Healer? A Trauma Informed Guide for Ministers to Understand the Mind of the Wounded

[73] Hanley Center.2023. Is There a Difference Between Emotional Abuse and Psychological Abuse?

[74] Ed Citronnelli Ministries SWAT Advanced Training

[75] See Torace D. Solomon. Finger of God p.27-8

[76] American Psychological Association. Episode 255. Speaking of Psychology; What's the difference between guilt and shame? With June Tangney, PhD.

[77] See Episode 255 with June Tangney, PhD

[78] Mulholland, Robert Jr. Invitation to a Journey: A Road Map for Spiritual Formation p. 56

[79] See Jackson, Da'Naia. Traumatized is God a Monser or Healer? A Trauma-Informed Guide for Ministers to Understand the mind of the Wounded p.19

[80] One of the early church heresies was Docetism, the belief that Christ had not really become human because of the insurmountable difference between the divine and human worlds. Some, therefore, thought that Jesus only seemed to be human but never gave up his divine nature or essence. See Helmut Koester, History, Culture, and Religion of the Hellenistic Age (Minneapolis: Fortress Press, 1995) p.414

[81] Richard J. Foster, Streams of Living Water: Celebrating the Great Traditions of Christan Faith (San Fransico: Harper,1998) p.189

[82] Sww Scazzero, Emotionally Healthy Discipleship p.12

[83] See Scazzero, Emotionally Healthy Discipleship p.12

[84] See, Torace D. Solomn, Finger of God

[85] See Torace D. Solomon, Finger of God p.29-30

[86] See Torace D Solomon, Finger of God p.i

[87] See, Torace D. Solomon, Finger of God p.i

[88] See Torace D. Solomon. Finger of God p.ii

[89] See Torace D Solomon Finger of God p.iii

[90] See, Solomon, Torace D. Finger of God p.68

[91] Jaxn, Derrick.2013. A Cheating Man's Heart, A Novel p.3

[92] See, What is Masking? Simplypsychology.org

[93] See, Solomon, Torace D. Finger of God p.66

[94] See, Solomon, Torace D. Finger of God p. 66

[95] Ed Citronelli SWAT Advanced Training p.9

[96] See, Mental Heal America Dissociation and Dissociative Disorders

[97] Jackson, Da'Naia. 2022. SYNTHESIS OF THE FOURTH GOSPEL: LIFE, FUTURE AND CREATION RENEWAL. Essay. Oral Roberts University

[98] Jackson, Da'Naia. 2022.Synthesis of the Fourt Gospel. Essay. Oral Robert's University

[99] See, Solomon, Torace D. Finger of God p.140

[100] See, Jackson, Da'Naia, Traumatized: Is God A Monster or Healer? A Trauma-Informed Guide for Ministers to Understand the Mind of the Wounded p.4

[101] Hill and Walton. Survey of the Old Testament p.173

[102] Jackon, Da'Naia. Traumatizes: Is God a Monter or Healer? p/4-7

[103] See, Jackosn, Da'Naia. Traumatized: Is God a Monster or Healer? p.4

[104] Mental Health America. Co-Dependency mentalhealthamerica.org

[105] See Jaxn, Derrick. 2013. A Cheating Man's Heart p.42-3

[106] See Jaxn, Derrick,2013. ACMH p.44

[107] See, Jaxn, Derrick.2013. ACMH p.44

[108] See, Jaxn, Derrick.2013. ACMH p.44

[109] KMD Law Classic Problems. Modern Solutions. July 07th 2021. Kmdlaw.com

[110] See, KDM LAW. July 07th 2021 publication kmdlaw.com

[111] Robert's, Oral. The Still Small Voice of God

[112] See, Solomon, Torace D. Finger of God p.140

[113] See, Solomin, Torace D. Finger of God p. 140

[114] See, Jaxn, Derrick ACMH p.41

[115] Ed Citronelli Ministries SWAT Advanced Training

[116] Ed Citronelli Ministries SWAT Advacned Training

[117] See, Jaxn, Derrick. ACMH p. 41

[118] See, Jaxn, Derrick. ACMH p.39

[119] Merriam-Webster Dictionary. Merriam-webster.com

[120] See, Jaxn, Derrick, ACMH p.39-40

[121] See, Jaxn, Derrick. ACMH p. 39-40

[122] See, Jaxn, Derrick. ACMH p.40-41

[123] See Jaxn, Derrick. ACMH p. 55

[124] See Jaxn, Derrick ACMH p.41

[125] See, Solomon, D. Torace. The Finger of God p.133

[126] See, Solomon, Torrce D., p.36

[127] Got Questions. Your Questions. Biblical Answers. gotquestions.org

[128] See, Solomon, Torace D. Finger of God p140

[129] See, Jaxn, Derrick. ACMH p.44

[130] The Jewish Study Bible 2nd Edition TORAH, NEVI'IM, KETHUVIM p.396

[131] See, Jaxn, Derrick. ACMH p.44

[132] Franklin, Devon. How to Tell the Difference between a Healthy Man and a Toxic Man https://www.instagram.com/reel/C68Nibgp31e/?igsh=Z2E1dWI0aHVxdnIz

[133] Cross Reference: Genesis 1:2;4:12;9:2; Ps 9:2; Genesis 4:7; Philippians 2:3,4; Ephesians 5:21-33

[134] See Genesis 3:8-13

[135] Merrit, James, Dr. August 1, 2022. The God Who Sees Me. Touching Lives with James Merrit. Touchinglives.org

[136] Cross Reference 2 Samual 6:20-23

[137137] Cross Reference Genesis 11:30; 25:21

[138] See, Merrit, James. The God Who Sees Me

[139] See, Merrit, James, The God Who Sees Me

[140] Rachman, S. Behav Res Ther. April 2010. Betrayal: A psychological analysis. National Library of Medicine

[141] See, Solomon, Torace D. Finger of God p.140

[142] Linder, N. Jason, PsyD. 7 Hidden Effects of Trauma and Complex Trauma. What many people don't know about trauma. October 12,2021. Psychology Today. Psycologytoday.com

[143] Herman, J. (2015). Trauma and recovery: The aftermath of violence—from domestic abuse to political terror. (3rd ed). Hachette UK.

[144] Van der Kolk, B. A. (2015). The body keeps the score: Brain, mind, and body in the healing of trauma. Penguin Books.

[145] See, Linder 7 Hidden Effects of Trauma and Complex Trauma; Shapiro, F. (2017). Eye movement desensitization and reprocessing (EMDR): Basic principles, protocols, and procedures. (3rd ed.). Guilford Press.

[146] Cvetek, R. (2008). EMDR treatment of distressful experiences that fail to meet the criteria for PTSD. Journal of EMDR Practice and Research, 2(1), 2-14.

[147] See, Linder, 7 Hidden Effects of Trauma and Complex Trauma

[148] Johnson, S. M. (2002). Emotionally focused couple therapy with trauma survivors: Strengthening attachment bonds. Guilford Press.

[149] Glover, Vivette. Adv Nerobiol. 2015. Prenatal Stress and its effects on the fetus and the child: possible underlying biological mechanisms. National Library of Medicine

[150] Glover, Vivette. Adv Nerobiol. 2015. Prenatal Stress and its effects on the fetus and the child: possible underlying biological mechanisms

[151] Madhusoodanan, Jyoti. September 30th, 2019. How Matenal Mood Shapes the Developing Brain

[152] See, Madhusoodanan, Jyoti. How Mental Mood Shapes the Developing Brain

[153] See, Madhusoodanan, Jyoti. How Mental Mood Shapes the Developing Brain

[154] See, Hammonds, Frank and Ida Mae. A Manual for Children's Deliverance

[155] Got Questions. You Questions. Biblical Answers. What is the Heart?

[156] See, Got Questions. What is the Heart? Gotquestions.org

[157] See,Got Questions. What is the Heart? Gotquestions.org

[158] Active Christianity. What is the Heart? Ctivechristianity.org

[159] Roberts, Oral. The Sickness Attitude. YouTube RichardRobertsMinistries

[160] Clinton, J. Robert. Dr. The Making of a Leader 2nd Editon Recognizing the lessons and stages of leadership development p.26

[161] See, Clinton, J. Robert. Dr. The Making of A Leader p.26

[162] Gift-mis is a term coined by Dr. C. Peter Wagner- a church growth theorist- in his book Your Spiritual Gifts Can Hel Your Church Grow. It describes the set of spiritual gifts a leader demonstrates in his ministry. Usually, leaders demonstrate more than one spiritual gift in their ministry. The identification if personality traits or natural abilities in leaders who have manifested know gifts suggests that perhaps there is a correlation between certain personality traits and certain kinds of gifts. Clinton, J. Roberts book *Unlocking Your Giftedness: What Leaders Need to Know to Develop Themselves and Others* explores this idea. Natal abilities may be reflected om a spiritual gift; that is, a spiritual gift may relate to or be based on a previously recognized natural ability. The Holy Spirit releases the gift through the individual in such a way that his natural ability is enhanced with the power of the Spirit.

[163] Informal training is a technical tern taken from leadership training models theory. Training can be categorized under three broad headings: formal, nonformal, and informal. Informal training models are defined as those non-programmatic models that makes deliberate use of life activities for closure training. See, Clinton, J. Robert manual *Leadership Training Models*, Chapter 9, which deals with informal training.

[164] *Imitation modeling* is a technical tern taken from leadership training model theory that usually refers to informal training models in which the person learns primarily by observing a role model and imitating skills, values and attitudes.

[165] Imitation modeling is a technical tern taken from leadership training model theory that usually refers to informal training models in which the person learns primarily by observing a rilerole model and imitating skills, values and attitudes.

[166] Mentoring refers to a low-key informal training model where a person with serving, giving, encouraging attitude (the mentor) sees leadership potential in a still-to-be-developed person (the protégé or mentoree) and is able to promote or otherwise significantly influence the protégé toward the realization of leadership potential. See also The Mentor Handbook: Detailed Guidelines and Helps for Christian Mentors and Mentorees, written by Clinton, J. Robert Dr., Clinton, Richard. Dr.

[167] Formal training, one of three broad categories of training models, refers to training that takes place in institutions set up to offer programmatic instruction leading to degrees or other recognized closure incentives, See Clinton, J. Robert Dr. Manual Leadership Training Models, Chapter 7, which deals with the Fromal Mode-especially centralized models

[168] See, Clinton, J. Robert. Dr. The Making of Leader p.2/

[169] Awwad, Johnny. 2011. "From Saul to Paul: The Conversion of Paul the Apostle." Theological Review 32 (1): 1–14. https://search-ebscohost-com.oralroberts.idm.oclc.org/login.aspx?direct=true&db=a9h&AN=60631654&site=ehost-live&scope=site.

[170] Jackson, Da'Naia.2022. Sauls Metamorphose to Paul: A Look at the Patterns, Methodology and Theology of Apostle Paul Essay p.1

[171] See, Awwad, Johnny. 2011. "From Saul to Paul: The Conversion of Paul the Apostle." Theological Review 32 (1): 1–14. https://search-ebscohost-com.oralroberts.idm.oclc.org/login.aspx?direct=true&db=a9h&AN=60631654&site=ehost-live&scope=site.

[172] Gundry, Robert H., 2012, A Survey of the New Testament, 5th ed. Grand Rapids: Zondervan. (Print ISBN: 978-0310494744, 0310494745) (eText ISBN: 9780310494768, 0310494761) p.86

[173] See, Awwad, Johnny.2011. "From Saul to Paul: The Conversion of Paul the Apostle p.

[174] See, Awwad. Jonny. 2011. P 6

[175] J. Christiaan Beker, Paul the Apostle: The Triumph of God in Life and Thought (Philadelphia: Fortress Press, 1980), 182-183

[176] Mathew, Thompson. 2017. Spirit-Led Ministry in the 21st Century. Bloomington, IN: WestBow Press. [Print ISBN: 9781512792317; Digital ISBN: 9781512792324]

[177] See, Jackosn, Da'Naia.2022. Sauls Metamorphose to Paul: A Look at the Patterns, Methodology and Theology of Apostle Paul Essay p.2

[178] Keener,51-165

[179] Avery-Peck, A.J., 2014, 'Farewell speech IV. Judaism A. Second temple and Hellenistic Judaism', in D.C. Allison, C. Helmer & V. Leppin (eds.), Encyclopedia of the Bible and its Reception (Essenes – Fideism), vol. 8, pp. 880–883, De Gruyter, Berlin.

[180] See Avery-Peck 2014 (889)

[181] Stenchke, Christoph W. 2020. "Lifestyle and Leadership According to Paul's Statement of Account before the Ephesian Elders in Acts 20:17–35." Harvard Theologies Studies 76 (2): 1–11. doi:10.4102/hts.v76i2.5901.

[182] See, Jackson, Da'Naia.2022. Sauls Metamorphose to Paul: A Look at the Patterns, Methodology and Theology of Apostle Paul Essay p.3

[183] Roberts, Richard. YouTube. Oral Roberts. The Sickness Attitude. https://www.youtube.com/watch?v=DjPSYNEAu_E

[184] Dissociation. Psychology Today. Psycholgytoday.com

[185] Got Questions. Your Questions. Biblical Answers. What Does The Bible Mean By "Dying to Self"? Gotquestions.org

[186] Shrier, Cahleen Ph.D. 2002. The Science of the Crucifixion. Azuza Pacific University. Adapted Tally (French '00) Flint. Apu.edu; also see, Cross Reference Matthew 26:36-46; Mark 14:37-42; Luke 22:39-43

[187] Shrier, Cahleen Ph.D. 2002. The Science of the Crucifixion. Azuza Pacific University. Adapted Tally (French '00) Flint. Apu.edu; also see, CrossRef- Matthew 26:67-75; Mark 14:61-72; Luke 22:54-23:25; John 18:16-27; Matthe 27:26-27; Mark 15:15-21; Luke 23:25-26; John 19:1-28

[188] Shock First Aid Treatment. Cleveland Clinic. Myclevelandclinic.org

[189] Shock First Aid Treatment. Cleveland Clinic. Myclevelandclinic.org

[190] Shock First Aid Treatment. Cleveland Clinic. Myclevelandclinic.org

[191] Kleber RJ. Trauma and public mental health: A focused review. Front Psychiatry. 2019;10:451.doi:3389/fpsyt.2019.00451

[192] Krause-Utz A, Frost R, Winter D, Elzinga BM. Dissociation and alterations in brain function and structure. Curr Psychiatry Rep. 2017;19(1):6.doi:10.1007/s11920-017-0757-y

[193] Gupta, Sanjana.2024. What to Know About Traumatic Shock. Medically reviewed by Daniel B. Block, MD. Verywellmind.com

[194] MIT Medical. Common reactions to traumatic events

[195] Lanius RA. Trauma-related dissociation and altered states of consciousness: a call for clinical, treatment, and neuroscience research. Eur J Psychotraumatol.2015;6:27905.doi:10.3402/ejpt.v627905

[196] El-Solh AA. Management of nightmares in patients with posttraumatic stress disorder: Current perspectives. Nat Sci Sleep.2018;10:409-420:doi:10.2147/NSS.S166089

[197] American Psychology Association. Trauma and Shock

[198] Boyer SM, Caplan JE, Edwards LK. Trauma-related dissociation and the dissociative disorders: Neglected symptoms with severe public health consequences. Dela J Public Health.2022;8(2):78-84.doi:32481/djph.2022.05.010

[199] See, Gupta, Sanjana.2024. What to Know About Traumatic Shock. Medically reviewed by Daniel B. Block, MD. Verywellmind.com

[200] Substance Abuse and Mental Health Services Administration. Key ingredients for successful trauma-informed care implementation.

[201] See, Solomon, D. Torace. The Finger of God p. 17

[202] See, Solom, Torace D. The Finger of God p.17

[203] Got Questions. Your Questions. Biblical Answers. What Does It Mean That "The Two Shall Become One Flesh" (Gen 2:24)

[204] See, Got Questions. What Does IT Mean That "The Two Shall Become Once Flesh"

[205] See, Dr. Cahleen Shrier Lecture on the Science of Crucifixion of Christ Lecture

[206] See, Dr. Cahleen Shrier Lecture on the Science of Crucifixion of Christ Lecture

[207] Florida Women's Law Group. March 15th, 2022, The Narcissist's Word Salad

[208] Florida Women's Law Group. March 15th, 2022, The Narcissist's Word Salad

[209] Streep, Peg. 5 Kinds of Blame-Shifting, and Why They Work. Psychologytoday.com

[210] BreakTheSilenceDV. Reactive Abuse: What it is and Why Abusers Rely On It. January 28th, 2019

Made in the USA
Columbia, SC
29 July 2024

39545535R00139